Liberal Politics and Public Faith

In the eyes of many, liberalism requires the aggressive secularization of social institutions, especially public media and public schools. The unfortunate result is that many Americans have become alienated from the liberal tradition because they believe it threatens their most sacred forms of life. This was not always the case: in American history, the relation between liberalism and religion has often been one of mutual respect and support. In *Liberal Politics and Public Faith: Beyond Separation*, Kevin Vallier attempts to reestablish mutual respect by developing a liberal political theory that avoids the standard liberal hostility to religious voices in public life. He claims that the dominant form of academic liberalism, public reason liberalism, is far friendlier to religious influences in public life than either its proponents or detractors suppose. The best interpretation of public reason, *convergence liberalism*, rejects the much-derided "privatization" of religious belief, instead viewing religious contributions to politics as a resource for liberal political institutions. Many books reject privatization—*Liberal Politics and Public Faith: Beyond Separation* is unique in doing so on *liberal grounds*.

Kevin Vallier is an Assistant Professor of Philosophy at Bowling Green State University.

Liberal Politics and Public Faith

Beyond Separation

Kevin Vallier

Routledge
Taylor & Francis Group

NEW YORK AND LONDON

First published 2014
by Routledge
711 Third Avenue, New York, NY 10017, USA

and by Routledge

2 Park Square, Milton Park, Abingdon, Oxfordshire OX14 4RN

First issued in paperback 2016

Routledge is an imprint of the Taylor & Francis Group, an informa business

© 2014 Taylor & Francis

The right of Kevin Vallier to be identified as author of this work has been asserted by him in accordance with sections 77 and 78 of the Copyright, Designs and Patents Act 1988.

Library of Congress Cataloging-in-Publication Data
Vallier, Kevin.
Liberal politics and public faith : beyond separation / Kevin Vallier. —
   1 [edition].
      pages cm
   Includes bibliographical references and index.
   1. Religion and politics.   2. Liberalism.   I. Title.
   BL65.P7V35 2014
   322'.1—dc23
   2014013494

ISBN 13: 978-0-415-78973-8 (pbk)
ISBN 13: 978-0-415-73713-5 (hbk)

Typeset in Minion
by Apex CoVantage, LLC

For My Grandmother, Reba Kirby Southwell
I did good

Contents

Acknowledgments

This is my first book and, as such, I owe enormous debts of gratitude not only to those who helped me with the book, but also to those who helped me become the sort of person that could write one. I have dedicated the book to my grandmother, who, with my mother, encouraged my theological and philosophical interests from an early age. I'm grateful to my wife, Alicia, and Jerry Gaus, my dissertation advisor, who supported my trek through graduate school and the writing of this book. I'm also grateful to my friends at the University of Arizona, especially John Thrasher, Kyle Swan, Keith Hankins, and Chad Van Schoelandt, who read this material in one form or another many times and always provided thoughtful and incisive help. David Schmidtz was gracious and supportive—financially, intellectually, and personally— throughout graduate school and my early career. I'm also thankful to Thomas Christiano and Steve Wall, who with Dave and Jerry, helped guide the dissertation that heavily influenced this book. I was unusually fortunate to have two excellent external committee members, Christopher Eberle and Nicholas Wolterstorff. Both went *far* beyond their duties in providing me with detailed comments and conversation throughout the dissertation. I was delighted that their help continued throughout the formation of the book.

A number of others read and commented on the manuscript, in whole or in part, including Robert Audi, Nathan Ballantyne, Jason Brennan, Corey Brettschneider, Christian Coons, Michael Cust, Fred D'Agostino,

Stephen Davies, Ryan Davis, Russell DiSilvestro, Ben Dyer, David Estlund, Jessica Flanigan, Chris Freiman, Bill Glod, Alex Gourevitch, Erik Herrmann, Ben Hertzberg, Javier Hildalgo, Charles Larmore, Mark LeBar, Jacob Levy, Andrew Lister, Roderick Long, Stephen Macedo, Adam Martin, Bryan McGraw, Mary McThomas, Ryan Muldoon, Mark Murphy, Carmen Pavel, Laura Phillips, Guido Pincione, Jeppe von Platz, Maura Priest, Jonathan Quong, Randy Reynolds, Micah Schwartzman, Danny Shahar, Daniel Silvermint, John Tomasi, Justin Tosi, Piers Turner, Tracy Vallier, Peter Vanderschraaf, Bas van der Vossen, Craig and Brandon Warmke, Paul Weithman, Fabian Wendt, Will Wilkinson, Paul Woodruff, Enrico Zoffoli, Matt Zwolinski, and two anonymous referees who reviewed the manuscript for Routledge and provided many helpful comments.

I would also like to thank everyone who helped me with copyediting and publishing the book, including Andy Beck and John Downes-Angus at Routledge and Harry David, who put together the index. I'm also grateful to several Bowling Green graduate students who reviewed the manuscript, including Ben Bryan and especially Andrew Erickson, my research assistant.

I've discussed issues covered in this book at a number of difference conferences and workshops. My thanks to two audiences at Brown University, one at a colloquium series and the other at a mini-workshop at Brown's Political Theory Project. I am also grateful to the audience at my research workshop at the University of Arizona held in the fall of 2013 and to the other summer research fellows at the Institute for Humane Studies during the summer of 2010. I have presented parts of the book at Wheaton College, Ohio State University, the University of Manchester, the University of Tennessee and meetings at the American Philosophical Association and the American Political Science Association. This book was written over the years with generous financial support from the Institute for Humane Studies, Brown's Political Theory Project, the University of Arizona's Freedom Center, the Arizona Arts, Humanities and Social Sciences Fellowship and the Harvey Fellows Program sponsored by the Mustard Seed Foundation.

Finally, some of the content of the book has appeared in previously published articles. Separate parts of Chapter 2 originally appeared in different forms in "Liberalism, Religion and Integrity" (in *The Australasian Journal of Philosophy*), "The Fragility of Consensus: Public Reason, Diversity and Stability," co-authored with John Thrasher, (in *The European Journal of*

Philosophy), and parts of Chapters 2 and 4 appeared in "Against Public Reason's Accessibility Requirement" (in *The Journal of Moral Philosophy*). Other parts of Chapter 4 appeared in "Consensus and Convergence in Public Reason" (in *Public Affairs Quarterly*). Some of the discussion contained in Chapters 1 and 4 draws on material I published with Fred D'Agostino in the Stanford Encyclopedia of Philosophy entry on Public Justification, others draw on an article I co-authored with Jerry Gaus, "The Roles of Religious Conviction in a Publicly Justified Polity: The Implications of Convergence, Asymmetry and Political Institutions" (in *Philosophy and Social Criticism*).

Introduction

I was born in 1982, in the midst of the contemporary American culture wars. As with so many in my generation, I have never known my country without the polarizing and socially destructive attempts by diverse groups to institutionalize their preferred scheme of values. Given the depth and pervasiveness of this struggle for culture dominance, taking sides has often proven irresistible. As with so many members of my generation who were attracted to the study of ideas, I played along, spending great time and energy on behalf of those who were Right and fighting against those who were Wrong (my intensity was not diminished either time I changed teams).

But as I thought through the social, cultural and religious issues that so deeply divide Americans (abortion, gay marriage, human origins, Christianity), I started to wonder whether a culture war was the inevitable result of these deep disagreements. I asked myself whether it was really impossible for Americans to live together without each side vying for the power to impose their views on the other. After all, Protestants and Catholics profoundly disagree over matters of great import to them. But in the United States, neither group thinks it has the authority to decide their disagreements through the exercise of government power. Granted, this theological truce was a long time in the making, but it came nonetheless.

Protestants and Catholics solved their problems by becoming *liberals*.[1] Broadly speaking, a liberal is someone who tries to convince people to agree to disagree rather than to come to blows.[2] From Locke on, the liberal has attempted to extract herself from the divisive political conflicts of her age and to provide an impartial framework for resolving them. When it came to state religion, liberals were spectacularly successful, convincing non-liberal people of faith that they could live together well without institutionalizing their respective theological views.

But liberals can no longer claim to stand above the fray. Instead, liberal claims to neutrality are widely regarded as a smoke screen by which liberals use political power to impose their views on others. With respect to religion, many believe that contemporary liberalism is wedded to secularism. Liberalism is thus identified with an aggressive secularization of social institutions, especially public media and public schools. The result: many citizens of faith regard liberalism as a threat to their most sacred forms of life. Sadly, many liberals have played along, happy to restrict religious influences in American politics.

I believe we do not have to fight, for there is a truly liberal solution to the culture wars, much as there was for the wars of religion. The point of this book is to develop a liberalism that provides such a solution. Of course, I cannot address every aspect of the culture wars. I will instead focus on the problem that animates it—the disagreement about the proper role of religion in American public life. Liberal and conservative culture warriors have strikingly different visions for the place of religion in politics. Liberals range between claiming that religion should be kept entirely out of politics to claiming that religion must be subordinated to secular concerns. Conservatives, especially Christian conservatives, reject liberalism for this reason and vie for the political establishment of civic theism, where our institutions explicitly recognize the moral and religious authority of God. Both sides see the other as the oppressor. And both claim the mantle of religious liberty as their own.

I. The Promise of Convergence Liberalism

But both sides are wrong. And they are wrong because they share a common assumption: that liberalism is fundamentally antagonistic to religious influences in public life. This book dissents by defending a form of liberalism that should prove attractive to citizens who believe that their religious convictions have a proper place in the public sphere.

The alternative, which I term *convergence liberalism*, can resolve the conflict over the role of religion in public life, striking at the root of the American culture wars.

Liberalism comes in many forms, and I cannot discuss them all. Instead, I shall focus on the dominant form of academic liberalism: public reason liberalism. Public reason liberalism combines traditional liberal commitments to civil and political liberties with the requirement that coercion be justified to all in terms they can reasonably be expected to accept. Public reason liberals are the most notorious defenders of the view that liberalism requires privatizing religious reasoning and expression in public political life.[3] Calls for privatization raise the ire of their religious critics, who argue that requiring religious citizens to privatize their convictions violates their integrity and treats them unfairly. I believe that the critics are right to reject privatization, but wrong to believe that public reason requires it. Convergence liberalism provides an effective response to these criticisms because, as we shall see, it holds that liberal commitments to freedom, equality and respect for diversity require rejecting religious restraint.

II. Post-secular Liberalism

Post-secularism is a bourgeoning research paradigm within sociology and political science that assumes that secularization is coming to an end, both nationally and internationally, and sees the secular as a sectarian domain of reasoning, discourse and political power rather than a neutral, dispassionate domain as it is traditionally understood. Like many post-secularists, I reject the double standard that liberals often apply to religious and secular reasons, treating religious reasoning as private, sectarian and irrational, and secular reasoning as public, universal and rational. Convergence liberalism accepts the permanence of religious influences in public life and views both secular and religious forms of reasoning as resources for constructing and maintaining liberal democratic institutions. In this way, convergence liberalism is a post-secular liberalism.

Why does it matter that convergence liberalism is post-secular? Despite the hopes of many secular liberals, modernity has not eliminated religion. Any fair-minded assessment of national and international religious movements must accept that religion is not going away. Instead, Christianity and Islam in particular are expanding dramatically worldwide, often in relatively liberal countries, and especially in the Global South. We may well be entering a new age of religious commitment and conflict. Liberalism originally sold itself to the West as a political program that could resolve religious conflicts. But over time liberalism has created a conflict of its own—between its adherents and citizens of faith. Liberalism not only needs to adapt for theoretical reasons, it needs to adapt for *practical* reasons. Liberals should develop a new political program that offers genuine resolutions to the conflicts between religious and secular citizens and between diverse peoples of faith. Liberalism must adapt if it is to survive an upsurge in religious belief and religious conflict.

III. The Plan of this Book

Liberal Politics and Public Faith: Beyond Separation defends a single thesis that spans its seven chapters—namely, that public reason liberalism, properly understood, realizes foundational liberal values while according religion a prominent and powerful role in public life. I claim that, in theory and practice, public reason liberalism is far friendlier to religion in public life than *both* its proponents and opponents believe.

Chapter 1 introduces public reason liberalism and characterizes its basic approach to religion in public life. Public reason liberalism is best understood in terms of a *Public Justification Principle*, the master principle of the book. The Public Justification Principle (PJP) holds that coercion is permissible only when each member of the public has sufficient reason to endorse the coercion. Public reason liberals use the Public Justification Principle to generate what I call *principles of restraint*, principles that require liberal democratic citizens to refrain from offering or acting upon private, religious reasons in their political activities. Restraint comes from public reason liberalism's concern about religious influences in public life. But while many public reason liberals take restraint to follow directly from the Public Justification Principle, the truth is more complicated.

Chapter 2 discusses the religious objections to public reason liberalism. The objections are leveled against restraint, but the religious critics share the public reason liberal's belief that the connection between restraint and public justification are tightly connected. Consequently, they reject the Public Justification Principle based on their concerns about restraint. I begin by constructing a *Master Argument* for restraint that splits the case for restraint into three premises, underscoring the distinction between the Public Justification Principle and restraint. If I can defeat one of these premises, I can free public reason liberalism from restraint. I then turn to assess the arguments against restraint. Religious critics advance two general arguments against restraint: the integrity objection and the fairness objection. The integrity objection holds that restraint requires religious citizens to violate their integrity, and the fairness objection holds that restraint places burdens on religious citizens not shared by secular citizens. After some refinement, I conclude that the objections successfully defeat restraint. I then address the common claim that restraint prevents social divisiveness and agree with the religious objectors that the divisiveness objection is inconclusive. I conclude the chapter by arguing that while the religious objections defeat principles of restraint, they fail to defeat the Public Justification Principle if the Master Argument fails. Thus, by denying that the Public Justification Principle entails restraint, we inoculate it against religious criticisms.

Chapter 3 develops a strategy for defeating the Master Argument by providing public reason liberals with decisive reason to reject restraint on their own terms. That is, I provide an *internal* critique of public reason liberalism's approach to religion in public life. To begin, I argue that the Public Justification Principle is ambiguous among multiple interpretations, some of which may not require restraint. If those interpretations can be vindicated based on considerations public reason liberals find significant, then public reason liberals will be committed to those interpretations by their own lights. To locate salient considerations, I analyze the sources of normativity on which the Public Justification Principle is based and which help to determine the legal scheme it validates. I distinguish two such sources: respect for integrity and respect for reasonable pluralism. To respect integrity is to allow citizens to live integrated lives based on their comprehensive doctrines and ideals. To respect reasonable pluralism is to permit citizens to govern themselves in accord with laws and norms on which they can converge from their diverse perspectives, that is, to respect the diverse judgments of the public as a whole. Public reason liberals must prefer interpretations of the Public Justification Principle that better respect integrity and reasonable pluralism, given that they endorse these forms of respect. They therefore have decisive reason to embrace interpretations of the Public Justification Principle that do not require restraint. If so, we have shown that the best version of public reason liberalism does not require religious restraint.

Chapters 4 and 5 execute the strategy developed in Chapter 3. Specifically, they develop an alternative interpretation of the mainstream conception of justifying reasons and idealization, themselves components of the Public Justification Principle. Chapter 4 defends a *convergence* conception of justificatory reasons, on which reasons offered to justify coercion need not be shared or even accessible to citizens. Instead, each member of the public may endorse liberal institutions for distinct, intelligible reasons. Thus, an *intelligibility requirement* limits the set of justificatory reasons to all and only those reasons that members of the public can see as justified for the person who has them based on the person's own evaluative standards. I criticize the dominant *consensus*, or shared reasons understanding of justificatory reasons, according to which justificatory reasons must be shared or accessible for all. I reject the consensus view on the grounds that it respects integrity less and restricts reasonable pluralism more than convergence. Specifically, consensus limits the integrity-based reasons to which citizens can appeal and often bars them from converging on norms they can all affirm in light of such reasons. Since convergence permits private (yet intelligible) reasons into the process of publicly justifying laws, citizens may employ their personal reasons in their political lives. These considerations render restraint indefensible even for public reason liberals.

But convergence loses its power if it is combined with a *radical* conception of idealization that ascribes justificatory reasons to citizens based on perfect rationality and full information. The resulting ascription of reasons may restrict respect for integrity and diversity by revising and homogenizing citizens' projects and principles. I address this concern in Chapter 5. I first outline the mainstream, radical conception of idealization and argue that while radical idealization has its attractions, it threatens to abstract citizens from their deeply held convictions and so justify restricting their integrity and preventing them from converging on common norms from diverse perspectives. For these reasons, we must reject radical idealization in favor of a *moderate* conception of idealization that attributes reasons to citizens on the basis of their deeply held principles and values. Moderate idealization identifies citizens' reasons by upgrading their rational faculties and information sets based on their present commitments. If coherent, moderate idealization is preferable to radical idealization, based on our two desiderata, and so protects convergence from the threat of radical idealization. Chapter 5 thereby completes the theoretical case against restraint by vindicating an interpretation of the Public Justification Principle that does not require restraint. However, to make convergence liberalism more plausible, we must draw out its implications for political practice.

Chapter 6 applies convergence liberalism to public deliberation and religious accommodation. Consensus liberalism requires that persons qua citizens prioritize public deliberation in shared terms over the pursuit of diverse values. But convergence gives priority to the diverse reasoning of citizens and permits religious reasons to play the role of defeaters for coercion. To demonstrate, I develop a *Principle of Intelligible Exclusion* (PIE) which holds that publicly justified institutions must not employ coercion for which citizens have intelligible defeaters. This principle demonstrates that restraint does not apply to citizens. I argue restraint applies to legislators by requiring that they support only those proposals they believe can be publicly justified based on intelligible reasons. Otherwise they may act on whatever reasons they like. Only judges must reason and rule in shared terms.

Intelligible Exclusion has implications for religious accommodation as well. I argue that public reason requires expansive religious accommodations, far beyond those protected by the standard, consensus view. I review three landmark court decisions, *Wisconsin v. Yoder, Employment Division v. Smith* and *Mozert v. Hawkins*. These cases illustrate the defeater reasons of religious citizens that require some legal body, judicial or legislative, to provide religious accommodation. On this basis, I argue that the plaintiffs in each case deserved religious accommodation. Along these lines, I agree with the *Yoder* decision and disagree with the *Smith* decision. And contrary to the arguments of mainstream public reason liberals, I argue that the *Mozert* parents merited legal accommodation. I conclude that convergence liberalism protects religious citizens from an overreaching liberal state and thereby treats religious citizens with appropriate respect.

Chapter 7 applies convergence liberalism to public education. I begin by again contrasting the convergence approach with the mainstream consensus view. Consensus liberals argue that the public education system is perhaps the most vital institutional component for promoting shared liberal democratic values. Public education helps reproduce consensus liberal citizens who can sustain liberal institutions in the future. But convergence liberalism prizes and protects diverse reasoning. Citizens' diverse, dispersed defeaters undermine attempts to publicly justify the uniform civic curricula endorsed by consensus liberals. I illustrate this point by addressing the teaching of intelligent design. The controversy over intelligent design indicates that many parents have defeaters for both highly secularized and relatively de-secularized educational curricula, especially because many parents are prepared to withdraw their children entirely from public schools they believe undermine the transmission of their moral and religious values. We shall see that religious and secular citizens jointly have defeaters for a wide range of value-based curricula required by consensus civic education. I conclude that convergence requires transforming American education into a school choice system where government retreats from the provision of public education. It instead provides a voucher-based safety net and imposing minimum educational requirements open to diverse interpretations of civic values. By allowing citizens to separate according to their values, a publicly justified polity can avoid unjustified coercion. In this way, Chapter 7 demonstrates that public reason liberalism provides extensive protections for religious and secular parents to raise their children in accord with their values. The conclusion of Chapters 6 and 7, then, is that convergence liberalism vindicates our thesis in practice as well as in theory.

IV. Hope

My goal in this work is to justify the hope that religious and secular citizens and their philosophical apologists can be reconciled in theory and practice. I believe that we can see our way out of this seemingly insuperable conflict through careful analysis of liberal political theory. The resulting account of liberal theory and practice should demonstrate that we can live together well despite our differences. I realize that I defend a controversial thesis. Perhaps my efforts will fail. But given what is at stake, it is surely worth a try.

Notes

1. At least when it came to institutionalizing theological doctrine.
2. In the academic and historical—not the popular and colloquial—sense.
3. As I contend in Ch. 1, because public reason liberalism replicates early liberal support for privatization, we can assess the social impact of liberalism generally by assessing public reason's approach to religion.

CHAPTER **1**

Public Reason Liberalism
Religion's Child and King

Freedom is the primary concern of the liberal tradition. Liberals assume that persons are naturally free and equal, such that the coercive restriction of freedom by equals requires justification. *Public reason* liberals holds that the required justification be *public*, in terms that all can accept.

Despite their emphasis on freedom, liberals, and public reason liberals specifically, are accused of trying to restrict religious influences in political life. This work declares liberalism innocent by answering the challenges that religious critics have raised against it, and does so by defending public reason liberalism against its religious critics. Yet public reason liberalism is a new branch of liberalism, barely thirty years old. So how could analyzing its approach to religion in politics enlighten us about liberalism's approach? The answer is that public reason liberalism's treatment of religion represents, in microcosm, the treatment offered by liberalism itself. If public reason liberalism is friendly to religion in public life, then perhaps liberalism is too.

To understand why liberalism is seen as hostile to religion in public life, we must appreciate the point of liberal political theory. Liberalism holds that persons are free and equal and recognizes that they inevitably disagree about what is right and good. The point of liberalism, then, is to develop institutions that allow these persons to live together despite their disagreements. Consequently, liberals want political institutions to be impartial among competing conceptions of the right and the good. Liberalism seeks what Thomas Nagel calls "higher-order impartiality," because it transcends disagreements among moral and religious views, hoping to resolve them in ways all regard as fair.[1]

In light of this aim, liberals have always faced the criticism that their ascent to transcendence fails. Liberals, say the critics, are as sectarian as anyone else. Admittedly, liberals have not always handled themselves with grace in response. Many insist that their critics are simply chafing under the restraints liberalism imposes on their authoritarian and unreasonable impulses. Moral and religious sectarians must "[g]row up!"[2] In the name of fairness, anti-liberals must restrain themselves from using religious reasons to support or oppose laws. Citizens of faith must *privatize* their religious commitments.

So while public reason liberals, as liberals, want to protect religious liberty, they also want to restrain the power of religion in the public square. Accordingly, they approach religion with a divided heart. A political order must be publicly justified to religious citizens while preventing them from imposing religiously based coercion on others.

Public reason liberalism's approach to religion in political life therefore displays a deep tension, as it claims to both serve and master religious forces in public life. Chapter 1 explains the source, ground and structure of public reason liberalism and outlines how its schizophrenic attitude toward religion derives from liberalism's theoretical structure. Restraint is not necessarily motivated by anti-religious bias, but rather by the attempt to balance a series of theoretical concerns. This is important: if we are to exonerate public reason, we must first explain how religious restraint is not rooted in secularist bias.

I.   Religious War and Social Contract

John Rawls, the dean of modern liberal political theory, introduces his *Political Liberalism* by arguing that liberal political theory developed under distinctively modern circumstances, specifically within political bodies that were historically characterized by a pervasive pluralism of religious belief and practice. Rawls illustrates this pluralism with a familiar narrative about the role religion played in the inception of Western liberal democracies:

> What the ancient world did not know was the clash between Salvationist, creedal, and expansionist religions. That is a phenomenon new to historical experience, a possibility realized by the Reformation. Of course, Christianity already made possible the conquest of people, not simply . . . to exercise power and dominion over them, but to save their souls. The Reformation turned this possibility inward upon itself.
>
> What is new about this clash is that it introduces into people's conceptions of the good a transcendent element not admitting of compromise. This element forces either mortal conflict moderated only by circumstance and exhaustion, or equal liberty of conscience and freedom of thought. . . . Political liberalism starts by taking to heart the absolute depth of that irreconcilable latent conflict.[3]

Rawls here appeals to a conventional liberal story about the origins of liberal democracy. Several centuries ago there existed a religio-political unity called "Christendom." Citizens of Christendom practiced some version of Christianity and took its basic tenets for granted. But once Christians were free to argue amongst themselves about which sect had the correct theology, they produced a century and a half of devastating military conflicts between Lutherans, Calvinists, Anabaptists and Catholics that culminated in the Thirty Years' War. This "holy cataclysm" consumed many lives until the Peace of Westphalia terminated the bloodletting, enshrining in Western culture and politics the core principle that religious difference never constitutes a just case for war.[4]

I am not sure whether this story is true. But liberals often tacitly accept it and have formulated their theories in response to this rather crude historical narrative. Many liberals see themselves as the first advocates of religious toleration as a political solution to war and disagreement.[5] Religious groups for centuries maintained that a stable social order was impossible when citizens were permitted to openly disagree about fundamental matters, especially theological ones. Liberal political theory responds by demonstrating that political order can be achieved despite wide differences in beliefs, even on matters as significant as religion. While Thomas Hobbes and John Locke supported attempts to stamp out (some forms of) Catholicism in England, they rank among the first figures to argue that social cooperation could be achieved by appealing to the common reason of all instead of the truth of a particular religious tradition.[6] Though a number of religious and political thinkers before them believed that political justification could be achieved through natural reason, these earlier figures did not grasp that natural reason leads to disagreement as often as it leads to agreement. Not until the seventeenth century did political theorists grapple with the problem of persistent disagreement over religious matters.[7]

The great social contract theorists (Hobbes, Locke, Rousseau and Kant) attempt to provide a nonsectarian justification of political order. They are concerned, first and foremost, with the conflict of *private judgments*. Private judgments inevitably conflict, and so we need some public method of resolving the ensuing disputes. As Hobbes famously wrote, "No one mans Reason, nor the Reason of any one number of men, makes the certaintie" and concludes that "when there is a controversy in an account, the parties must by their own accord, set up for right Reason, the Reason of some Arbitrator, or Judge, to whose sentence they will both stand."[8] Hobbes knew personally the threat posed by those fanatical individuals who would co-opt coercive power to impose their views on others.[9] The core problem of *Leviathan* is to provide a justification for a political order in light of the challenges posed by such persons. As Gerald Gaus has noted, many think that Hobbes is most concerned with the "foole" or the man who claims there is no such thing as justice.[10] But in reality, the large majority of *Leviathan* is devoted to showing how those who believe in justice and follow their interpretation of it still cannot resolve their disagreements without the steady, awesome hand of the state. Hobbes tried to show that practical rationality requires transcending one's religious view and accepting a public social arrangement where disputes would be decisively resolved, even with respect to religious practices and beliefs.

Locke identified a similar problem, though he believed state power should be substantially more limited. Nonetheless, Locke was just as concerned as Hobbes about moral and religious disagreement. Even though natural law is generally clear to all "rational Creatures," they will still be "biased by their Interest, as well as ignorant for want of studying it, [and] not apt to allow of it as a Law binding to them in application of it to their particular Cases."[11] We have reason to leave the state of nature because of the conflict among private judgments, for in civil society "all private judgment of every particular member being excluded, the community comes to be umpire, by settled standing rules, indifferent, and the same to all parties," with the result that those empowered by the community decide "all the differences that may happen between any members of the society concerning any matter of right."[12] Note the strength of Locke's claim: *all* private judgment about political matters requires substituting public for private judgment. Both Locke and Hobbes sought to show that the practical rationality of each person, their private reason, requires submission to public reason. Private conviction is both the source of conflict and the source of resolution. It is because we disagree that we must transcend private judgment, and thus it is individually rational to take a public point of view.

Locke and Hobbes were so concerned about religious war and disagreement that they sought to modify Christian theology to neutralize its threat to stable political order. Hobbes's long excursus into Christian theology and Biblical exegesis in Parts III and IV of *Leviathan* were arguably meant to show that Christianity was compatible with giving the Sovereign authority over private judgments about theological matters. Locke tried to transform Christians' understanding of the social implications of Christianity. His *Reasonableness of Christianity* sought to inoculate Christian society against Christianity's more "virulent" forms. The *Letters* were impassioned pleas for toleration, but included controversial claims that churches were mere voluntary associations and that doctrinal differences amongst Protestant Christians were unimportant. Locke even denies that religious knowledge is possible. On matters of religion, there is only mere belief. Locke advances this view in his famous *Essay* but repeats it in the *Letter*.[13] Liberals must tame religion before unleashing it within the social order.

Much could be said about Rousseau and Kant, but for now it is enough to recognize that the social contract theorists saw themselves as responding to religious war and disagreement.[14] These liberal political theorists sought to both respect and *sustain* religious diversity by limiting the reach of religiously motivated politics. But let us follow history onward.

II. The Liberal Approach to Religion in Public Life—Rawls as Exemplar

Despite intellectual successes in the seventeenth and eighteenth centuries, in the nineteenth century social contract theory was replaced by utilitarianism, Hegelianism and Marxism. Social contract theory was not revived until after the Second World War, first in the United States.

The most prominent figure in this revival is John Rawls. Rawls's engagement with social contract theory led him to develop the intellectual foundation for the contemporary liberal treatment of religion and politics, though the standard treatment preceded him in both culture and legal practice. His treatment of religion in public life is best illustrated by the factors that led him to transition from *A Theory of Justice* to *Political Liberalism*. We shall see that his political theory (the first version of public reason liberalism) displays the tensions characteristic of liberalism's treatment of religion in public life. Fair warning: what follows contains new and controversial Rawls exegesis. I offer it because I believe that focusing on Rawls's view will help identify the source of liberalism's attitude towards religious influences in politics. Those familiar with newer readings of Rawls or those less interested should feel free to skip this section.

As is well known, Rawls argues that a society is just when its basic structure is regulated by principles that would be selected by parties to an original position, constrained by the veil of ignorance. The selection process is a contracting procedure that chooses Rawls's two principles of justice. The foundation for the principles is the subject of Part I of *Theory*. Part II covers their institutionalization. In the much unexplored Part III, Rawls attempts to demonstrate that the two principles and their institutionalization are compatible with a plausible conception of personal good. For Rawls, Part III was critical to the project of *Theory* as a whole. Rawls modified his political philosophy in *Political Liberalism* because he was dissatisfied with the account of stability in Part III.[15] For this reason, let us focus for a moment then on *Theory's* conception of stability.

The idea of stability is central to all social contract theories. From Hobbes to Rawls, social contract theorists have attempted to demonstrate that social order is possible in a diverse and contentious social world. They claimed that the adoption of common principles allows diverse individuals to resolve their disputes in a productive and cooperative manner. This means that citizens must do more than accept such principles; they must reliably act upon them. To be stable, then, political principles must have the continual, motivated assent of the citizenry. Without stability, political principles must be imposed by the sheer use of force.

Part III of *Theory* develops Rawls's conception of stability. Rawls distinguishes between two types of stability: "inherent" and "imposed."[16] Stability is imposed when a society's institutional structure stabilizes itself independently of (and even despite) the reasons of its citizens, perhaps through the imposition of political power by a sovereign state. Inherent stability is obtained when a "society that is well-ordered . . . generally maintains itself in a just general equilibrium and is capable of righting itself when the equilibrium is disturbed."[17] A conception of justice is inherently stable when citizens comply with principles of justice for moral reasons and out of moral motives, not merely from accidental or pragmatic considerations. Thus, as Paul Weithman has argued, Rawlsian stability is a "condition of general equilibrium" where "everyone knows that everyone else acts justly, and each replies to the justice of others by being just himself."[18] Rawls dislikes imposed stability because it bases politics on force alone; in contrast, Rawls hopes to demonstrate that inherent stability is possible.[19] Inherent stability is attractive because it bases institutional power on citizens' reasons, enabling the state to respect their natural freedom and equality.

The object of stability is Justice as Fairness. Part III of *Theory* holds that members of a well-ordered society will come to affirm Justice as Fairness as regulative of their lives as a whole. It is thus inherently stable; divergence from it is self-correcting because citizens endorse it via their sense of justice. But Rawls openly wonders whether members of the well-ordered society have reason to maintain their sense of justice, given that others might prefer to free-ride on their compliance. He tries to solve this assurance problem by arguing that citizens have independent reason to maintain their sense of justice apart from the benefits of stability. This independent reason is that endorsing their sense of justice is part of their good. Rawls calls this process congruence, which links "the concepts of justice and goodness."[20] Congruence is obtained when each citizen endorses her sense of justice from within her "thin theory of the good"—her conception of the good is separable from her sense of justice. The case for congruence is conditional. It is only rational to maintain one's sense of justice when others do the same.[21] Rawls writes that "even with a sense of justice men's compliance with a cooperative venture is predicated on the belief that others will do their part."[22] Weithman argues that this mutual expectation of compliance leads members of the well-ordered society into a Nash equilibrium, where each citizen has reason to act in a certain way because it is the best response to the actions of everyone else.[23] In a well-ordered society, one where a society's basic structure is regulated by a shared conception of justice, individuals will have no incentive to deviate from

Justice as Fairness. Given that Justice as Fairness is inherently stable, all citizens have reason to comply with it.

Rawls's shift from *Theory* to *Political Liberalism* was based on his dissatisfaction with the story above. If we understand the reasons for the shift, then we will understand why Rawls wanted to restrain religious influences in public life. We can also sidestep the considerable confusion about how to interpret Rawls's principle of restraint, the duty of civility, if we understand why Rawls endorses it. If we are clear about why a liberal like Rawls defends restraint, and the character of the restraint he endorsed, then we can explain the general liberal ambivalence about religion in public life.

Rawls came to believe that *Theory*'s idea of a well-ordered society was unrealistic because it assumed that citizens share the ideals associated with Justice as Fairness, namely the conceptions of the good that led citizens to endorse their sense of justice.[24] In order to share these conceptions of the good, members of a well-ordered society must share a common conception of the person[25] and the partially comprehensive philosophical doctrine associated with it.[26] If they do not, then inherent stability will break down. Rawls came to believe that reasonable members of a well-ordered society would not share a common conception of the person because of "the fact of reasonable pluralism." Thus, the fact of reasonable pluralism renders the account of inherent stability in *Theory* unrealistic because it assumes too much agreement among members of a well-ordered society. The fact of reasonable pluralism threatens Rawls's political project.

What is reasonable pluralism? It is the state of a society that obtains when rational, honest and thoughtful individuals disagree about even the most significant matters in life. Rawls believed that reasonable pluralism was the natural "outcome of the free exercise of free human reason under conditions of liberty."[27] Rawls identified the "burdens of judgment" as the cause of reasonable disagreement.[28] Among these burdens are the conflicting and complex evidence we have for our differing views, the challenges we face when weighing differing considerations to arrive at common judgments, the naturally vague and indeterminate political concepts we must employ in discussion and so on.[29] Due to reasonable pluralism, citizens will not converge on a shared conception of the person. Instead, citizens will have many different, but reasonable, conceptions of the good, conceptions of the person and so on. Given the ubiquitous presence of the burdens of judgment, seeking agreement on a conception of the person is a fool's errand. Any account of stability that depends on such agreement is implausible.

The challenge of reasonable pluralism led Rawls to convert Justice as Fairness into a "political conception of justice."[30] A political conception of justice is a set of principles whose normative force does not depend on the truth or unique reasonableness of any one comprehensive doctrine. A political conception thereby provides a focal point on which two or more comprehensive doctrines can converge.[31] In this way, a political conception of justice becomes the object of an "overlapping consensus" when citizens endorse the political conception from within their distinct but reasonable points of view. In a well-ordered society, each reasonable view is "either congruent with, or supportive of, or else not in conflict with, the values appropriate to the special domain of the political as specified by a political conception of justice."[32] The reasons provided by the political conception should "normally outweigh" comprehensive values and principles that might contradict or undermine them.[33] But in general, Rawls hoped that in an overlapping consensus citizens would deny that prioritizing the political renders them disloyal to their comprehensive doctrines.

The idea of a political conception of justice provides a new conception of inherent stability because the political conception is endorsed from a plurality of reasonable perspectives based on differing conceptions of the person. Thus, liberal social institutions are inherently stable, or stable for the right reasons, when the political conception is endorsed by each reasonable comprehensive doctrine.

Like *Theory*, *Political Liberalism*'s account of stability requires that citizens be assured that others will abide by and internalize a public conception of justice. Stability in *Political Liberalism* requires that citizens endorse the political conception based on shared ideals that are "political" and not comprehensive.[34] If members of a well-ordered society find the ideals associated with the political conception worth adopting for their own sake, then they have reason to accept and internalize Justice as Fairness as regulative of their actions, even if they think others may not do the same. For this reason Rawls argues, "[A] political conception assumes a wide role as part of public culture" and contains a "certain conception of citizens as free and equal."[35] The political conception includes at the least an "ideal of citizenship" learned under conditions of "full publicity."[36] In brief, Rawls has given up assuming a shared conception of the *person* for a shared conception of the *citizen*.

Thus, it is critical to the project of *Political Liberalism*, and therefore to Rawls's project as a whole, to flesh out an ideal of democratic citizenship shared by members of a well-ordered society. Such an ideal is critical because it provides citizens with independent reasons to endorse the political conception of justice, rendering stability for the right reasons a feasible social goal.

Rawls maintains that reasonable pluralism does not undermine a shared conception of the citizen. But even so, an assurance problem remains. Rawls must show that in his model of a well-ordered society, citizens will know that (nearly) everyone else accepts the political conception. Widespread suspicion that the political conception is not widely endorsed can undermine assurance, even if no one actually rejects it. For this reason, Rawls postulates that our shared ideal of citizenship requires that we engage in a process of political justification. Liberal democratic citizens seek to justify the use of coercive political power to one another in terms they can reasonably be expected to accept. When citizens do so, they comply with what Rawls calls *the liberal principle of legitimacy*, which holds that political power is justified only when it is compatible with a constitution that all can "endorse in light of principles and ideals acceptable to their common human reason."[37] If citizens follow the principle, then assurance is easier to generate because political justification occurs in commonly accepted terms. In this way, citizens can tell that others affirm the political conception because they act upon and speak in terms of shared political ideals.

When citizens act upon and speak in terms of shared political ideals, Rawls says that they employ *public reasons*, or reasons that reasonable people can accept or share. Public reasons are reasons that are based on shared political values. The use of public reasons provides assurance in two ways. First, by offering one another public reasons, citizens display their commitment to liberal democratic principles because they reason on the basis of the shared values that support those principles. If their political arguments and activities rely primarily on unshared reasons, like religious reasons, citizens suggest to others that their comprehensive reasons are most important and that in cases of conflict, their private, sectarian reasons win out. If they reason in shared terms, they suggest otherwise.[38] But for Rawls, citizens must do more than signal that they prioritize the political over the comprehensive, because citizens rightly prioritize their comprehensive doctrines in many cases. Consequently, the use of public reasons must also demonstrate that citizens do not believe their comprehensive doctrines conflict with the political conception. For Rawls, doubts are "put to rest" when "leaders of the opposing groups . . . present in the public forum how their comprehensive doctrines do indeed affirm [the] values [of the political conception]."³⁹ The use of public reason demonstrates a commitment to the political conception both because citizens appear to accept it and because they are willing and able to illustrate how their comprehensive doctrines warrant that acceptance.

The use of public reasons is governed by the *duty of civility*. The duty of civility is a moral, not legal, duty to provide public reasons in a public forum and to restrain one's use of comprehensive reasons when constitutional essentials are at stake. Before we articulate the principle, it is important to note that Rawls changed the content of the duty twice. He initially took an "exclusive view" of the duty of civility, such that "on fundamental political matters, reasons given explicitly in terms of comprehensive doctrines are never to be introduced into public reason."⁴⁰ Rawls then adopted the "inclusive view," which permits "citizens . . . to present what they regard as the basis of political values rooted in their comprehensive doctrine, provided they do this in ways that strengthen the idea of public reason itself."⁴¹ Rawls later rejected even the inclusive view for the "wide view," which holds that citizens can introduce comprehensive reasons into political discussion so long as "in due course proper political reasons . . . are presented that are sufficient to support whatever the comprehensive doctrines introduced are said to support."⁴² All three versions of the duty of civility were designed such that compliance with the duty will assure citizens that each person affirms the political conception.

Rawls moved towards the wide view because he thought it important that citizens demonstrate the connection they draw between the political conception and their comprehensive doctrines. The wide view permits the use of comprehensive reasons, which gives it an advantage, as "the mutual knowledge of citizens' recognizing one another's reasonable comprehensive doctrines bring[s] out a positive ground for introducing such doctrines."⁴³ The wide view permits diverse procedures for providing assurance. For instance, the wide view permits "reasoning by conjecture" whereby citizens with one reasonable comprehensive doctrine can engage those with distinct and conflicting reasonable comprehensive doctrines on the latter's own terms.⁴⁴ Citizens can reason in private terms to help other citizens to embrace the political conception from their own point of view. This means that the wide view permits the use of religious reasons.

Further, since the wide view permits some appeal to religious reasons, the duty of civility imposes fewer restrictions on religious citizens than it may initially appear. Weithman interprets the wide view to permit citizens to rely on their comprehensive doctrines (including their religious doctrines) "without adducing public reasons in support of their positions, so long as their doing so does not lead others to doubt that they acknowledge the authority of the public conception of justice"; instead, if doubts do not arise, the proviso is *never triggered*.[45] Citizens need only comply with the wide view if they think assurance is genuinely required.[46]

Assuming that the wide view is the proper interpretation of the duty of civility, how does it apply in practice? Rawls is clearest on this matter in his discussion of Martin Luther King, Jr. King's writings demonstrate that his Christian commitments suffused his thoughts and drove his actions. Of significance to Rawls, King often advocated racial equality on explicitly Christian grounds. But Rawls's initial exclusive view of the duty of civility seemed to render King's advocacy inappropriate. Rawls saw this as a disadvantage of the duty of civility because the appeal to Christian doctrine helped to bring about more just laws. Furthermore, it just seems wrong to conclude that King acted in an illiberal fashion, and Rawls wanted his duty of civility to account for that considered judgment. Thus, the wide view permits King and those that follow him to appeal to their comprehensive values in supporting laws and policies.

However, even the wide duty of civility is restrictive: a liberal democratic citizen must be willing and prepared to offer public reasons for her positions on constitutional matters when her allegiance to society's fundamental political principles and institutions is in doubt. Further, she should restrict her use of comprehensive reasons if she is concerned that the law or policy she supports may not turn out to have a political or public ground.[47] Religious reasons, on this model, are second class. They are insufficient to generate political justification. If matters pertaining to constitutional essentials are based merely on comprehensive reasons, then political justification is deficient. Rawls requires citizens to prioritize shared values over comprehensive values. I will discuss how burdensome this is in the next chapter. For now, take note of the fact that the duty of civility places concrete restrictions on the use of comprehensive reasons, including religious reasons.

Rawlsians follow Rawls in restricting political discourse to public or shared reasons. Stephen Macedo is perhaps the most prominent second-generation Rawlsian to affirm a shared reasons standard, and Jonathan

Quong is perhaps the most prominent third-generation Rawls to do the same.[48] Doctrines of restraint vary considerably in content, but the duty of civility is their template. Rawlsians nigh universally accept that our shared conception of the citizen includes a principle akin to the duty of civility. To be a good Rawlsian citizen, one must speak in public terms. She must transcend her sectarian perspective and reason from a public point of view.

III. Four Tensions in the Liberal Approach to Religion in Public Life[49]

Rawls's approach to religion in public life exemplifies the approach of social contract liberalism as a whole: religious influences must be restricted to protect liberal institutions. But there is a good reason to accept this approach, such that the motivation for restraint need not depend upon arbitrary bias or discrimination. Social contract theory requires a conception of stability and, accordingly, assurance mechanisms. These mechanisms will often take the form of civic norms that govern citizens by requiring them to engage in certain lines of conduct. *All* social contract theorists thought that these norms included restrictions on religious influences in politics. For example, Rawls's focus on public reason harkens back to Hobbes and Locke's emphasis on the need for a system of public adjudication of disputes. While Hobbes and Locke did not focus on deliberative duties, they thought that private judgments must be set aside to construct a stable and free political order. And while Rawls allows for more liberty of private religious practice than Hobbes or Locke, he shares their fundamental concern about religious disagreement.

But the common focus on a system of public judgment creates some important tensions in social contract liberalism's approach to religion in public life. Understanding these tensions begins with the recognition that religious reasons play multiple roles in the justification of a social contract. For Hobbes, Locke and Rawls, religious commitments provide reason to *accept* a system of public judgment. They argue that it is rational from each person's private perspective to submit to a public system of adjudication. Thus, they contend that practical rationality requires submission to religious restraint, *even for religious citizens*. Here we meet the first tension in liberalism's approach to religion in public life. According to the social contract liberals,

(1)   Religious citizens are rationally committed to
       transcending their religious commitments.[50]

Social contract theorists believe that some persons can have rational religious beliefs and rationally engage in religious practices, but they maintain that citizens are committed to setting religion aside when it comes to politics. This is not to undermine religion, but to save it. One reason to take a public perspective is to resolve disputes fairly so that citizens can trust that their freedom to live their private lives is protected. But note how odd this is. On the one hand the social contract theorists affirm the rationality of (some) religious belief and defend the freedom to act on religious commitments. On the other hand, they argue that religious citizens are rationally committed to refrain from acting on their religious commitments in the critical social domain of politics. But what if these demands conflict? The social contract theorists maintain that a full examination of the structure of practical rationality will reveal that most conflicts of this sort are illusory.

The second tension concerns the use of political power:

(2)   Religion is best protected if its political power
       and influence is restricted.

Tension (2) may seem less strange than (1), as religious toleration seems to be the best way to defend religious liberty generally. But I submit that this only seems obvious in societies where religious toleration is the norm. From the adherent's perspective, the best way to protect her religion is to ensure its political dominance. With enough power and influence, one's religious view might prevail, with all its attendant benefits. One convincing ground for (2) is purely empirical, namely that real-world protection is best ensured through political toleration. But the deeper liberal ground for (2) is that religion is *morally* protected when its political power and influence is restricted. The social contract theorists expect religious citizens to accept moral limitations on their religious freedom. Only citizens who recognize that the rule of a particular religious sect (even one's own) is oppressive will be willing to restrict the political power of their own religion. Consider an analogy with a moral doctrine. Is it obvious that one's *moral* view is best protected if its adherents ensure that it is not politically dominant?

Liberals wish to both restrict the role of religion in public life and safeguard it at both the institutional level, as embodied in (2), and at the level of individual practical rationality, as embodied in (1). A third tension in liberal thought follows:

(3)   Religious commitment is both a resource
      and threat to liberal institutions.

For the social contract liberal, religious commitment provides part of the justification for liberal institutions, institutions that restrict religious liberty. But she also recognizes that religious commitments can provide citizens with reasons to reject a system of public judgment that may excessively restrict their religious activity, as social contract liberals often see religious believers as especially committed to co-opting political power to promote their own conceptions of transcendent goods (though many secular doctrines may do the same). This disposition threatens to destroy the legitimacy and stability of the social order.

The standard liberal response to (3) is to construct a political order and a conception of citizenship that are neutral among religious commitments and often override them. The liberal hope is to create a shared space within which all citizens can resolve their disagreements. If so, liberals can neutralize the threat of religious commitment, while still drawing on it to create and sustain liberal institutions. This is why liberals want a neutral or *secular* (essentially nonreligious) political realm. The state must be largely devoid of religious influences if it is to serve as a neutral arbiter. Few liberals believe that the creation of a shared political space requires that the state restrict religious speech and expression. Instead, the restrictions are part of the ethics of citizenship, an ethic to which all citizens are rationally committed. We arrive at an explanation for the popular liberal tropes about the separation of church and state and the privatization of religion, generating our fourth and final tension:

(4)   Religious citizens are rationally committed
      to a secular public sphere and secular state.

This tension is explicit in Locke and Rawls. The father of liberalism and the father of public reason agree that the best response to religious disagreement is to privatize religion. Public reason is both the fruit of religious disagreement and an attempt to master it. Public reason liberalism is both Western religion's child and king.

IV. Public Reason Liberalism—Its Contemporary Structure

We now shift gears. Rawls's *Political Liberalism* is simply the first and most prominent member of what is today called *public reason* or justificatory liberalism.[51] Public reason liberalism holds that state coercion is permitted only when each person has sufficient reason to accept it. When all citizens have such reasons, the coercion in question is *publicly justified*. Let's unpack this idea.

The family of public reason liberal political theories can be categorized in accord with a master principle that I call the *Public Justification Principle* (PJP), defined as follows:

> *Public Justification Principle (PJP)*: A coercive law L is justified only if each member *I* of the public P has some sufficient reason(s) R_i to endorse L.[52]

The Public Justification Principle contains many aspects open to various interpretations, but I shall cover six: (i) grain of coercion, (ii) conception of legitimacy and authority, (iii) scope of the public, i.e. those subject to coercion, (iv) conception of sufficiency, (v) conception of justificatory reasons and (vi) conception of idealization.[53] The specification of the Public Justification Principle will vary according to the value of these variables.

Let me make two things clear before I proceed. First, throughout the rest of the chapter I offer only a *generic characterization* of public reason views. I do not defend my own interpretation of public reason until Chapter 4. So in this chapter and the next I also outline how the Public Justification Principle varies among public reason liberals. I need to provide a characterization of public reason general enough to show that the tradition has been widely misunderstood even by its proponents, so I cannot be too specific in characterizing the view lest I leave out some major figures.

Second, contrary to what some claim, public justification is implicitly understood as a social *state* achieved when coercive actions bear a certain relation to those coerced. Specifically, public justification is a three-place relation between the object of justification, the subject of justification and the justifiers in question (a relation between a law, a person and her reasons to accept the law). Many understand the idea of public justification as a process (typically a deliberative process) by which citizens present reasons to others as justifications. That is *not* the most general specification of the idea of public justification. Instead, it is simply one way to understand how the Public Justification Principle is satisfied or how a public justification is brought about. Public justifications may be brought about in other ways as well (see Ch. 5, Sec. VI, for a discussion of three other methods). It is for this reason that I will often speak of a law being publicly justified *for* a person rather than *to* a person, as the notion of a law being publicly justified *to* a person suggests an actual act of justification. For a law to be publicly justified, no such act needs to take place.

(i) Public reason liberals universally assume that members of a publicly justified political order can agree on a sufficient number of paradigmatic cases of coercion to engage in public justification. However, there is an important issue concerning the thickness or grain of the coercion that must be addressed. Rawls holds that public justification applies merely to "constitutional essentials" and that public justification is required only when "basic questions of justice" are at stake.[54] But Jonathan Quong argues that public justification applies first and foremost to laws, a more finely grained unit of coercion.[55] Gerald Gaus holds that the justification of coercion applies to laws that lack "strong interactive effects" with other laws.[56] I have articulated the Public Justification Principle in terms of laws with the L variable, but L can be read at a coarser grain to apply only to constitutional essentials.

(ii) Rawls understands the idea of public justification as part of the theory of legitimacy. For Rawls, a regime is legitimate when its use of coercive political power is at least morally permissible.[57] Thus, when a law is publicly justified to a member of the public, the state is morally permitted to apply the law to that member. On the traditional Hohfeldian scheme, A has a liberty-right (or privilege) to φ if and only if A has no duty not to φ. So when law L is publicly justified, state A has a liberty-right to impose L on member of the public B. Other public reason liberals take a stronger view, holding that when a law is publicly justified, those coerced also have a duty to comply with the coercion.[58] Thus when law L is publicly justified to a member of the public, the state has a claim-right to coercion. On the traditional Hohfeldian scheme, A has a claim-right that B φ if and only if B has a duty to A to φ.[59] In this way, public justification is thought to concern political authority. I take it that A has authority over B to demand that B φ just when A has a claim-right that B φ. Thus, to publicly justify a law to B is to show that state A has a claim that B comply with law L such that B has a duty to the state (or perhaps to the body politic, rather than the government specifically) to comply with L.

Note that the Public Justification Principle does not refer to legitimacy or authority. Instead, it identifies when a law is *justified*, so it is silent on exactly what normative statuses are involved. As we have seen, it is neutral about whether the state merely has a liberty-right to coerce or whether it has a claim-right to coerce.[60] What's more, it is silent on whether subjects must merely comply with the coercion applied to them or whether they have a duty to refrain from interfering with coercion the state justifiably applies to others.

In the book, I will focus on the public justification of claim-rights held by the state to coercively impose publicly justified law because I see public reason liberalism as an attempt to explain how free and equal persons can have authority over one another. Since I am only concerned with the justification of legal claim-rights, I will use both terms "legitimacy" and "authority" to refer to claim-rights. So throughout the book, when I say that law L is justified for a person, I mean that the law is legitimate and authoritative because citizens are obligated to comply with it.

For what it is worth, I personally think that public justification also entails that those other than the coerced individual have duties to permit the state to coerce that citizen and to permit the citizen to comply with the coercion in question. Since laws typically apply to a large group, such deference is required partly out of equality and reciprocity: publicly justified law is a great good, and people will rationally want to insist on the same amount of deference from that citizen when it comes to the application of the law to them. Furthermore, I think public justification generates decisive duties, ones that are not overridden by competitors, for since public justification occurs in terms of sufficient reasons, contrary reasons do not override them. If a law is publicly justified for a member of the public, John, and the law requires that John engage in some action Φ, then John has an undefeated duty to Φ.

Now, let me stress once more that public reason liberals typically say much less about what it means for a law to be publicly justified. So for the purposes of the book, I shall remain officially neutral about whether public justification requires mutual deference or generates decisive duties.[61] The book is not intended to settle the matter.

(iii) The scope of the public determines which persons are the subjects of justification for coercion. By and large, public reason liberals consider the public to include all members of a traditional nation-state. This is largely due to the need to simplify but also due to what some identify as an implicit nationalism within the public reason tradition. For instance, Rawls is well known for confining his theory of justice to members of a nation to which no one could be added or subtracted except by birth or death, though he later developed an account of public justification for international groups.[62] There is also controversy concerning whether future generations are parties to public justification, and if so, how they should be built into the relevant justificatory model. I shall leave these issues aside by focusing on present adult members of a nation-state. My main line of argument does not depend on how I answer this question.

(iv) On public reason liberalism, a coercive law L is justified when members of the public have *sufficient* reason to endorse L. But the concept of sufficiency can be cashed out in different ways. At a minimum, sufficient reasons must be undefeated.[63] A reason R is sufficient for X only if X lacks other reasons that rebut or undercut reason R. But a sufficient reason must be more than an undefeated reason, as reason R may not favor an endorsement of the law. For example, I may lack a defeater reason for a law that bans my marketing raw milk, but that does not mean I have sufficient reason to endorse the law that bans marketing raw milk. I simply lack reasons that count for *or* against the law.[64] Sufficient reasons, then, rationally *require* endorsement. Despite the importance of the idea of sufficiency, few public reason liberals provide an account of it. Gaus is the most prominent exception, understanding sufficiency in terms of open justification, which holds that a reason is sufficient when it can be derived via sound methods of inference from our present beliefs and value affirmations.[65] I shall understand sufficiency in terms of epistemic justification later on (Ch. 4, Sec. I), but for now I set epistemological issues aside.

Sufficient reasons must also be understood as driving the endorsement of a law against a coherent alternative. The standard alternative is to have *no law at all* regulating the issue in question. For instance, if we ask whether a law prohibiting the use and sale of marijuana is publicly justified, we ask whether it is publicly justified with respect to having no law regulating the use and sale of marijuana. If the sufficient reasons of members of the public hold that a law regulating the use and sale of marijuana is superior to no law at all, then the law may be publicly justified. Note that I say the law *may* be justified, because there may be other competing laws that members of the public also regard as superior to no law at all. In that case, either law may be publicly justified. In cases of a conflict between two laws superior to no law, public reason liberals typically appeal to social decision procedures (see Ch. 3, Sec. IV, and Ch. 5, Sec. VI for further discussion).[66]

(v) A justificatory reason is a reason that counts toward the justification of a law or policy. Justificatory reasons are not by themselves sufficient reasons. Instead, justificatory reasons are all and only those reasons that can enter into the process of public justification, i.e., the assessment of reasons that count for or against a law. Thus, justificatory reasons may fail to be sufficient; and, importantly, they may even serve as defeater reasons for proposed laws.

A conception of justificatory reasons specifies the variable R_i in the Public Justification Principle by identifying a subset of the set of reasons possessed by each individual member of the public I. To clarify, suppose that there are only two members of the public, John and Reba, and that they each have sets of reasons, John with set $J = \{J_1 \ldots J_n\}$ and Reba with set $R = \{R_1 \ldots R_n\}$. A conception of justificatory reasons is a *subset* of the conjunction of set J and set R. The narrowest conception of justificatory reasons, the shared reasons standard, identifies as justificatory the reasons found in both sets J and R, that is, reasons with the same content.[67] For example, perhaps John and Reba both have reason to support a policy banning the sale of raw milk. In that case, their reason to support the ban is shared. All other conceptions of justificatory reasons are broader than the shared reasons, though they all exclude *some* of a person's personal reasons.

Public reason liberals disagree about the appropriate conception of justificatory reasons. The overwhelmingly dominant conception of reasons is the *consensus* conception, which depends either on the *shared* reasons requirement or the *accessible* reasons requirement.[68] In contrast to the shared reasons requirement, the accessible reasons requirement holds that the set of justificatory reasons members of the public regard as justified for one another be based on common evaluative standards.[69] An accessible reason might be drawn from a scientific theory that all can evaluate, but all do not accept, such as climate change models that generate specific predictions about how much, say, sea levels will rise due to increased carbon emissions. In these cases, accessibility requirements identify a larger set of reasons as justificatory than shared reasons requirements.

The *convergence* conception, by contrast, holds that the set of justificatory reasons includes all reasons that citizens can see as justified for some member of the public according to her own evaluative standards, even if other members of the public do not accept those evaluative standards. On this *intelligible* reasons requirement, a reason can be justificatory even if some members of the public believe it is based on false evaluative standards. For instance, some atheist members of the public will reject as invalid reasons based on divine revelation. But they may still regard revelation as a reasonable, if false, evaluative standard. On convergence, then, reasons based on divine revelation can count as justificatory, whereas on consensus revelatory reasons lack justificatory status.

So when I contrast consensus and convergence *liberalism*, I'm contrasting variants of public reason liberalism that adopt consensus and convergence conceptions of justificatory reasons respectively.[70]

(vi) A reason can only be justificatory if a member of the public would endorse it at the right level of *idealization*, as described by the P variable. Idealization is the practice of identifying citizens' reasons based on adequate information and inference. I understand idealization in terms of members' *belief-value set*. An agent's belief-value set includes all of her beliefs, desires, goals and plans, i.e., everything she thinks and wants.[71] An agent is idealized when theorists change the beliefs, desires, goals and/or plans in her belief-value set according to some criteria. Theorists typically alter belief-value sets along two dimensions, rationality and information; that is, they alter the informational sets and rational capacities of members of the public when determining what reasons they have. For example, Rawls's veil of ignorance models members of the public by blocking information from their deliberations that would undermine their impartiality.[72] Jürgen Habermas accepts deliberative conditions without such abstract idealization, instead favoring constraining the form of discourse between actual individuals.[73] David Gauthier endorses a bargaining scenario where individuals know the characteristics of persons but are unaware of which person they are.[74]

Idealization is typically employed on the grounds that an individual's justificatory reasons may differ from the reasons she actually affirms, as her actual affirmations are likely based on poor information, flawed reasoning and incoherent beliefs and desires. The actual affirmation view is sometimes termed justificatory populism.[75] Populist conceptions of idealization are widely regarded as flawed, since people can "withhold their assent because of obstinacy, selfishness, laziness, perversity, or confusion."[76] Actual consent theorists accept populist views. In response, public reason liberals tend to *radically* idealize.[77] They rid belief-value sets of *all* rational inconsistencies and relevant ignorance. In this way, radical idealization pushes the rationality and information dimensions to their upper bound. The other-worldly quality of radical idealization has raised concerns.[78] In response, some public reason liberals defend moderate idealization, a set of standards that permit errors and ignorance to remain in members' belief-value sets.[79]

Yet regardless of whether public reason liberals embrace radical or moderate conceptions of idealization, they all idealize citizens as *reasonable*.[80] The idea of the reasonable is typically understood as a disposition to engage in reciprocal interactions with others, following norms if others will too, and recognizing that reasonable people disagree.[81] The issue of reasonableness is somewhat vexed, as it is arguably the most abused term of art in the public reason literature. But, perhaps surprisingly, I do not think many of the issues addressed in this book depend on a particular conception of reasonableness, so long as that conception is suitably modest. For this reason, I will defer a discussion of reasonableness to Chapter 5, Section I.

Finally, note that the Public Justification Principle only specifies a restriction on the use of coercion. It does not explain why coercion is undesirable or how to remedy unjustified coercion. A number of normative principles might provide an explanation, such as a consequentialist norm that requires that unjustified coercion be minimized in the name of promoting well-being. I adopt a presumption in favor of liberty (and against coercion) as the relevant supplementary principle. What I shall call the Liberty Principle is usefully specified, following Feinberg's formulation, as follows:

> *The Liberty Principle*: Liberty should be the norm . . . coercion always needs some special justification. Unjustified coercion is pro tanto wrong.[82]

The Liberty Principle explains why coercion is undesirable and what to do about unjustified coercion: unjustified coercion is pro tanto wrong, and it should therefore cease in the absence of justification. The point of the Liberty Principle is to further explain the normative force of the

Public Justification Principle. Its normative power is that it explains the only way to meet the presumption in favor of liberty; the presumption is met when a coercive law is publicly justified.

The conception of liberty at work in the Liberty Principle is negative liberty. That the Liberty Principle is based on negative liberty should not render it controversial, as it does not forestall a role for other forms of liberty in public reason liberalism. The reason to adopt the Liberty Principle is simply the intuition that people should not have their negative liberty restricted without a good reason (or in our case, a justificatory reason). A good reason might be that the restriction of negative liberty might promote some other form of freedom. Therefore, by embracing the Liberty Principle, public reason liberals are not barred from regarding other forms of freedom as valuable or independently plausible.

The Liberty Principle has many prominent defenders, including Rawls. Rawls endorses a presumption in favor of liberty in his liberal principle of legitimacy; while he does not use the term coercion in *Political Liberalism*, he refers to "political action," which he understands as a form of coercive power, since "political power is always coercive power."[83] Given that political power is coercive power, Rawls clearly endorses a presumption against the use of coercion. And Rawls explicitly endorses such a presumption in *Justice as Fairness*, where he writes that "there is a general presumption against imposing legal and other restrictions on conduct without a sufficient reason."[84] Some liberals who reject the Public Justification Principle also endorse a version of the Liberty Principle. Stanley Benn defends a presumption against interference, claiming that "the burden of justification falls on the interferer, not on the person interfered with."[85] We can add Feinberg to this list as well.[86]

V. Why Public Reason?

All defenses of public reason liberalism appeal to three basic moral concepts: (i) liberty, (ii) equality and (iii) respect for persons. Liberalism has always assumed that persons are naturally free and equal in the sense that no one is born under the natural authority of others. As Locke famously claimed, "The *natural liberty* of man is to be free from any superior power on earth, and not to be under the will or legislative authority of man. . . ."[87] Rawls follows Locke in assuming that persons are "free and equal" in precisely this way.[88] In this way, both classical and contemporary liberals assume that persons are equal because they share this natural liberty to act as they see fit. Liberals also assume that persons have an intrinsic worth that merits respect. Recognizing their worth also means accepting their natural freedom and equality.

Based on this conception of the natural freedom, equality and worth of persons, liberals develop a theory about how equals can respectfully restrict each other's freedom. The social contract liberals argued that coercive laws must be justified from each person's point of view. Recognizing our fellows as free and equal means recognizing them as persons to whom a justification is owed. The public reason liberal argues that the Public Justification Principle provides the best interpretation of this ideal of mutual justification. Equals can respectfully restrict the natural freedom of their fellows only if those restrictions are publicly justified. Thus, Christopher Eberle, a prominent critic of public reason views, rightfully claims that "[r]espect for others requires public justification of coercion: that is the clarion call of [public reason] liberalism."[89] Stephen Macedo, one of the most prominent political liberals, rightly claims that the project of public justification is the "moral lodestar of liberalism," as a political tradition rooted in the recognition of persons as naturally free and equal and worthy of respect.[90]

Defenses of the Public Justification Principle conjoin the moral concepts of liberty, equality and respect with the recognition of reasonable pluralism. Reasonable pluralism is taken to motivate our need to justify coercion to others by their own lights. Since free societies display reasonable pluralism, many of our fellow citizens will substantially disagree about what is right and good. Consequently, we cannot simply appeal to our own reasons as sound justifications for coercion. Instead, we must appeal to the distinct reasons of others. Thus, reasonable pluralism motivates the need to address unique justifications to others.

Yet nearly all contemporary liberal political philosophers accept that persons are naturally free and equal and that coercion requires a justification. Public reason liberals are distinguished by their claim that the justification must be *public*. Why is this? The basic thought is that unless others can see for themselves the reason that they are being coerced, the coercion is authoritarian and disrespectful. Consider Gaus, who argues that "a moral order of free persons rejects appeal to the natural authority of some people's private judgments over those of others." In contrast, a moral order that allows an elite to make moral demands that other free and equal persons cannot see reason to acknowledge "is *authoritarian.*"[91] While Gaus here speaks of moral demands generally, what he says holds for coercion as well. For Gaus, there is a deep connection between whether coercion is authoritarian and disrespectful and whether those coerced can comprehend and accept the reasons for the demand. If John forces Reba not to sell raw milk, and she can recognize no reason to comply with his request, then John simply browbeats and oppresses her.[92] Coercive laws must somehow have rational uptake with citizens if they are to be compatible with citizens' freedom, equality and worth. Thus, in general, the reason that the justification of coercion among free and equal persons must be public is because those coerced must recognize the coercion as valid if such coercion is to be compatible with the natural equality of persons.[93]

A small point before moving forward. Common arguments for the Public Justification Principle to some extent elide an additional foundational question about whether it is an objective moral principle or based in some process of construction. Rawls, perhaps the most famous constructivist, bases the requirement of public justification on our shared conception of ourselves as free and equal (first as persons, then as citizens).[94] Rawls does not want his conception of justice and legitimacy to rule out realist groundings or realist views of ethics and politics in general.[95] But the normative force of public justification derives from our shared ideas and conceptions, according to his view. Charles Larmore has provided the most prominent moral realist grounding for public reason liberalism. For Larmore, a commitment to publicly justifying coercion rests "upon a principle of respect for persons whose validity must be understood as antecedent to the democratic will."[96]

VI. Public Reason Liberalism's Approach to Religion in Public Life

The standard public reason approach to religion in public life holds that citizens must refrain from employing religious reasons as bases for political deliberation and decision making, or at least subordinate religious reasoning to secular or shared (i.e., public) reasoning. Thus, public reason liberals nigh universally hold that good liberal democratic citizens will restrain themselves from offering and acting upon religious reasons in public life. Restraint comes in two strengths—prohibition and subordination. Some principles of restraint prohibit the use of religious reasons, whereas weaker principles merely require that citizens subordinate religious reasoning to public reasoning. Restraint has two general domains of application, discourse and action. Restraint might restrict religiously based speech or it may prohibit citizens from acting on religious reasons when they organize or vote. Restraint only applies to the public sphere, not private life. No public reason liberal imposes restraint on discussions or actions that do not bear directly on political decisions. Rawls's duty of civility scores well on all these dimensions. It subordinates the use of religious reasoning to public reasoning in both discourse and action, but only when constitutional matters are at stake.

Restraint is tied to the consensus conception of reasons. All present principles of restraint restrict the use of *private* reasons, i.e., reasons that are neither shared nor accessible.[97] These principles waver between principles that prioritize shared reasons and more permissive principles that appeal to accessible reasons.[98] The primary reason that restraint and consensus are so tightly tied together is that most public reason liberals think that shared and accessible reasons exhaust the category of public reasons. Public reasons *just are* shared or accessible reasons, depending on the theorist. Thus, if respect for persons requires the public justification of coercion, then in deliberation, justification must proceed in public, that is, shared or accessible, terms. Consider Rawls again as an exemplar. The duty of civility requires that citizens prioritize the use of reasons drawn from the political conception of justice, i.e., reasons drawn from shared political values. The duty of civility permits the use of comprehensive reasons only if the proposals they support can be justified in purely political (shared) terms.

Principles of restraint do not single out religious reasons; instead, they bar appeal to all private or "comprehensive" reasons. In Rawls-speak, this means that liberal democratic citizens may not solely rely on reasons derived from their comprehensive doctrines. In broader terms, restraint bars or restricts appeal to any unshared or inaccessible reason, depending on the principle in question. Religious reasons are restricted indirectly because, as a matter of course, religious reasons appear unshared and inaccessible in religiously diverse societies. Thus, in one sense, restraint is not about religion at all. However, in practice restraint applies most prominently to religious citizens because the reasons they appeal to are less likely to be shared or accessible than the reasons appealed to by secular citizens.[99]

Defenses of restraint appeal to the Public Justification Principle and the conceptions of freedom, equality and respect on which it is based. A common argument for restraint runs as follows: because we recognize that we are all free and equal but reasonably disagree about conceptions of the good, we should speak to one another in public terms. Charles Larmore adds instructive detail to this common argument by claiming that restraint is a corollary of the Public Justification Principle. If we should not impose coercive laws on others unless they have sufficient reason to accept them, then we should not appeal to reasons they reject when we make our case for the laws in question. Larmore:

> In discussing how to resolve some problem (for example, what principles of political association they should adopt), people should respond to points of disagreement by retreating to neutral ground, to the beliefs they still share in order either to (a) resolve the disagreement and vindicate one of the disputed positions by means of arguments that proceed from this common ground, or (b) bypass the disagreement and seek a solution of the problem on the basis simply of this common ground.[100]

When citizens reasonably disagree, they should speak in common terms out of mutual respect. A good citizen understands that others reject doctrines she holds dear. If she is to treat them as equals, she must speak to them in terms they can both accept or at least understand.

But an astute critic of restraint will detect a gulf between the requirement of public justification and restrictions on deliberation. The fact that laws must be publicly justified tells us nothing about what citizens can talk about by itself. Arguments for restraint frequently overlook the distinction between public justification and public *deliberation*. As we have seen, public justification is essentially a relation between persons, laws and reasons—a social state that obtains when each person has sufficient reason to endorse a law. But most public reason liberals identify public justification with the *process* of deliberatively justifying our preferred political proposals. Jonathan Quong draws this connection when he claims that "the idea of public reason entails a particular version of *democratic deliberation*," which occurs when both citizens and officials advocate political proposals only when they genuinely think that their decisions are justifiable based on "considerations that each person can reasonably endorse in their capacity as a free and equal citizen, that is, they only support laws that can be justified by appeal to *public reasons*."[101] But public deliberation and public justification must be connected by *argument*, rather than by definition; and public reason liberals rarely set the argument out in detail.

I believe that the standard public reason approach to religion in public life is based on a tie between deliberation and justification that has yet to receive adequate articulation. From what I can tell, public reason liberals implicitly defend the connection on two grounds. The first argument is stability based: speaking and acting upon public reasons helps to promote social stability of some sort. Micah Schwartzman holds that restraint promotes the public justification of laws. For Schwartzman, citizens should be *sincere* by offering public reasons for their positions because "sincerity is an important condition of public deliberation . . . and deliberation is necessary to evaluate, criticize and improve the quality of public justifications."[102] Ideally, citizens and public officials should be able to determine which laws are publicly justified. Schwartzman's principle of restraint is meant to aid this process, which in turn promotes stability for the right reasons.[103] Christopher Eberle analyzes two stability-based arguments, the "Argument from Bosnia" and the "Argument from Divisiveness." These arguments claim that without restraint, liberal democratic societies will experience social disruption, disharmony, or perhaps even religious strife and warfare.[104] Thus, restraint promotes public justification by providing for social stability as such, and not merely stability for the right reasons.[105]

The second type of argument is based on respect for persons and takes two forms. The first form maintains that a commitment to the Public Justification Principle conceptually entails a principle of restraint. An argument of this sort might hold that the ideal of public justification can only be achieved through deliberation in terms of public reasons. If so, restraint will serve as a constitutive means towards public justification. One could read Larmore in this way. The goal of public justification is to ensure that the shared justification for each law is laid bare and widely accepted. Reaching this goal requires retreating to neutral ground in the face of reasonable disagreement, not merely as an instrumental means but as a proper part of the justificatory process.[106] Another form of respect-based argument derives restraint directly from respect for persons, bypassing the Public Justification Principle itself. On this view, respect for persons both requires that laws be publicly justified and that citizens engage in mutual justification in public terms. On the latter view, the Public Justification Principle does not entail restraint, but the ground for it, respect for persons, entails a principle of restraint. I am not aware of anyone who understands him or herself as making this claim, however, so I will set it aside.[107] If respect requires deliberative restraint, it is widely thought to do so by means of the Public Justification Principle.

My main point is that restraint is grounded in the Public Justification Principle. A commitment to public justification is widely assumed to include a commitment to deliberating about the use of state power in terms of shared or accessible (public) reasons. The standard public reason approach to religion in public life, then, is characterized by restraint on the use of religious reasons. The approach is well motivated given the structure of public reason liberalism. The priority that public reason liberals often assign to shared and often secular bases of reasoning therefore need not be motivated by some secularist bias, but merely by a commitment to public justification.[108]

We can now see that public reason liberalism's approach to religion in public life is characteristic of the liberal tradition. Accordingly, it contains the same four tensions in its approach to religion in public life. On the standard interpretation of the Public Justification Principle,

(1) Religious citizens are rationally committed to transcending their religious commitments.
(2) Religion is best protected if its political power and influence is restricted.
(3) Religious commitment is both a resource and threat to liberal institutions.
(4) Religious citizens are rationally committed to a secular public sphere and secular state.

First, public reason liberalism follows liberalism in maintaining that religious citizens are rationally committed to transcending their religious commitments despite having sufficient reason to affirm their religious beliefs and values. In other words, religious citizens are both required to act in accord with their religious convictions *and* to engage in religious restraint. Public reason is grounded in a moral requirement of respect for persons as free and equal. Public reason liberals believe, therefore, that any rational moral agent will acknowledge the great weight of this imperative. And the best conception of respect for persons requires that citizens not coerce one another without public justification, which in turn requires religious restraint.

Religious citizens are also committed to restraint in virtue of the fact that restraint promotes their ends. If religious citizens are willing to set aside their sectarian proposals for coercion, then they can rightfully demand that others do the same and so protect their religious liberty. If religious groups co-opt the state to promote their own goals, then they create a divisive political culture that will ultimately make them worse off. Alternatively, if religious citizens will lay down their political arms, then the liberal state will protect their freedoms against those who would limit them. Public reason liberalism in this way reflects the second tension in liberal thought because the bonds of public reason ensure respect for religious freedom.

Consequently, public reason treats religion as a resource and a threat in both theory and practice. Public justification must be compatible with citizens' religious reasons for citizens to converge on laws from diverse religious and secular points of view. Thus, religious considerations can contribute to public justification. However, religious commitments may also defeat the case for liberal laws and policies, as religious citizens may have reason to reject liberal institutions. So religious reasons can strengthen and weaken commitment to liberal institutions. Religious reasoning can both sustain and erode practical support for liberal institutions as well. Sometimes religious political activism promotes publicly justified laws, such as religious political activity during the civil rights movement. Yet religious political activism might impose illiberal laws perhaps like those defended by the American religious right.[109]

This conflicted attitude towards religion in public life leads public reason liberals to conclude that even religious citizens should embrace a largely secular public sphere. Restraint requires that citizens sideline or subordinate their use of religious reasons in public life, thereby stripping public discourse of religious voices. The second-class justificatory status of religious reasons may also require religious citizens to accept a secular state that is insensitive to their distinctively religious complaints. This is puzzling. Shouldn't religious citizens attempt to politically institutionalize their faith commitments? Not so, say public reason liberals. Instead, the *opposite* is true: religious citizens must aid the secularization of their own political institutions.

VII. Conclusion

We have seen that public reason liberals are the direct descendants of the social contract tradition. They retain its tolerant yet privatizing spirit. And while public reason's religious critics often argue that its approach to religion in public life issues from secularist bias, it is well-motivated by public reason liberalism's foundational values and theoretical framework. In order to undermine the case for restraint, therefore, we must do more than insist that public reason liberals play fair. We must surgically alter public reason liberalism's skeletal structure.

We now turn to religious criticisms of public reason. Religious critics claim that restraint inequitably burdens religious citizens and violates their integrity. I argue that these objections are successful, though only against restraint, not the Public Justification Principle. This mixed result motivates the search for a new interpretation of the Public Justification Principle that can rescue public reason liberalism (and indeed, liberalism itself) from these powerful objections.

Notes

1. Nagel 1991, p. 216.
2. Macedo 2000b, p. 35.
3. Rawls 2005, pp. xxv–xxvi.
4. Philpott 2001, p. 81.
5. There is some question about this. See Amartya Sen's discussion of toleration in India under the rule of Ashoka in the third century B.C. Sen 2011, pp. 75–7.
6. For standard examples of the "intolerance" of social contract liberals, see Hobbes 1994 [1668], pp. 411–88; Locke 2003 [1690], p. 245; Rousseau 1997 [1762], p. 151. Pincus 2009 contends that only some forms of Catholicism were deemed intolerable in seventeenth- and eighteen-century England.
7. There is a notable absence of concern with political implications of disagreement throughout the great works of political philosophers, even into the seventeenth century. Pierre Bayle and Roger Williams stand out as rare exceptions. See Bayle 2000, p. 235; Williams 2008.
8. Hobbes 1994, p. 23.
9. Ibid., p. 490.
10. Gaus 2012.
11. Locke 2003, p. 327.
12. Ibid., p. 137.
13. See Wolterstorff 1996, pp. 118–33 for a discussion of Locke's religious epistemology.
14. Perhaps Rousseau's most well-known take on the separation of politics and religion can be found in Book IV, Chapter 8 of *The Social Contract*. See Rousseau 1997, pp. 142–51. I find Kant's view considerably more complicated. For a recent overview, see DiCenso 2011.
15. Rawls 2005, pp. xv–xvi.
16. Weithman 2010, p. 44.
17. Ibid., p. 45. In *Political Liberalism*, inherent stability becomes stability for the right reasons. Rawls 2005, p. xli. I shall use these terms interchangeably.
18. Weithman 2010, p. 44.

19. Rawls 1971, p. 436.
20. Ibid., p. 498. I employ the idea of congruence for my own purposes in Ch. 3, Sec. IV.
21. Weithman 2010, p. 67.
22. Rawls 1971, p. 336.
23. Weithman 2010, p. 64; Rawls 1971, p. 103.
24. Weithman 2010, pp. 234–69; Rawls 1971, Sec. 86.
25. Rawls 1999, p. 293.
26. Rawls 2005, p. xviii. Broadly speaking, a comprehensive doctrine is similar to a worldview or a philosophy of life.
27. Ibid., p. 144.
28. Ibid., p. 54.
29. Ibid., pp. 56–7.
30. Ibid., p. 134.
31. Ibid., p. xix.
32. Ibid., p. 169.
33. Ibid., p. 156.
34. Weithman 2010, p. 271.
35. Rawls 2005, p. 71.
36. Ibid., p. 71.
37. Ibid., p. 137.
38. I first argued for this claim in Thrasher and Vallier 2013, but see Ch. 2, Sec. VI.
39. Ibid., p. 249.
40. Rawls 2005, p. 247.
41. Ibid.
42. Rawls 1999, p. 591.
43. Ibid., p. 593.
44. Ibid., p. 594.
45. Weithman 2010, p. 330.
46. Ibid., p. 331.
47. It is possible to read the duty of civility as only requiring that citizens offer comprehensive reasons for proposals that will eventually turn out *in objective fact* to be supportable based on public reasons alone, but on such an objectivist reading, the duty would ratify political behavior based on factors inaccessible to citizens' cognitive faculties. For this reason it is more plausible to read Rawls as claiming that citizens can offer comprehensive reasons for proposals that *they reasonably believe* will turn out to be supportable based on public reasons alone.
48. Macedo 2000a, p. 37; Quong 2011, Ch. 9.
49. I shall refer to the "liberal approach" to religion in public life without specifying that I am talking about the liberalism of the social contract or Rawlsian liberalism. I acknowledge that there are liberals, like John Stuart Mill, who did not base liberalism on a social contract. Further, Hobbes is a paradigmatic social contract theorist but a proto-liberal at best.
50. To put it more precisely, if less elegantly, religious citizens are committed to what follows clearly from what they justifiably hold to, namely to transcending their religious commitments. I thank Robert Audi for this point.
51. The term "justificatory liberalism" derives from Gaus 1996.

52. I phrase the Public Justification Principle as a necessary condition on the use of coercion. While I think it is also a sufficient condition, none of my arguments require me to endorse this latter claim. I thank Danny Shahar and Chad Van Schoelandt for this point.
53. One variable concerns the type of practical reasoning, or a conception of the telos of public justification, such as reaching agreement, a bargain or an evolutionary equilibrium. I will discuss this matter in Ch. 5, Sec. VI.
54. Rawls 2005, p. 140.
55. Quong 2011, pp. 233–50.
56. Gaus 2011, p. 495. Gaus also links interactive effects with "justificatory dependency," a related standard. For an extended discussion of grain, see Lister 2010.
57. Rawls 2005, p. 137.
58. Gaus 2011, pp. 465–70. Gaus argues that publicly justified states also have normative powers to create duties, but I leave that complexity aside here.
59. Wenar 2010. The existence of a claim-right entails the permission to coercion, or in Hohfeldian terms, a liberty-right to coercion.
60. For a discussion of the relationship between political authority and the duty to obey the law, see Raz 1986, pp. 99–105.
61. Given these foundations, a natural worry about my view is why we should make such a big deal about justifying coercion when we must also justify authority. What explains why they go together? The short answer is that I think the best foundations of public reason begin by publicly justifying *moral authority* and then showing how coercion must be justified insofar as members of the public want the coercion they use against one another to have moral authority. This also implies that if we wish to coerce *without* moral authority, we may not need to publicly justify that coercion. I think such cases are rare with respect to the vast majority of human beings, since our moral emotions lead us to care that our demands have authority over others. The view in the literature most like my own is Gaus's authority-based defense of the right against legal coercion. See Gaus 2011, pp. 479–90. Since this book concerns the justification of coercion and not moral authority generally, I shall leave these complex issues to the side. I thank Mark Murphy and Chad Van Schoelandt for pressing me for specifics on these matters.
62. Rawls 2002.
63. Pollock and Cruz 1986 has an excellent discussion of epistemic defeaters, or reasons or beliefs that undermine or rebut the epistemic justification of other reasons or beliefs.
64. This distinction might collapse if we recognize that moralizing or enforcement always has a cost in virtue of depriving someone of an option. If so, we always need endorsement-favoring reasons to outweigh the cost. I thank Chad Van Schoelandt for this point.
65. Gaus 1996, p. 30. Gaus has since moved beyond open justification to a more social conception of sufficiency. See Gaus 2011, pp. 244–50.
66. On the use of decision procedures in public reason, also see Gaus 1996, esp. Ch. 11 and Ch. 13.
67. Jon Quong appears to go further, arguing that not all shared reasons are public reasons, only shared reasons derived from liberal political values. Quong 2011, p. 180.

68. D'Agostino 1996, p. 30 restricts consensus views to the shared reasons standard, but I shall use the term more broadly to include the accessible reasons standard as well. See Ch. 4, Sec. I. For further discussion see Nagel 1987, p. 232; Eberle 2002, pp. 252–86.
69. I will further distinguish the shareability and accessibility requirements in Ch. 4, Sec. I.
70. Though also coupled with a conception of idealization, convergence liberalism adopts both an intelligibility requirement and a moderate degree of idealization. See Ch. 5 for a defense of moderate idealization.
71. The notion of a belief-value set derives from Bernard Williams's conception of a subjective motivational set. See Williams 1981, p. 102.
72. Rawls 1971, p. 118.
73. Habermas 1999, p. 198. Deliberative conditions must be free, in particular, of inequalities of power.
74. Gauthier 1986, p. 245.
75. Eberle 2002, p. 200.
76. Gaus 1996, p. 121.
77. Though not in specific personal situations where idealized agreement is not normatively efficacious, such as consent to sexual intercourse. See Estlund 2009, p. 46.
78. See Ch. 5, Sec. VII for a discussion.
79. The most prominent example of moderate idealization can be found in Gaus 2011, pp. 235–43.
80. I should qualify this a bit: most public reason liberals do not care about justifying coercion to psychopaths, even if they're idealized. So not all members of the public are always idealized as reasonable. I thank Chad Van Schoelandt for this point.
81. Rawls 2005, pp. 48–53. I explore reasonableness further in Ch. 5, Sec. I.
82. This is Joel Feinberg's formulation. See Feinberg 1987, p. 9. Feinberg's formulation does not necessarily entail public justification as a special justification, but it does suggest that some account of justification is needed.
83. Ibid., p. 68. Also see ibid., p. 217.
84. Rawls 2001, p. 44.
85. Benn 1988, p. 87.
86. Feinberg 1987, p. 9. While Benn is concerned with interference and Feinberg with coercion, their presumptions are otherwise similar.
87. Locke 2003, p. 110.
88. Rawls 1971, pp. 225–6.
89. Eberle 2002, p. 54.
90. Macedo 1990, p. 78.
91. Gaus 2011, p. 16. Emphasis in original. Gaus speaks of social morality in general.
92. Gaus 1996, p. 123.
93. For much more discussion, see Gaus 2011, pp. 14–35.
94. Paul Weithman argues that Rawls's defense of political liberalism is "conception-based." See Weithman 2010, pp. 353–62.
95. Rawls 1999, p. 434.
96. Larmore 2008, p. 140.

97. While present principles of restraint apply to reasons, I defend a principle of restraint for *proposals*. See Ch. 6, Sec. II.
98. I take the set of accessible reasons to be a superset of the set of shared reasons. I will explore these requirements in detail in Ch. 4, Sec. I.
99. And even if this claim is false, in virtue of the fact that secular persons appeal to private reasons drawn from their particular, ideological interpretation of shared political ideals, like equality and welfare, religious reasons are still seen as the paradigmatic unshared reasons and are often used as examples by mainstream public reason liberals as such, so they can serve as particular, vivid examples of private reasons. I thank Chad Van Schoelandt for this point.
100. Larmore 1999, p. 135.
101. Quong 2011, p. 256. Also see Cohen 1989, p. 21.
102. Schwartzman 2011, p. 4.
103. Schwartzman does not defend his principle of sincerity, solely on the ground that it promotes stability for the right reasons.
104. Eberle 2002, p. 153.
105. See Ch. 2, Sec. VI for further discussion.
106. I employ the language of "constitutive" and "instrumental" means, following Schmidtz 1996. Instrumental means are familiar, such as the use of a piano to play a particular piece, but a constitutive means towards some end partly constitutes achieving that end, such as playing a particular measure in the composition in question as a means towards playing the piece in its entirety. On Larmore's view, restraint appears to be a constitutive means towards the achievement of public justification.
107. Though one might interpret Larmore in this way in passages like the one I have cited.
108. The standard public reason approach to religion in public life also covers religious accommodations. It allows for extensive accommodations, though its consensus commitment sometimes prevents religious reasons from defeating proposed coercion. I leave discussion of accommodation to Ch. 6, as it has not been a central concern in academic debates about liberalism and religion in public life.
109. I do not endorse this characterization of the religious right, though it is common among public reason liberals.

CHAPTER 2

The Religious Objections
The Faithful Revolt

In this chapter, we examine three objections to religious restraint. The *integrity objection* holds that restraint compels religious citizens to violate their integrity. The *fairness objection* holds that restraint places more burdens on religious citizens than secular citizens, and is therefore inequitable. And the *divisiveness objection* holds that restraint is not required for social stability. I believe these objections succeed: the first two by establishing a conflict between restraint and public reason liberalism's foundational commitment to liberty and equality, and the latter by showing that divisiveness arguments are too inconclusive to justify restricting the freedom and equality of religious citizens.

However, religious critics contend that the Public Justification Principle is refuted if the case for restraint is refuted. To vindicate public reason liberalism, I must decouple restraint and the Public Justification Principle. What I shall call the Master Argument shows that the Public Justification Principle entails restraint only if three premises hold, two of which I shall reject. Specifically, the Public Justification Principle only entails restraint if it is combined with a consensus conception of justificatory reasons and what I shall call a principle of exclusion.

Citizens of faith understandably resent public reason liberalism. Restraint is genuinely objectionable on liberal grounds. Fortunately, public reason liberalism does not require restraint.

I. Preliminaries

We first need to wade through a number of important caveats and definitions. It bears noting at the outset that the cases for and against restraint apply to nonreligious moral doctrines. The case for restraint is based on concerns about giving *any* comprehensive doctrine unrestricted public influence.[1] I focus on religion because it is of enormous social significance. Accordingly, I will set aside a number of criticisms of public reason liberalism advanced by religious critics that do not directly concern religion or the features religions share with other comprehensive doctrines. For example, Nicholas Wolterstorff has argued that public reason liberalism unfairly privileges the value of noncoercion over other competing values.[2] Kent Greenawalt argues that public reason liberalism is "incomplete," and therefore lacks the resources to resolve many important political problems.[3] I also sideline concerns about liberal neutrality. Instead, I interpret the ideal of liberal neutrality as the ideal of public justification. Publicly justified institutions resemble the "neutral" institutions that liberals traditionally endorse.[4]

I now provide working definitions of terms like "religion," "religious commitment" and "faith." Robert Audi identifies nine characteristics of a religion, none of which is strictly necessary but which generally accompany our use of the term. Religions often include:

(1) Appropriately internalized belief in one or more supernatural beings (gods);
(2) Observance of a distinction between sacred and profane objects;
(3) Ritual acts focused on those objects;
(4) A moral code believed to be sanctioned by the god(s);
(5) Religious feelings (awe, mystery, etc.) that tend to be aroused by (2) and (3);
(6) Prayer and other communicative forms concerning the god(s);
(7) A worldview according the individual a significant place in the universe;
(8) A more or less comprehensive organization of life based on the worldview;
(9) A social organization bound together by (1)–(8).[5]

As shorthand, I take a "religion" to be a comprehensive doctrine with a core set of principles about the supernatural that prescribe social organization, practices, rituals, norms, beliefs and actions. A "religious commitment" is a commitment to affirm doctrines about the super-natural and to act in accord with the prescribed practices and social institutions associated with the religion in question.[6]

My definition of religion relies on a conception of the supernatural. I take supernatural claims to have two components, both of which deny naturalism. Naturalism is the conjunction of a metaphysical thesis and an epistemological thesis. Metaphysical naturalism holds that the set of extant entities is describable by physics. Epistemological naturalism holds that the only propositions that can be known are those that concern the physical world and the laws of nature, mathematics and logic. Supernaturalism conjoins the converse theses. Metaphysical supernaturalism holds that the set of extant entities includes both the set describable by physics and a set of nonmaterial, nonconceptual entities, such as souls, angels, demons, gods or the God of classical theism. Epistemological supernaturalism holds that one can know the truth of propositions that concern the beliefs, attitudes, will, thoughts, reasoning, commands, actions and/or testimony of at least one nonmaterial, nonconceptual entity.

Faith must be carefully defined in light of the above definitions. First, faith should not be defined in terms of its epistemic status. Faith is frequently taken to essentially involve irrational or evidentially unsupported beliefs. Others hold that faith includes believing proposi-tions that go beyond reason that are not inconsistent with it. Yet many religious believers hold that their beliefs about the supernatural are sup-ported by reason. To respect reasonable pluralism, then, public reason liberals must employ a definition that allows that faith can be rational.

I shall understand faith in terms of supernatural content. Specifically, I shall argue that faith consists in beliefs about the supernatural. At the simplest level, one can have faith "in God" by believing that God exists. Further, in the major monotheisms faith is often compared to *trust*, especially in the promises that God makes to humanity. In Christian-ity, for instance, faith is often understood to include a belief in Jesus's promise to save believers. Thus, I will assume that having faith requires affirming doctrines about the supernatural and trusting in the testi-mony or revelation of supernatural beings.

I recognize that my conception of religion is tied to the major mono-theisms. One can reasonably deny this tie.[7] But the clash between liberalism and religion *is* tied to the major monotheisms. And since that clash is our focus, we can confine ourselves to those religious traditions and philosophical doctrines that raise the problem.

As far as I am aware, Patrick Neal has made the only attempt to systematically classify religious objections to public reason liberalism.[8] While Neal's concern is with Rawls's political liberalism, his classification system generalizes. Neal groups the objections into four categories: incompleteness objections, fairness objections, integrity objections and denial of truth objections. I reproduce Neal's description of the last three objections:

(1) *The Integrity Objection* is perhaps the most prevalent argument made against Rawls from the point of view of religious belief. The heart of this argument is that the Rawlsian idea asks the religious citizen to "split" himself in a way that does, or can do, damage to the moral and/or religious integrity of the person. In being asked to conduct his political activity in accordance with public reason, and to treat his religious views as being fundamentally nonpolitical, the citizen, so it may be claimed, is being asked to repress or deny a fundamental part of himself when he enters the public realm.

(2) *The Fairness Objection* seeks to hoist the Rawlsian argument on its own petard. The claim is that rather than embodying the principle of fairness, the doctrine of public reason is itself an expression of unfairness insofar as it subjects religious citizens to restraints that are not applied to nonreligious citizens.

(3) *The Denial of Truth Objection* challenges public reason on the grounds that it seems mistaken to require the citizen to avoid stating claims of truth as truth. The charge is advanced not so much in terms of alleged damage to the person (as in the integrity objection), but rather in terms of the social costs of encouraging hypocrisy and/or dissembling over the profession of truth as one sees it.[9]

Neal's list is incomplete, as it omits a response to what Christopher Eberle calls the "argument from divisiveness," which holds that religious restraint is required to avoid "disruption and disharmony" among citizens.[10] I shall call the objection to the argument from divisiveness the *divisiveness objection*:

(4) *The Divisiveness Objection* holds that religious restraint does not significantly reduce social disruption and disharmony. Instead,

either restraint produces no significant increase in divisiveness or produces more divisiveness than no restraint. Restraint therefore cannot be justified on stability-based grounds.

Each of these objections deserve critical scrutiny, though I shall set (3) and (4) aside after this chapter. Concerns about objections (1) and (2) span the book.

Before analyzing these objections, however, I want to again stress that these religious objections are *not unique to religious citizens*, but instead can be raised by adherents of *any* comprehensive doctrine, such as J.S. Mill's utilitarianism or Ayn Rand's Objectivism. Restraint targets all comprehensive doctrines, not just religious ones. I focus on religious citizens for three reasons. First, the vast majority of people affected by principles of restraint are citizens of faith. As a matter of empirical fact, secular citizens tend not to stress the reasons that make them distinct as often as religious citizens do. Second, focusing on religious citizens aids ease of presentation. Third, and most importantly, I focus on religious citizens because I want to resolve problems for public reason raised by people of faith for faith-friendly critics of public reason.

II.   The Master Argument for Restraint

The standard arguments for restraint fail to link the Public Justification Principle to restraint, but I believe we can formulate a Master Argument for restraint that is capable of doing the job. To begin, let's revisit the Public Justification Principle:

> *Public Justification Principle (PJP)*: A coercive law L is justified only if each member I of the public P has some sufficient reason(s) R_i to endorse L.

The principle holds that the presumption in favor of liberty is met when the coercive restriction of liberty is publicly justified. Again, by itself, it says nothing about restraint. To derive restraint, we first require an interpretation of reasons R_i. The religious objectors, like mainstream public reason liberals, interpret reasons R_i as the claim that justificatory reasons must be shareable or accessible (that is, that R_i is specified by a consensus standard). So the first premise of the Master Argument must be:

(1)   Public Justification Principle → Accessibility/Shareability Requirement

Premise (1)—which I shall call the *justificatory premise*—explains why principles of restraint prioritize shared or accessible reasons, and is a critical premise in any argument for restraint. But more premises are required. We have still said nothing about deliberation.

The second premise assumes that citizens' reasoning can be regulated in two ways. Reasoning may be regulated as bases of deliberation and action via principles of restraint. Alternatively, reasoning may be regulated in their role as *justifiers*. The latter form of regulation determines the set of reasons to which publicly justified institutions must be sensitive. *Principles of exclusion* regulate such reasons. To illustrate, contrast restraint with the Establishment clause of the United States Constitution. Restraint regulates how one should act or talk politically, whereas the Establishment clause precludes certain considerations from counting as bases of coercion. Restraint concerns the *practice* of justification, exclusion the justification itself.

The distinction is important—a reason expressed in the public sphere on behalf of a proposal does not necessarily overlap with the reasons that justify or defeat the proposal in question. The reasons that John offers Reba to support a law may differ from the reasons Reba has to support the policy. Laws must be sensitive to Reba's reasons to support or reject a policy in order to be publicly justified, but they need not be sensitive to the reasons John and Reba *offer one another in conversation*. Thus, if the Public Justification Principle is to imply restraint, the advocate of restraint must show that exclusion requires restraint.

Principles of exclusion arguably follow from conceptions of justificatory reasons and the Public Justification Principle. If respect requires the public justification of coercion in terms of shared or accessible reasons, then laws can only be publicly justified if each citizen has sufficient shared or accessible reason to accept the law. A principle of exclusion therefore specifies that laws must be sensitive to some reasons and not to others. Thus premise (2) of the Master Argument:

(2)   Accessibility/Shareability Requirement → Principle of Exclusion

Premise (2) derives a principle of exclusion from a conception of justificatory reasons. I take this to follow as a conceptual truth. If justificatory reasons are just those that satisfy an accessibility or shareability requirement, then the only laws that can be justified are those supported by accessible or shareable reasons. Consequently, given the assumption that we should not coerce one another without justification, an assumption embodied in the Liberty Principle (Ch. 1, Sec. V), then we should not coerce one another without sufficient accessible or shareable reason. In other words, we should *exclude* inaccessible and shareable reasons from figuring into a public justification.

We have *still* not justified restraint. Premise (3) completes the justification:

(3)   Principle of Exclusion → Principle of Restraint

Defenses of restraint divide into respect-based and stability-based arguments (Ch. 1, Sec. VI), which we can now interpret as partial defenses of (3). Respect-based arguments hold that citizens should speak primarily or solely in consensus terms because respect for persons requires the justification of coercion via public reasons; justificatory discussions must occur in terms of public reasons, with private reasons excluded. Stability-based arguments hold that practicing restraint will aid the process of excluding private reasons from the process of public justification, in turn promoting social stability or stability for the right reasons. If citizens primarily speak and act based on public reasons, liberal democratic institutions will more easily produce publicly justified laws and policies, generating stability of one or the other form.

The connection between exclusion and restraint requires distinguishing two approaches to exclusion. A *direct* method of exclusion advances principles of restraint that drive citizens to explicitly restrain their use of excluded reasons. Through their political actions, citizens directly attempt to exclude reasons that are not employed to impose coercive law. In contrast, an *indirect* method allows citizens to forgo explicit attempts in political deliberation and action to bar excluded reasons from playing a justificatory role. The indirect approach focuses instead on regulating the behavior of politicians and the structure of political institutions to ensure that excluded reasons do not generate publicly unjustified law. Briefly, the indirect approach lets excluded reasons into the political process but does not let them leave.[11] The Master Argument selects the directness of exclusion by asking which principles of restraint effectively bar publicly unjustified law based on excluded reasons. If a direct approach is required for effective exclusion, then the Master Argument will justify a direct approach, and otherwise not.

We can now formally state the Master Argument:

(1) Public Justification Principle → Accessibility/Shareability Requirement
(2) Accessibility/Shareability Requirement → Principle of Exclusion
(3) Principle of Exclusion → Principle of Restraint

The Master Argument is the pivot around which I situate the arguments advanced by public reason liberals and their religious critics. All the religious objections are aimed at restraint. As a result, the religious objectors can only undermine the Public Justification Principle if all three entailments hold. If the objections succeed and the premises are true, then the religious objector acquires a defeater for the Public Justification Principle by modus tollens. Conversely, if the objections fail and the premises are true, then the case for restraint is compelling.

I believe that the case for premise (3) is inconclusive. Stability-based arguments for premise (3) such as arguments from divisiveness are unconvincing, as are arguments based on a conception of stability for the right reasons. However, I shall focus on arguing that premise (1), the justificatory premise, is false. If premises (1) and (3) are false, then we can amputate restraint from public reason liberalism and vindicate our thesis.

III. Principle of Restraint—The Specifics

The Master Argument is an argument for generic restraint, not a specific principle of restraint. For this reason, we should examine some prominent principles of restraint from the literature. I will focus on principles defended by Larmore, Rawls and Audi.

I have already introduced Larmore's principle (Ch. 1, Sec. VI), but recall that it holds that "[a] commitment to treating others with equal respect forms the ultimate reason why in the face of disagreement we should keep the conversation going, and to do that . . . we must retreat to neutral ground."[12] If two citizens disagree on some important political matter, then respect requires that they begin to speak in shared terms. To resolve their disagreements, citizens should not base their arguments on considerations their interlocutors cannot recognize as valid. This restriction applies to religious reasons because they are often unshared.

Larmore defends his principle by arguing that in a well-ordered society, good citizens will do more than simply announce to each other "the conclusions they each have derived from their own first principles" and then using the political process to forcibly resolve their disagreements. Instead, "they reason from what they understand to be a common point of view; their aim is to adjudicate disagreement by argument."[13] The critical idea is that the point of public justification is to adjudicate disagreements by argument. If citizens recognize each other as free and equal, then they will endeavor to construct a social order by using shared reasons, as this is the best way to reach agreement. For if citizens set out to agree, they must appeal to considerations they both regard as valid, indeed, considerations that they both accept. Larmore puts a finer point on the shared reasons requirement, as the aim of public justification is to select principles of justice that "each person [has] both sound *and identical* reasons to embrace."[14] This is an extreme consensus view, but it is motivated by the interpretation of public justification as requiring agreement. Citizens must agree on the same principles of justice and on the reasons for selecting them. Only then has true agreement been reached.

Larmore's principle applies to a limited social domain, so it requires less of citizens than one might think. First, as we have seen, restraint only applies when citizens cannot otherwise resolve their disagreements. Second, restraint does not apply to the entire public sphere. Larmore distinguishes between two arenas of public debate: "open discussion" and "decision-making." In the former, citizens dialogue merely as citizens, whereas in the latter they discuss issues as participants in a government body. Open discussion should not be regulated by restraint. For one thing, restraining open discussion will obscure citizens' convictions and discourage them from changing their minds. Further, and important for our purposes, a central feature of many religious perspectives on the point of human life is that "their adherents ought to do their best to persuade others . . . to heed the vital truths about the human good they believe they have seen."[15] Restraining open discussion, therefore, would be both "unjustly discriminatory" and "an unacceptable abridgement of the free exercise of religion."[16]

Restraint applies to public decision making because it has an essentially coercive character. The reasoning of public decision makers directly affects who is coerced, and so such reasoning must be regulated by a principle of public reasoning. Diverse reasoning is "beside the point when citizens are engaged in authoritatively deciding what principles governing the basic structure of society shall have the force of law."[17] But even if it were relevant, "basing one's decisions . . . upon divisive ideals of the human good must *always* be inappropriate."[18]

Larmore denies that such restraint is inequitable because political decision making requires that all persons, secular or no, refrain from appealing to their divisive ideals of the human good. It is therefore no more burdensome on religious citizens than secular citizens.[19] However, he is clear that such restraint is burdensome: "public reason amounts to a *demanding form of self-discipline* that the citizens of a liberal democracy are called upon to exercise" out of a commitment to fairness.[20]

Turning to our second example, recall Rawls's principle of restraint, the duty of civility. The duty of civility holds the comprehensive considerations can be introduced into political discussion in the public sphere whenever one likes, so long as "in due course proper political reasons— and not reason given solely by comprehensive doctrines—are presented that are sufficient to support whatever the comprehensive doctrines introduced are said to support."[21] For Rawls, then, citizens may offer one another comprehensive reasons for their preferred policies. But if political reasons do not support the relevant proposals, offering comprehensive reasons is morally defective.

Nonetheless, the duty of civility permits three supplementary uses of comprehensive reasons: declaration, witnessing and reasoning from conjecture.[22] When a citizen makes a declaration, she states her comprehensive doctrine. Declaration expresses comprehensive views in order to aid mutual comprehension of each other as citizens. Citizens witness when "some citizens feel that they must express their principles [and] dissent from existing institutions, policies or enacted legislation."[23] To witness is to publicly and discursively resist some law or policy. Finally, citizens reason from conjecture when we "argue from what we believe, or conjecture, are other people's basic doctrines, religious or secular, and try to show them that, despite what they might think, they can still endorse a reasonable political conception that can provide a basis of public reason."[24] Reasoning by conjecture occurs when citizens take on the assumptions of their interlocutors for the sake of mutual understanding.

The duty of civility remains somewhat ambiguous. Weithman provides perhaps the most permissive interpretation, where the duty of civility only requires that citizens speak in political terms when other citizens doubt their allegiance to the political conception (Ch. 1, Sec. II). I will stick to Weithman's "double-wide" interpretation for economy of argumentation. If the religious objections refute the double-wide view, then they should refute more stringent readings as well.

Before we examine Audi's principle of restraint, I should stress that Audi is not a public reason liberal. Furthermore, he does not derive restraint from any public justification principle but from independent principles of liberty, equality and neutrality.[25] However, we should examine Audi's approach to restraint for two reasons: (i) because he has produced the most extensive specification and defense of restraint available and (ii) because we can evaluate his approach from within the perspective of public reason. In other words, we can assess his approach to restraint as if it were grounded in a foundational commitment to public justification.

Audi is well known for his principle of restraint, the *principle of secular rationale*, which in its present form holds that

> Citizens in a democracy have a prima facie obligation not to advocate or support any law or public policy that restricts human conduct, unless they have, and are willing to offer, adequate secular reason for this advocacy or support (e.g., for a vote).[26]

The principle of secular rationale (PSR) includes two key concepts, secularity and adequacy. A secular reason for an action or a belief is "one whose status as a justifier of action (or belief) does not evidentially depend on (but also does not deny) the existence of God; nor does it depend on theological considerations."[27] The secularity of a reason is therefore determined by its epistemic relation to other reasons, not by its content. As a result, secular reasons can include limited appeals to theologically informed notions of human worth; secular reason can also be understood as "natural reason."[28] An adequate reason for an action or a belief is one that meets some threshold of epistemic justification; it "evidentially justifies" the action or belief in question.[29] An adequate reason for some action or belief implies that the "action or belief based on the reason is . . . rational."[30]

The PSR is a prima facie obligation. Its force is "defeasible" and "may be overridden by a competing obligation." For Audi, some political contexts require using reasons in ways that violate the PSR. For example, protecting one's institutions against a dangerous external threat may justify appealing to religious reasons to keep religious political bodies in one's defensive coalition.[31] Audi also stresses that the PSR is "non-exclusive" because it permits citizens to appeal to religious reasons for their positions. So even in normal cases citizens can appeal to religious reasons so long as they have an adequate secular reason for their actions and beliefs.

The PSR has two more notable features. First, Audi claims that the PSR "does not . . . rule out having *only* religious reasons for lifting oppression or expanding *liberty*."[32] In other words, the PSR only applies to imposing coercion, *not* to repealing it. The PSR only concerns coercion, which accords with "the idea that freedom is the default position in a liberal democracy."[33] Most public reason liberals do not distinguish between reasons to propose and reasons to reject coercion.[34] Restraint typically applies to both. But Audi rejects what I shall call the symmetry requirement (Ch. 4, Sec. II), which allows him to restrain only reasons to propose coercion. Audi also emphasizes that his principle does not require "that adequate reasons must be shared by everyone," but instead only need to be "accessible to rational adults." Such reasons need only be "appraisable . . . through using natural reason in the light of facts to which they have access on the basis of exercising their natural rational capacities."[35] Audi emphasizes that when citizens are properly informed and "fully rational," we should expect that they will "tend to agree on whether a consideration is a reason for a law or public policy," but that this is no guarantee.[36] So Audi adopts an accessibility requirement, not a shareability requirement.[37]

As a result, the PSR is considerably less demanding than its critics have often supposed. First, a great deal of religious political activism is aimed at securing legal exemptions. If so, religious citizens can fight for exemptions solely on the basis of religious reasons, even on constitutional matters, actions barred by Larmore and Rawls in many cases. Furthermore, even when proposing coercion, citizens need not share reasons. Their reasons need only be accessible.

But what Audi gives religious citizens he somewhat takes away with his supplementary principle of religious rationale, which requires that religious citizens not advocate coercive laws and policies "unless they have, and are willing to offer, adequate religious reason for this advocacy or support."[38] This principle imposes an additional requirement on religious citizens, that they have adequate *religious* reason to support the restriction of human conduct. And Audi does not stop there, as he advocates a principle of ecclesiastical political neutrality, which requires that churches must not support candidates or laws that "restrict human conduct, particularly religious or other basic liberties," without a secular rationale.[39] Audi even adds a principle of participatory neutrality that applies specifically to clergy.[40] So while in some respects Audi's principles are permissive, their scope is quite broad. The resultant conception of civic virtue is both detailed and stringent.

I should stress that Audi's principles of restraint can be grounded in the Public Justification Principle, as his arguments for restraint will have force for public reason liberals. Audi offers three arguments for the PSR. First, compliance with the principle "supports democracy and religious liberty," second, it "helps to prevent religious strife, since it limits coercion to kinds justified on grounds acceptable to any adequately informed, fully rational citizen," and finally that ". . . adherence to it is needed to achieve the reciprocity among citizens. . . . Rational citizens may properly resent coercion based essentially on someone *else's* religious convictions."[41] These defenses fit the Master Argument. The first two arguments connect exclusion and restraint on stability-based grounds. The third argument provides a respect-based connection. Thus, while Audi is not a public reason liberal, his principles of restraint can be defended in their terms.

IV. The Integrity Objection

The integrity objection is lodged against restraint, but to understand it we must first understand the philosophical concept of integrity that the objection rests upon. Integrity comes in many conceptions.[42] I employ Bernard Williams's "identity" conception of integrity.[43] Reba has identity integrity when she is true to her character, projects, plans and beliefs. On this view, "integrity means fidelity to those projects and principles that are constitutive of one's core identity."[44] By a "principle" I mean a commitment to some comprehensive ideal of life or a corollary or implication of it.[45] "Fidelity" to these ideals requires acting in concert with them and reliably not violating them. Projects are more complex. Loren Lomasky describes a project as possessing three primary characteristics: (i) persistence, (ii) centrality and (iii) structure.[46] Projects are persistent insofar as they extend over long periods of time. A project has centrality when it "help[s] explain a life" or when it is the focus of many other goals.[47] A project's structure means that it produces "stability" in an individual's life by uniting her actions.[48]

Martin Luther is an extreme example of a person with integrity, due to his willingness to die for his principles. When accused of heresy at the Diet of Worms, Luther stood in front of the power elite of the Holy Roman Empire and famously refused to recant, saying "I cannot and will not retract anything, since it is neither safe nor right to go against conscience. May God help me. Amen."[49] By all accounts, he expected that his refusal would result in being burned alive. Luther's behavior at the Diet of Worms demonstrates that his belief in "justification by faith" constituted his core identity; it helps to explain who Martin Luther was. We can contrast Luther with someone who lacks integrity, in this case because he lacks life projects. Consider Frederic Moreau from Gustave Flaubert's *Sentimental Education*. Moreau is a romantic who is never satisfied with what he has. While in the beginning of the novel he pursues Madame Arnoux with great passion, he periodically loses interest. His unwillingness to commit to her, or any other woman, leaves him with four conflicting love interests. Moureau's professional life follows the same pattern: he drops out of law school, quickly abandons his political aspirations and is unable to make firm, honest life choices. He is constantly busy, but he lacks clear projects, and so, on Williams's view, lacks integrity.[50]

Three caveats. First, the identity view includes corporate bodies. Roman Catholic readers, who may be partial to collective or institutional conceptions integrity, are not excluded by the identity view. Second, persons focused on a single project do not necessarily have more integrity than those who pursue several smaller projects. Thus persons of religious integrity need not have a single core set of commitments.[51] Finally, I will resist assigning especially zealous citizens more integrity than others. Having integrity is not identical with being a fanatic.[52]

Integrated persons are united by the fact that reasons issuing from their projects and principles possess great normative force and thereby generate strong claims to noninterference. Public reason liberalism requires formal recognition of these claims because citizens have the capacity to pursue a conception of the good and live up to their individual ideals. Consequently, public reason liberals must ascribe integrity serious moral weight and so allow reasons of integrity to play a justificatory role. A critic might worry that I must say more to show that personal integrity has moral value; I point that critic to Chapter 3, Section II.

Now consider Nicholas Wolterstorff's classic statement of the integrity objection:

It belongs to the *religious convictions* of a good many religious people in our society that *they ought to base* their decisions concerning fundamental issues of justice on their religious convictions. They do not view it as an option whether or not to do so. It is their conviction that they ought to strive for wholeness, integrity, integration, in their lives. . . . Their religion is not, for them, about *something other* than their social and political existence; it is *also* about their social and political existence.[53]

Michael Perry similarly suggests that to "bracket" one's religious convictions is tantamount to "[annihilating] essential aspects of one's very self."[54] In both Perry and Wolterstorff's descriptions, we are introduced to people with identity integrity, those who build their lives around fidelity to core projects and principles. The integrity objection maintains that public reason liberalism requires individuals to repress or privatize those religious aspects of their identities that require them to engage in political activity. For Perry and Wolterstorff, such a requirement is objectionable. Asking citizens to privatize their beliefs is manifestly unjustified to them and so privatization cannot be required to treat others with respect as public reason liberals maintain. From the perspective of many theistic citizens, for instance, public reason liberalism requires them to violate their duties to God. For theists, though, genuine respect for persons cannot require disobeying God and so cannot require restraint. Consequently, liberal calls for privatization amount to little more than bossing religious citizens around.

The integrity objection may initially appear to be a kind of psychological objection—that principles of restraint frustrate religious citizens, breed resentment, hurt their feelings, etc. But the psychological interpretation faces difficulties, as public reason liberals can reply by telling their religious critics to toughen up. Stephen Macedo says as much when he advises citizens who wish to institutionalize their religious views to "grow up!"[55] On this view, the integrity objection smacks of whining—the religious critic objects to restraint on the grounds that citizens of faith are psychologically fragile. In light of these disadvantages, we should opt for a normative interpretation of the integrity objection. The normative interpretation holds that religious citizens have *no reason* to engage in integrity-violating restraint. Properly understood, the integrity objection asks whether religious citizens have reason to endorse restraint. It is concerned not with what citizens of faith *can* handle but what they can *reasonably be required* to handle.

To refute public reason liberalism, then, integrity objectors must do more than cite costs to integrity—impositions that bar citizens from acting on their integrity-related reasons. All political theories prevent citizens from pursuing their projects and principles in some cases. A successful integrity objection identifies morally significant integrity costs. Religious objectors typically argue that restraint imposes morally significant integrity costs because it requires that religious citizens "split" their identities as persons of faith. To split an identity is to corner off the social space in which individuals can act in accord with their own judgments. Thus, political theories that split identities prevent citizens from acting on their convictions in some vital domain of life. Since activity in that domain is of great import, restraint threatens to alienate citizens from their values and principles.

But even split identities do not by themselves create a problem for public reason liberalism. Liberal society splits the identity of a mobster; mobsters often use violence to get their way and liberal societies demand that they not do so. A better example is the split between a person acting in her office as judge and her private life. Surely there is no problem with *this* public-private splintering.[56] If a religious judge claimed that the restrictions of her office violate her integrity because they require her to only deliberate on admissible evidence, we would rightly balk. Liberalism will inevitably make some forms of life impossible, such as being a mobster or being a judge who rules based on her private reasons; such restrictions are not a bad thing. The power in the integrity objection is rooted in the dis-analogy with the judge and the mobster: the religious citizen seems burdened *without sufficient reason.*

Public reason liberals will undoubtedly reply that the reasons for restraint are strong enough to justify the integrity costs to which many object. The duty to treat others as free and equal trumps the integrity-related reasons of citizens of faith and requires privatization. Evaluating who is right may prove difficult. To strengthen the integrity objection, we should try to show *how* integrity costs are imposed when citizens abide by restraint in political practice and then explain how restraint threatens to split their identities.

For this reason, let us try to develop a more empirically oriented argument, one that focuses more on the dynamic, sociological impact of widespread compliance with restraint. Paul Weithman's work can help us to do so. Weithman argues that American churches have played a positive role in promoting democratic action and political participation.[57] For instance, from the Civil Rights Era to the present day, black churches have played a fundamental role in introducing members of black communities to politics. Weithman claims that African Americans are one among many cultural and ethnic groups whose members develop their citizenship by participating in religious organizations. The good brought about by such participation is "realized citizenship," a full involvement in politics that is a morally praiseworthy achievement, both socially and politically.[58] For Weithman, churches contribute to realized citizenship, especially for the poor and minorities. They serve as "venues of discussion," educate citizens about policy and candidates, and teach them organizational and discursive skills applicable to politics. Citizens thereby achieve self-worth through their political participation, which in turn helps them ally with their fellow citizens. Churches provide "the ability to participate in and to recognize debate as *public* debate."[59] Without this ability, one cannot achieve realized citizenship and the well-being associated with it.

On this basis, one can argue that restraint is objectionable in part because it closes off viable avenues towards realized citizenship.[60] Restraint impairs citizens' social and political development and prevents them from learning to deliberate based on considerations that could advance their interests, such as religious reasons. Some churches help form their parishioners' identities both as people of faith and as citizens. We can argue that these parishioners have no reason to accept norms that impede the development of their religious identity, even if obeying such norms will obstruct the development of their identities as citizens. Again, many citizens receive their political education in church and think about political problems in religious terms; inhibiting citizens' acting on religious considerations thereby discourages them from political participation. To illustrate, suppose that African American churches during the Civil Rights Era had accepted principles of restraint and so refrained from publicly defending civil rights on religious grounds. Since many African Americans attained realized citizenship through public expressions of religious commitment mediated by their churches, principles of restraint would have likely limited these substantial achievements.

That said, no public reason liberal believes that citizens should not discuss their religious reasons or organize politically in church.[61] Instead, they merely require that when voting or arguing in the public sphere, citizens should rely primarily on nonreligious considerations. For this reason, it is hard to see how identity-development and political participation could be substantially set back by restraint. Some burden may be placed on churches' abilities to promote political participation, but it is not clear how significant the burden would be in practice. It is surely true that principles of restraint *can* restrict identity-formation and political participation, but it is not clear that restraint *must* have this effect. Our updated, empirically oriented version of the integrity objection therefore seems to rely on complex sociological judgments based on inconclusive evidence. Accordingly, the strength of our reconstructed integrity objection is unclear.

Nevertheless, if widely accepted, principles of restraint would have some of the effects Weithman describes. If citizens recognize that acting primarily on religious reasons in the public sphere is considered immoral or inappropriate, they will be less inclined to act in accord with their religious identities for fear of public sanction.[62] Consequently, should they choose to participate in politics on religious terms, they must bear the costs of being alienated from some sectors of their society. A number of real-world cases vividly illustrate this point, but let us focus on the role of religious conviction in the fight against apartheid in South Africa.

During the latter half of the twentieth century, South Africa was ruled by an apartheid government whose brutal crimes killed tens of thousands and created many more refugees. In 1990, Nelson Mandela was freed from a several-decade prison sentence for protesting apartheid; in 1994, he was elected president of South Africa and started to reverse the social and political damage caused by apartheid. In the process, he formed the South African Truth and Reconciliation Commission, led by Anglican Archbishop Desmond Tutu. The Truth and Reconciliation Commission (TRC) was designed to expose the human rights abuses of the apartheid regime; amnesty was offered to those who committed serious human rights abuses in exchange for public admission of their misdeeds. The TRC embraced a conception of *restorative* justice that realizes justice by reintegrating perpetrators into their communities through confession and forgiveness. While the commissioners were politically, ethnically and religiously diverse, the philosophy of the TRC had an explicitly Christian emphasis.

Throughout his book *No Future Without Forgiveness*, Tutu stridently defends the restorative justice approach pursued by the TRC on Christian grounds, arguing that no human, no matter how wicked, should be given up on. Christian theology reminded Tutu that perpetrators "remained children of God with the capacity to repent, to be able to change."[63] For Tutu, "It was theology that enabled me to assert that this *was* a moral universe. That theology undergirded my work in the TRC." When Tutu was challenged by journalists for bringing his Christian convictions into the commission, he remarked that he had been selected because he was a religious leader and that there was no point in pretending that he was someone else. Instead, he acted as a religious leader and was accepted as such by the TRC. The clear implication is that "theological and religious insights and perspectives would inform much of what we did and how we did it."[64]

Let us reconsider the integrity objection in light of Archbishop Tutu's example. Tutu defended the TRC on explicitly Christian terms in innumerable public places. His Christian commitments directly influenced his role as the leader of a prominent and public institution responsible for healing deep rifts in a nation. If the principles of restraint advocated by public reason liberals were widely acknowledged within South African society, Tutu's witness would have been substantially muted. Again, Tutu "could not pretend [he] was someone else."[65]

Given that Rawls's principle of restraint is the weakest of the three we examined, if we can show that even Rawls's principle threatens Tutu's accomplishments, then the integrity objection should apply to all three principles we discussed. Remember Rawls holds that when citizens can only employ comprehensive reasons, the proposals they are used to defend will, in due course, turn out to be defensible in political terms. If Tutu is to be a good Rawlsian citizen, then he must restrain himself if he doubts whether his advocacy can be fully or adequately supported outside of his Christian commitments. By his own account, Tutu could publicly reach many South Africans only through Christian values. Or at least, his appeals to Christian values were most effective. Thus in some cases, a Rawlsian Tutu may not have been as effective an advocate— advancing his arguments in terms of a reasonable balance of political values could have easily fallen flat given the power and centrality of religious considerations in the lives of many South Africans.[66] Restraint seems to needlessly interfere with effective political activism on behalf of social justice. In Tutu's case, public reason liberal handwringing seems like pointless interference, vaunted language about respect for persons aside.[67] Tutu surely had nonreligious reasons for his actions, but restraint seems to nonetheless significantly restrict his freedom in ways that seem objectionable.

Let's now turn our focus to those underprivileged persons Tutu represented. Tutu brought many into the fight for social justice in South Africa who otherwise would have never found their political voices. Principles of restraint would have made this already difficult process more burdensome for those Tutu represented. Weithman argues that good Rawlsian citizens must be able to make "complex judgments ... to determine when public reasons are called for" and to have the sophisticated ability to "respond appropriately when offered the right or wrong kinds of reasons."[68] Tutu could make such judgments with little effort, but acquiring this capacity would be unduly onerous for these severely oppressed citizens. Public reason liberals should be impressed that those who endured so much had the capacity to engage in political dialogue on *any terms at all*. In South Africa, restraint would have closed off many avenues towards realized citizenship, and thus to the development of associated political identities.

The South African case illustrates the costs of religious restraint. Restraint might not be onerous for secular, college-educated citizens of Western liberal democracies, or perhaps even for intellectual leaders like Tutu. But when restraint is applied outside of this privileged group, its restrictiveness is clear. Lest someone reply that restraint can be suspended in cases of severe oppression, we need merely assume that some ordinary voters in liberal democracies face similar hurdles to the process of realizing citizenship, specifically hurdles involved in learning how to engage in the complex reasoning processes required by restraint. If restraint is suspended even for these citizens, then it starts to seem like a spare wheel, as it will only apply to those who have little difficulty complying with it.[69] I suspect that the real targets of restraint are the well-educated religious citizens of liberal democracies, whose politics public reason liberals abhor. But attempts to tailor restraint for these citizens would be ad hoc and biased.

Thus, the integrity objection wields great force. Perhaps, then, the burdens to integrity imposed by restraint are substantial enough to provide religious objectors with reason to reject public reason liberalism. Public reason liberalism is objectionable to the extent that it requires restraint. Religious objectors therefore have reason to reject the Public

Justification Principle by modus tollens, assuming the premises of the Master Argument hold.

We would be remiss not to consider a reply to the integrity objection. Audi emphasizes that his principle of secular rationale does not bar the employment of religious reasons, so that religious language can be used whenever one likes, even when it comes to political persuasion.[70] Unlike public reason liberals, Audi argues that many religious reasons are properly accessible and so count as adequate bases of political action. Second, he claims that religious reasons can play an important role in deliberation even if citizens comply with his Principle of Secular Rationale (PSR). Religious reasons can serve as evidence, clarification, sources of persuasion and motivation.[71] Finally, Audi also reminds his reader that the PSR is only a prima facie duty and does not apply to the lifting of coercion.

Audi's adjustments to the PSR certainly reduce the integrity costs they impose. Deeply religious citizens face no restraint when objecting to coercion and can supplement their attempts to coerce with religious reasons, so long as they have adequate secular reasons. But as we saw above, Audi defends a number of principles of restraint in addition to the PSR. Widespread social compliance with these principles could impose substantial costs on citizens by requiring that they develop and exercise the complex capacities needed to distinguish types of reasons— religious and secular reasons, adequate and inadequate reasons—and to identify the contexts where they apply.

We can read Audi's principles in two ways: either they impose morally significant constraints on political action or they do not. If Audi's principles rarely require restraint, then indeed the integrity objection is defused. But religious objectors should be happy with this outcome: restraint by and large does not affect religiously committed citizens. After all, even Christopher Eberle, one of the foremost religious critics, advocates a principle of restraint—the ideal of conscientious engagement—that is intended to impact citizen behavior.[72] On the other hand, if Audi's principles impose substantive restrictions, I submit that the integrity-based concerns raised by Perry, Wolterstorff and Weithman still apply. The internalization of Audi's principles requires significant effort due to their remarkably cognitive emphasis. In other words, they must be capable of a high degree of introspection with respect to which reasons are sufficient to justify their actions. To be a good citizen, on Audi's view, a citizen likely needs to be able to *explicitly determine* whether her nonreligious reasons for political action are epistemically adequate. Otherwise, it is not clear how she could comply with the PSR in good faith. In this way, compliance with Audi's many principles of restraint could easily restrain the realization of citizenship. Consequently, while Audi may have provided an adequate defense of his principles from within his own philosophical framework, no such rationale is available from within the framework of public reason, given the restraints and barriers to engaging in political action with integrity.

Let us now briefly turn to the denial of truth objection, which holds that restraint is objectionable because it requires citizens to deny the truth as they see it. While Neal separates this objection from the integrity objection, I think its normative force is entirely derived from the integrity objection, which is why I address it here. The basic concern is that it is strange to ask citizens not to speak out based on what they believe to be true. William Galston agrees, arguing that to treat others as free and equal, we are only obligated to offer others "what we take to be our true and best reasons for acting as we do."[73] As Neal notes, we often think persons are virtuous based on the fact that they state the truth as they see it. If public reason tells us not to do so, then so much the worse for public reason.[74]

The denial of truth objection typically targets Rawlsian political liberalism, which many believe requires that citizens not appeal to their truth claims in public life. But Rawls permits truth claims so long as *the fact that citizens' claims are true* is not used as a justification for coercion. Rawls argues that "holding a political conception as true, and for that reason alone the one suitable basis of public reason, is exclusive, even sectarian, and so likely to foster political division."[75] His point is that citizens' truth claims do not ground political authority over others, even if these claims are correct. To the extent they agree with Rawls, public reason liberals need not require that liberal democratic citizens deny the truth as they see it.

In response, the religious objector might argue that restraint only requires that the religious citizen *act* inconsistently with the truth as she sees it. But this is a version of the integrity objection. The wrongness of forcing someone to act inconsistently with her principles does not depend on whether those principles are true.[76]

V. The Fairness Objection

The fairness objection holds that restraint imposes inequitable burdens on citizens of faith, treating them as inferior to secular citizens. Since the Public Justification Principle requires restraint, public reason liberalism necessitates treating citizens of faith as second class. Therefore, public reason liberalism's commitment to respecting persons as free and equal is belied by its commitment to restraint. I argue that fairness objections successfully rebut arguments for restraint, though only after clarification and reconstruction.

In a discussion of Thomas Nagel's views on liberal impartiality and neutrality, Michael Perry advances a standard version of the fairness objection, arguing that in political discussion Nagel might be allowed to rely on most and maybe all of his relevant beliefs, including those that he considers most important, whereas Perry would be permitted to rely on a fraction of his and not the ones that he considers most central, specifically what his religious convictions tell him about the good life for man.[77] Thus, Nagel's claim to defend impartial political justification is false, because political justification is not impartial between secular liberals like Nagel and religious liberals like Perry. Consequently, at least one version of public reason liberalism is said to privilege secular beliefs, despite advancing putatively impartial criteria for acceptable political justifications.[78] It requires the inequitable treatment of religious citizens, as religious citizens (like Perry) cannot rely on their most cherished beliefs in their political lives, in contrast to secular citizens (like Nagel). Wolterstorff expresses a similar complaint when he claims that barring citizens of faith from basing their political dialogue and action on their religious convictions infringes "*inequitably*, on the free exercise of their religion" since if left to choose for themselves, they would act on their religious beliefs.[79] If given a choice, religious citizens will rely on their religious beliefs, that is, their most important beliefs, in their political lives. But restraint permits secular citizens to act on *their* most important beliefs, despite the fact that many secular doctrines will be similarly restrained in principle.

We can better evaluate the fairness objection by elaborating its premises and determining which ones are under contention. I interpret the fairness objection as follows:

(i) Public reason liberalism (the PJP) requires restraint. (The Master Argument)
(ii) Restraint requires privileging shared/accessible reasons over religious reasons.
(iii) Privileging shared/accessible reasons over religious reasons imposes greater burdens on religious citizens than on secular citizens.

(iv) These greater burdens are inequitable.
(C) Restraint is inequitable. (ii, iii, iv)
(C2) The Public Justification Principle is inequitable. (i, C)

Since premise (i) is based on the Master Argument for Restraint, let us grant it for the sake of argument. Our analysis of principles of restraint (Sec. III) gives us reason to grant premise (ii). The contentious premises are (iii) and (iv).

Religious critics can defend (iii) by claiming that many religious citizens rely primarily on their religious reasons in their political lives. Secular citizens, on the other hand, often prioritize shared or accessible reasons, given that secular reasons are more often shared than religious reasons. In religiously pluralistic societies, religious reasons are almost never shared and may be mostly inaccessible. The main argument here, it must be admitted, is contingent and sociological. The claim is that under present social conditions, secular citizens tend to rely on shared considerations more than religious citizens. But there may be circumstances where secular citizens prefer to rely on their comprehensive moral doctrines; such secular reasons would not be so privileged on the whole. That may weaken the appeal of (iii) but if it is true, and (iv) is plausible, then we have a compelling argument against restraint and the Public Justification Principle.

Perhaps the most important attempt to deny something like premise (iii) is offered by Jürgen Habermas. He counters (iii) by providing an account of the relevant burdens that restraint imposes on religious and secular citizens and then claims that, as a matter of course, the burdens are not unequal. He pursues this strategy vis-à-vis his own principle of restraint.[80] His *translation requirement* holds that "all enforceable political decisions must be formulated in a language that is equally accessible to all citizens, and it must be possible to justify them in this language as well."[81] Habermas recognizes that the translation requirement may run afoul of fairness worries. If so, his associated theory of legitimacy, by emphasizing equality and reciprocity, contradicts itself if it imposes a political ethos on citizens that "distributes cognitive burdens unequally between secular and religious citizens."[82] We can see, then, that he accepts premise (iv), making (iii) the key premise he must deny.

Habermas substantiates his argument against (iii) by claiming that religious citizens in liberal democracies have already endured the relevant cognitive burdens due to the historic challenges of modernity.

These burdens include the religious person's encounter with pluralism, which requires her to revise and reform her convictions in light of challenges from other faiths, and the pressure to figure out how to separate secular and sacred beliefs such that the development of secular inquiry and science will not contradict her faith.[83] Last, and most significantly, a religious citizen must recognize the priority of secular reasons in politics by engaging in the (arguably Herculean) cognitive task of drawing a connection between the ideas of equality and individuality on which modern law and morality is based, and her comprehensive doctrine.[84]

For Habermas, the only way that these burdens can be fair is if secular citizens bear equivalent cognitive burdens. In light of this, Habermas argues that secular citizens must accept that that they inhabit a post-secular world where religious communities will continue to exist, and this requires mental burdens "*no less cognitively exacting* than the adaptation of religious awareness to the challenges of an ever more secularized environment." Secular citizens must come to reasonably expect conflict with reasonable religious citizens.[85] Furthermore, secular citizens must engage in a complex cognitive process by which they reconstruct their conception of democratic citizenship that includes religious people, and this alteration is "no less demanding than the corresponding mentality of their religious counterparts."[86]

Habermas, in effect, offers two replies to the charge that his conception of public justification is biased in favor of the secular: (a) religious citizens have already endured the relevant cognitive burdens, such that the cognitive costs of inhabiting a secular public sphere are relatively low and (b) secular citizens face a similar cognitive cost by adjusting to life in a post-secular society. The translation requirement appears to impose heavier cognitive burdens on religious citizens, but the costs are both lower than they appear and equivalent to those borne by secular citizens.

Habermas's description of the relative cognitive burdens of religious and secular citizens is mistaken. For the sake of argument, assume that religious citizens have already paid the cognitive costs Habermas identifies. They must still develop a conception of how their faith relates to political issues as they arise. Further, they must exert the cognitive energy required to reconcile their religious faith with their conception of the political sphere as secular. The process of secular reasoning is not learned all at once. Secular citizens pay far fewer costs in admitting that religious communities are not going away and that religious citizens might have something reasonable to add to public discourse. Religious citizens must effectively teach themselves political theology, whereas secular citizens need only admit that religious citizens are A-OK. Now, importantly, Habermas stresses that secular citizens must search for core moral values embedded in religious reasons advanced by their religious peers to help them figure out how to translate religious reasons into politically appropriate reasons. But this search, however construed, does not match the burdens faced by religious citizens.

Furthermore, it is not obvious that religious citizens have already paid the cognitive costs Habermas identifies. Many religious citizens, if not the vast majority, have not inherited a worldview shaped by the relevant social and ideological developments. While a handful of theologically liberal elites may have grappled with the fact of religious pluralism in the way Habermas suggests, most religious citizens have not. Theological conservatives often explicitly refuse to make such adjustments, and the vast majority of religious parishioners have probably rarely engaged in the relevant cognitive processes. Habermas's translation requirement imposes significant cognitive burdens on both groups, far more than it imposes on secular and theologically liberal citizens. The fairness objection retains its force.

Let us assume then that premise (iii) holds, at least as a matter of contingent and sociological fact in liberal democracies. Public reason liberals might then argue against premise (iv). One plausible line of criticism would be to hold that the burdens are not inequitable because restraint only needs to be impartial in intent and not in practice. In general, public reason liberals deny that publicly justified principles and laws must be impartial or neutral with respect to the costs they impose on citizens. Rawls was clear that his conception of state neutrality, based in public reason, was merely procedural.[87] So long as all reasonable comprehensive doctrines have equal normative capacity to determine the structure of the law, political liberalism is sufficiently impartial or neutral. Rawls grants that political liberalism and its associated constraints may render some forms of life more difficult than others. But he claims that neutrality in effect is too demanding, since any liberal political theory will impose more burdens on some than others. Along the same lines, public reason liberals could argue that restraint is no worse for wear if it imposes more burdens on religious citizens than secular citizens.

Perry and Wolterstorff preempt this response by arguing that the public reason criterion for identifying justificatory reasons is implausible.

Perry argues that public reason liberalism relies on a conception of practical rationality called the linear model, which holds that epistemology should assume that "the structure of knowledge [rests] on some favored class of statements."[88] Wolterstorff blames the inequitable treatment of religious reasons on an "independent source" epistemology.[89] On the independent source view, citizens ". . . are to base their political debate in the public space, and their political decisions, on the principle yielded by some source *independent of* any and all religious perspectives to be found in the society."[90] These two conceptions of epistemic rationality straightforwardly privilege secular beliefs over religious ones. If they are implausible, then so is the case for restraint. Attacking the criterion of justificatory reasons, however, cannot effectively buttress the fairness objection. If public reason liberals have an inadequate account of justificatory reasons, their whole theory is threatened. In order to substantiate the fairness objection, religious objectors should find an alternative defense of premise (iv).

I defend premise (iv) on the grounds that, while neutrality of effect is a defective ideal, the unequal burdens of restraint are still just cause for resentment on behalf of citizens of faith and so sufficient to reject restraint on egalitarian grounds. In the end, what public reason liberals propose are restraint norms that everyone knows fall harder on citizens of faith than secular citizens, even if the inequality is due to contingent sociological factors. The religious critics can grant that public reason liberalism need not be neutral between all doctrines, but argue that if public reason systematically privileges the reasoning of secular citizens, that on this basis they have reason sufficient reason to reject the view. In other words, the religious objectors are perfectly entitled to reject public reason liberalism, via restraint, based on egalitarian concerns.

Public reason liberals might also reply to the fairness objection by arguing that its normative force derives entirely from the integrity objection. To see how this reply might go, suppose that the restraint imposes unequal burdens on religious and secular citizens. We can equalize costs in two ways: (c) decrease the burdens imposed on religious citizens, or (d) increase the burdens imposed on secular citizens. It is fair to assume that the religious objectors will prefer (c) to (d) due to the integrity objection. They wish all citizens to be free from restraint so that they can live integrated lives. If the fairness objection has independent normative force, however, it should generate at least *some* reason to prefer (d) to an inequality of burden. In other words, religious objectors will have reason to *level down* the freedom of secular persons. But leveling down is morally unattractive, since it hurts some and benefits no one. Inequality, therefore, does not seem to be the issue. The real concern is that excessive burdens are placed on citizens of faith.

I admit that the fairness objection provides some reason to level down, but this fact alone does not defeat it. The integrity objection arguably overrides leveling down, as imposing restraint on them would violate the integrity of secular citizens. Consequently, the fairness objection cannot justify leveling down even if it can add to the case against restraint.

In sum, restraint treats religious citizens as inferiors, since they must endure the recognition that secular citizens face fewer restrictions than they do. Integrity objections, then, cannot fully account for the moral ugliness of restraint. Accordingly, the fairness objection adds to the case against restraint.

VI. The Divisiveness Objection

The divisiveness objection is a reply to stability-based arguments for restraint.[91] Stability-based arguments support premise (3) of the Master Argument by linking exclusion and restraint. If restraint promotes stability, then one could plausibly maintain that it promotes publicly justified outcomes by excluding private reasons from the process of public justification. Restrained public discourse excludes private reasoning from the justificatory process. Thus, restraint promotes exclusion by generating stability. Stability-based arguments take two forms: (i) unrestrained societies tend to be fractious, and (ii) unrestrained societies cannot be stable for the right reasons. I shall call these arguments the *empirical* and *normative* stability-based arguments for restraint, or the empirical stability and normative stability arguments. I claim that both arguments fail.

Christopher Eberle has provided an extensive analysis of the empirical stability argument. He divides the argument into two grades, the stronger "argument from Bosnia" and the weaker "argument from divisiveness."[92] Examining these options will help to establish two different options in the literature.

The argument from Bosnia holds that failing to privatize religious belief produces "quite debilitating social and political dysfunctions."[93]

Defenders of the argument frequently point to the Thirty Years' War and contemporary conflicts in Bosnia to illustrate the damage that religious conflict can do. Consider Lawrence Solum's argument that allowing political competition between religious groups may undermine religious toleration and thus produce more religious conflict, since we can see that "world history and contemporary experience reveals that seemingly unshakeable stability can rapidly degenerate into strife and even chaos."[94] Or consider Richard Rorty, who claims, "Contemporary liberal philosophers think that we shall not be able to keep a democratic political community going unless the religious believers remain willing to trade privatization for a guarantee of religious liberty."[95] The argument from Bosnia holds, therefore, that a lack of restraint can destroy liberal democratic social orders.

This argument is misguided. The idea that a contemporary liberal democratic order can be undermined if some of its citizens fail to comply with principles of restraint is flatly implausible. Religious conflict can be dangerous, but no empirical evidence demonstrates that restraint helps to prevent it. Religious violence can be explained by other factors, perhaps by states that employ their coercive power to promote religious conversion, to restrict dissent and compel participation in rituals.[96] It is more likely that attempts to co-opt state power to further religious ends produce violence and unrest rather than a failure to engage in religious restraint.

Public reason liberals should retreat to the argument from divisiveness, which holds that the refusing to privatize religion may not produce outright religious conflict but will have other negative outcomes that are more probable in situations where religiously motivated political action is unrestrained.[97] The argument from divisiveness is stronger than the argument from Bosnia, because we citizens of liberal democracies are more familiar with the divisiveness erupting from religious discord than serious political instability and violence.[98]

Consider two examples of the argument from divisiveness. Abner Greene claims that legislation based on religious arguments "takes on a religious character, to the frustration of those who don't share the relevant religious faith and who therefore lack access to the normative predicate behind the law."[99] Kent Greenawalt argues that publicly advocating one's political positions in religious terms "promotes a sense of separation between the speaker and those who do not share his religious convictions and is likely to produce both religious and political divisiveness."[100] Given these cases, Eberle structures the argument from divisiveness as follows:

(A) A morally responsible citizen won't engage in divisive activity.
(B) A widespread refusal to privatize religion is divisive.
(C) Hence, a morally responsible citizen will privatize her religious convictions.[101]

Eberle points out that the term "privatize" is vague. I will appeal to the principles of restraint identified in Section III to make the term more precise. To privatize religion, then, is to comply with a principle of restraint. A successful divisiveness argument must therefore show that good social consequences flow from widespread compliance with these particular principles. Let us reformulate the argument:

(A) A morally responsible citizen won't engage in divisive activity.
(D) A widespread refusal to comply with X's principle of restraint is divisive.
(E) Hence, a morally responsible citizen will comply with X's principle of restraint.

X can refer to any principle of restraint, like Rawls's, Audi's, Larmore's or Habermas's.

The problem with the revised argument is that premise (A) is false. Responsible citizens will sometimes engage in divisive activity if it is required to advance a valuable and just proposal. As Eberle notes, those who fought against segregation in the American South were divisive and that was a *good* thing. In response, Eberle replaces premise (A) with a weaker premise attuned to the trade-offs of practicing restraint.[102]

(A*) Given two alternative activities, a responsible citizen will engage in the alternative that renders the community morally better off, all things considered.
(D*) Widespread compliance with X's principle of restraint will render the political community morally better off, all things considered, than a refusal to privatize.
(E*) Hence, a morally responsible citizen will comply with X's principle of restraint.

(A*) is more plausible than (A), but it requires that citizens have the implicit or explicit capacity to make fine discriminations between alternative political states of affairs. Such discriminations require significant cognitive exertion, enough to make the associated account of liberal democratic citizenship philosophically unattractive. (D*) is quite hard to establish. To do so, the public reason liberal must add up all of the morally significant costs and benefits that would result from a failure to privatize vs. successful privatization. Then she has to determine whether her country will be better off with privatization, all else equal.[103] This is a tall order, so tall that we can safely conclude that the modified argument from divisiveness fails.

While the divisiveness argument has considerable prima facie plausibility, it is weak. None of the arguments for restraint we have discussed establishes (D*). While defenders of restraint often argue that a lack of restraint causes divisiveness they *never* (yes, *never*) count the opportunity costs of restraint.[104] The morally relevant costs of privatization are all but ignored. Second, and along the same lines, arguments from divisiveness rarely take into account the discord caused by restraint.[105] Hostility to religious restraint is widespread and has arguably alienated many from liberal political thought and liberal political institutions. Restraint plainly causes controversy. Thus, the empirical stability argument fails.

So let's turn to the normative stability argument, which bases the case for restraint on its capacity to generate stability *for the right reasons.* Recall from Chapter 1 that Rawls's duty of civility serves as an assurance mechanism. If citizens of a well-ordered society comply with the duty of civility, they will be disposed to provide political reasons for their positions on constitutional matters when their allegiance to the political conception of justice in their society is in doubt. The duty of civility ensures that a political conception is stable for the right reasons, meaning that it is based on the free assent of rational and reasonable, free and equal persons.[106]

My assessment of the argument depends on three assumptions. First, I shall assume that a powerful reason to create institutions that are stable for the right reasons is to ensure that laws are publicly justified and thus compatible with respect for persons as free and equal. Good institutions will sustain laws that are publicly justified and repeal or reform laws that are not. If so, they are normatively stable. Second, I shall assume that the principles of restraint required to produce stability for the right reasons resemble the duty of civility. If we can show that the duty of civility cannot ensure stability for the right reasons, then we can assume that other principles will fail for similar reasons, at least in lieu of an argument to the contrary. Third, I shall assume that Weithman's "double-wide" interpretation of the duty of civility is correct and that, as such, ordinary citizens may never find themselves in situations where the duty is triggered.

John Thrasher and I have argued that the duty of civility is a fragile assurance mechanism.[107] We defend an alternative correlated equilibrium model of assurance that does not require restraint that I shall not discuss here.[108] Instead, I will review our arguments against the duty of civility.

For Rawls, normative stability requires *common knowledge* that members of a well-ordered society will abide by the requirements of the political conception of justice. In other words, citizens must not only know that they affirm the political conception but they must know that others affirm it and *why* they affirm it. The shared rationales for the political conception must be public knowledge. Everyone must know that everyone else knows. But recent work by Herbert Gintis shows that common knowledge can only be maintained in a small class of settings.[109] Consequently, common knowledge is fragile and liable to disintegration even under favorable conditions. Rawls's model of common knowledge production is thereby problematic. The problem is enhanced by the fact that Rawls requires that citizens assure one another directly in their deliberations. But direct assurance is undermined by the social phenomena of noise and drift.[110] Here's why.

The introduction of private reasons into the public sphere makes it hard to tell when citizens are advancing public reasons, which generates deliberative noise. Nonpublic reason exchanges may conceal the use of public reasons. Since citizens signal their allegiance to the political conception of justice through the public use of justificatory reasons, these signals must be easily distinguishable from noise. But on the double-wide view, they probably will not be. The use of private reasons is extensive, and so private deliberations will be loud.

Noise is amplified as interactions continue via a phenomenon known as informational drift. Small errors, when repeated, can quickly lead to a cascade of misunderstanding, miscommunication and divergence in interpretation. These "informational cascades" undermine mutual assurance equilibria.[111] An informational cascade occurs "when initial decisions coincide in a way that it is optimal for each of the subsequent individuals to ignore his or her private signals and follow the established pattern."[112] That is, a signaling error can become a public norm. This susceptibility is present among members of a well-ordered society. Citizens in the public forum base their public signals of assurance on their private interpretations of the content of the political conception. The citizens who interpret these signals will also rely on divergent interpretations and may not know the source of the signal. This is a recipe for confusion.

The duty of civility permits noisy signaling amplified by informational drift in a well-ordered society for the reason that the phenomena can occur even if all citizens are reasonable and well informed. Accordingly, the duty of civility is a poor assurance mechanism. These arguments apply with full force to other principles of restraint as well. For example, both Larmore's and Audi's principles permit the widespread use of private reasons.

The obvious response is to tighten up principles of restraint so as to exclude some private reasoning. But as we attempt to cleanse the public sphere of private (including religious) language, the integrity and fairness objections become more pressing. The ethical restrictions required to fully tame noise and drift problems could be substantial and so prove to be enormously restrictive of religious citizens' integrity and further add to the appearance of inequity. Furthermore, the basic liberal commitment to freedom and equality will likely bar the justification of any principle strong enough to stop substantial private reasoning from entering the public sphere. Stronger principles of restraint are for this reason unattractive. Restraint can neither guarantee nor even reliably produce normative stability. Like their empirical brethren, normative arguments for stability fail.

VII. Conclusion

The integrity objection, the fairness objection and the divisiveness objection (specifically, the *failure* of the argument from divisiveness) undermine the case for restraint, but not the Public Justification Principle. This is due to the fact that we can refute premises of the Master Argument, which provide the critical link between restraint and the Public Justification Principle. Public reason liberals and their critics accept the Master Argument, though they interpret it differently. Public reason liberals argue by modus ponens: because the Public Justification Principle is true and the premises hold, religious restraint is required by respect for persons. The religious critics argue by modus tollens: since religious restraint is objectionable, so is the Public Justification Principle.

I take a third approach by rejecting two premises of the Master Argument.[113] The case against premise (3), which links exclusion and restraint, is complete due to the fact that restraint does not improve the quality of public justifications by producing empirical or normative stability. Since stability arguments fail, we have little reason to think that exclusion requires restraint. At this point, I could declare victory against the Master Argument, but public reason liberals can respond to premise (3) in other ways. First, they may be able to buttress the empirical stability argument with sociological research or defend the normative stability argument with a formal model that demonstrates that restraint is required to generate stability for the right reasons. Second, and more likely, they may simply insist that premise (3) can be defended via a deontological argument that respect requires restraint.

I will therefore refute premise (1), the justificatory premise. A refutation of the justificatory premise could produce a decisive case against restraint, even if premise (3) holds. To do so, I will defend convergence against the mainstream consensus view based on the claim that convergence better manifests a commitment to the values that ground the Public Justification Principle. Before I can do so, however, I must develop a strategy for attacking the justificatory premise that both parties to the debate will recognize as valid. I will do so in Chapter 3.

Notes

1. Rawls 2005, p. 13.
2. Wolterstorff 2007, p. 139. I addressed this concern indirectly in Ch. 1, Sec. IV, where I claimed that public reason liberalism's presumption against coercion is not a method of assigning coercion a high weight vis-à-vis other values, but instead structures justificatory practices.
3. Kent Greenawalt (1988, pp. 98–172) advances this objection. For replies, see Reidy 2000 and Schwartzman 2004. Ch. 4, Sec. III, argues that the convergence conception of reasons is complete.
4. I follow Rawls in this: "I believe, however, that the term *neutrality* is unfortunate; some of its connotations are highly misleading, others suggest altogether impracticable principles. For this reason I have not used it before in these lectures." Rawls 2005, p. 191. Gaus 2003 constructs an interpretation of liberal neutrality in terms of a concern for public justification.
5. Audi 2011, p. 72. Audi draws from Alston 1964, p. 88.

6. My conception of religious commitment is somewhat distinct from others in the literature. Perry 1991, p. 119, defines religious commitments to include any answers about the ultimate meaningfulness of existence, whereas Eberle 2002, p. 71, employs the narrower notion of theistic content.

7. See Bellah 2011, pp. 1–44, for a discussion of the most general conceptual features of religion. He argues that supernaturalism is a modern component of religion.

8. Neal 2009.

9. Ibid., pp. 155–6.

10. Eberle 2002, p. 153.

11. For the direct-indirect distinction, I thank Andrew Lister.

12. Larmore 1987, p. 67.

13. Larmore 2008, p. 205. Larmore is focused on Rawls in this passage. Note that, like Rawls, Larmore is focused on the determining basic matters of justice and not necessarily the justification of particular laws. This complication is not relevant for our purposes.

14. Ibid., p. 205. Emphasis mine.

15. Ibid., p. 211.

16. Ibid., p. 211.

17. Ibid., p. 215.

18. Ibid., p. 215. Emphasis in original.

19. Ibid., p. 212.

20. Ibid., p. 213. Emphasis mine.

21. Rawls 1997, pp. 764–5.

22. Schwartzman 2011.

23. Rawls 2002, p. 155, nn. 57, 156.

24. Ibid., p. 156.

25. For an admirably condensed statement of Audi's conception of ethics and the foundations of his political philosophy, see Ch. 1 of Audi 2011. For a statement of his foundational principles, see pp. 39–48.

26. Ibid., pp. 65–6. Audi's view has arguably changed over the years. See Audi and Wolterstorff 1997, and Audi 2000 for detailed statements and defenses of his earlier views.

27. Audi 2011, p. 67.

28. See Audi 2009a for a development of this idea.

29. Audi 2011, p. 67.

30. Ibid., p. 68.

31. Ibid., p. 66.

32. Ibid., p. 68. Emphasis in original.

33. Thus Audi accepts a version of the Liberty Principle (Ch. 1, Sec. III).

34. Gaus and Vallier 2009 made one of the first such distinctions in the literature.

35. Audi 2011, p. 70.

36. Ibid.

37. I will further address the accessibility-shareability distinction in Ch. 4.

38. Audi 2011, p. 89.

39. Ibid., p. 95.

40. Ibid., p. 97.

41. Ibid., p. 76.

42. Harry Frankfurt understands integrity as self-integration. See Frankfurt 1988. Others understand integrity as involving unconditional commitments. Someone has integrity when she will never violate her commitments. See Calhoun 1995.
43. Cox, La Caze and Levin 2008, Sec. 2.
44. Calhoun 1995, p. 235.
45. I provide a more comprehensive conception of integrity in Ch. 3, Sec. III. See esp. n. 40.
46. Lomasky 1987, p. 26.
47. Ibid.
48. Ibid.
49. Luther is often thought to have said, "Here I stand. I can do no other," at this meeting, but scholars doubt this. See Brecht 1985, p. 460.
50. Flaubert 2004.
51. I thank Robert Audi for pressing me to stress this point.
52. Gaus 2003, p. 185.
53. Wolterstorff 1997a, p. 105. Emphasis in original.
54. Perry 1988, pp. 181–2.
55. Macedo 2000b, p. 35.
56. I will revisit judicial integrity in Ch. 6, Sec. III.
57. These arguments can be found in Weithman 2002. Weithman 2010 seems to endorse the double-wide duty of civility. However, Weithman does not provide reason to reject his earlier arguments.
58. Weithman 2002, p. 22.
59. Ibid.
60. It is not clear to me whether Weithman means to offer an integrity objection, rather than merely to complain about the loss of realized citizenship. So I construct an integrity objection from the materials he has provided.
61. Though recall that Audi is a partial exception to these claims in various respects.
62. Audi's Principle of Secular Rationale allows religious reasons to have motivational primacy, so in his case the effects arise insofar as citizens must recognize that acting *solely* on religious reasons is morally problematic. I thank Audi for encouraging me to make this distinction.
63. Tutu 1999, p. 87.
64. Ibid., p. 82.
65. Chad Van Schoelandt raises an important complication here: supposing that Tutu's language was required to heal racial tensions in South Africa, then that fact alone might prove to be a sufficient non-religious reason to support institutions like the TRC, with its characteristic practices. My reply is that principles of restraint will restrict Tutu's language, even if the consequences of his public speech help to produce publicly justified outcomes. Defenses of restraint are largely deontological or respect-based, not consequentialist.
66. Rawls 2005, p. 243.
67. Of course, it is true that Tutu may have had non-religious reasons for his positions—undoubtedly he did. The point is rather that restraint interferes with Tutu's free political actions in ways that seem objectionable.
68. Weithman 2002, pp. 206–7.
69. Though Ch. 6 develops principles of proposal restraint that have important effects, despite the fact that they only apply to political officials (always a small group vis-à-vis the citizenry as a whole).

70. Audi 2011, p. 91.
71. Ibid., p. 92.
72. Eberle 2002, pp. 104–8. See Ch. 4, Sec. IV, for a discussion of Eberle's principle of restraint.
73. Galston 1991, p. 109.
74. Neal 2009, p. 153.
75. Rawls 2005, p. 129.
76. I recognize that some liberal perfectionists may find this claim objectionable. See Wall 2010 for the claim that Gaus's version of public reason liberalism makes the case for coercion too independent of external or objective reasons.
77. Perry 1991, p. 15.
78. Let "secular beliefs" denote reasons deriving from doctrines of a non-religious character.
79. Wolterstorff 1997a, p. 105. Emphasis mine.
80. Habermas 2006.
81. Ibid., p. 12.
82. Ibid., p. 13.
83. Ibid., p. 14.
84. Ibid.
85. Ibid., p. 15. Emphasis mine.
86. Ibid., p. 18. A lot depends on this failure.
87. Rawls 2005, pp. 192–3.
88. Perry 1991, p. 54.
89. Wolterstorff 1997a, p. 78.
90. Wolterstorff 1997b, p. 166.
91. So in contrast to the integrity and fairness objections, which directly target restraint and the Public Justification Principle, the divisiveness objection seeks to undermine an argument for restraint based on the claim that unrestrained discourse is divisive and destabilizing.
92. Eberle 2002, p. 153.
93. Ibid., p. 166.
94. Solum 1990, p. 1096.
95. Rorty 2009, p. 137–8.
96. Eberle 2002, p. 161.
97. Ibid., p. 167.
98. Ibid., p. 169.
99. Greene 1993, p. 1630.
100. Greenawalt 1988, p. 219.
101. Eberle 2002, p. 168. I have converted premise numbers to letters so as not to overlap with premises of other arguments in the chapter.
102. I use "*" to denote Eberle's alterations. While Eberle does not employ premises (D) and (E), I have modified them along the same lines.
103. Eberle 2002, p. 173.
104. A few examples: Greene 1993, p. 1035; Greenawalt 1988, p. 219; Greenawalt 1995, p. 157; Rawls 2005, p. 129; Audi and Wolterstorff 1997, p. 32.
105. Eberle 2002, pp. 182–3, discusses Eberle's version of this concern.
106. I shall use the terms "stability for the right reasons" and "normative stability" interchangeably.
107. This discussion owes much to our collaboration.

108. Thrasher and Vallier 2013.
109. Gintis 2009, p. 153.
110. It is worth pointing out that we, like Rawls, are not really concerned with how the assurance equilibrium is attained; we are only concerned with the question of whether the equilibrium is stable once attained.
111. For an influential account, see Bikhchandani, Hirshleifer and Welch 1992.
112. Anderson and Holt 1997, p. 847.
113. Not premise (2), which ties a conception of justificatory reasons to a principle of exclusion. I take premise (2) to be a conceptual truth.

CHAPTER 3

Reconciliation in Theory
A Strategy

To vindicate my thesis, I must defeat the justificatory premise of the Master Argument, the claim that the best conception of justificatory reasons includes an accessibility or shareability requirement (Ch. 1, Sec. V). Chapter 3 identifies the considerations capable of doing so.

Here's how I will proceed. First, I will try to explain why the present debate between public reason liberals and their religious critics is at a philosophical impasse. In short, religious objectors have defeaters for restraint, but public reason liberals appear to lack them. I argue that we can break the impasse by denying the justificatory premise and disputing the mainstream conception of justificatory reasons (Sec. I). I then develop desiderata for adjudicating disputes about the appropriate conception of justificatory reasons grounded in public reason's foundational values. I identify two such values: respect for personal integrity and respect for reasonable pluralism and diversity. They serve as desiderata by ordering interpretations of the Public Justification Principle, showing which interpretations are superior to others (Sec. II). I then identify an ambiguity in this strategy between whether a publicly justified legal scheme *minimizes* or *eliminates* restrictions on personal integrity and reasonable pluralism. A *modus vivendi* approach holds that a publicly justified legal scheme minimizes legal restrictions on the integrity of citizens, whereas a *congruence* approach seeks elimination. I defend congruence on the grounds that it avoids the social and psychological costs associated with accepting a conflict between one's personal integrity and the publicly justified rules that allow diverse persons to live together on free and equal terms (Sec. III). I then discuss some familiar mechanisms for resolving apparent failures of congruence (Sec. IV). I conclude that if respect for integrity and diversity can be used to order conceptions of the Public Justification Principle, then I can use them to show that public reason liberals have defeaters for restraint. If even public reason liberals have defeaters for restraint, then the case against restraint is sound.

The deeper, more aspirational aim of this book is to reconcile liberal and religious citizens and their respective philosophical advocates. If we can show that public reason does not require restraint, we can bring these two groups much closer together. But reconciliation requires sacrifice: not only must public reason liberals reduce their hostility to religion in public life, but the religious critics must discard some of their most powerful objections to public reason.

I.   The Religion and Politics Debate at an Impasse

The religious objectors have three defeaters for restraint: the integrity objection, the fairness objection and the divisiveness objection. Restraint requires that citizens violate their integrity, inequitably restricts the freedom of religious citizens and does not appropriately promote social stability. When combined with the Master Argument, the religious objections provide public reason's religious critics with sufficient reason to reject the Public Justification Principle. Importantly, rejecting it does not mean denying that public justification has value. Christopher Eberle argues that while religious citizens have sufficiently strong reason to advocate for laws that are not publicly justified, he still holds that citizens have a duty to pursue public justification insofar as they can.[1] Rejecting the Public Justification Principle instead implies that publicly unjustified coercion is often permitted.

The standard response to the religious objections is to double-down on restraint and the Public Justification Principle and attempt to dispel the objections. As we have seen, Audi denies that his principle of secular rationale imposes significant integrity costs on citizens. Habermas tries to rebut the fairness objection by arguing that religious citizens have already paid the relevant cognitive costs. Steve Macedo insists that public reason's religious critics simply get over their scruples and deal with the fact that they live in a free, liberal society.[2] These replies are not *obviously* objectionable, even Macedo's. Every political theory has drawbacks, after all. So, public reason liberals might admit that restraint sometimes violates integrity and is in some ways inequitable, but insist that respect for persons is paramount.[3]

The religion and politics debate is at an impasse because each side pursues what appears to be a reasonable balance of reasons for and against restraint and often admit that the other side's concerns have force. Based on the present dialectic, it is unclear how to move forward. I believe the impasse can be bypassed if we can show that the Master Argument fails, specifically by showing that the values on which the Public Justification Principle is based give us reason to reject the justificatory premise. If I am right, a commitment to respect for persons and the public justification of coercion *doesn't require restraint*. Consequently, I maintain that public reason liberals have misunderstood the implications of their commitment to the public justification of coercion.

To decisively refute the justificatory premise, and so the Master Argument, we need desiderata whose force public reason liberals already regard as especially powerful. These desiderata should be based in values public reason liberals commonly affirm, such as respect for individual liberty, treating persons as equals, recognizing reasonable diversity among conceptions of the good life, preserving citizens' integrity, publicizing political principles and so on. If restraint-requiring conceptions of justificatory reasons poorly express a commitment to these fundamental values, then public reason liberals are required by their own lights to embrace alternative conceptions, if they are available. Therefore, we should try to identify some of public reason liberalism's fundamental values.

II. Two Foundational Values in Public Reason

A foundational value in public reason liberalism has two functions: (i) counting in favor of or *grounding* the Public Justification Principle and (ii) shaping the structure of law ratified by the Public Justification Principle.

Regarding (i), we have already reviewed a number of these foundational values (Ch. 1, Sec. V), specifically the ideas of natural human freedom and moral equality, along with the recognition that free and equal persons live under conditions of reasonable pluralism. One should accept the Public Justification Principle because it expresses recognition of the fact that persons have no natural duty to obey one another and that they are in this way free and equal. Accordingly, if we recognize the fact of reasonable pluralism, we will see that justifications for political authority must consist in considerations that each person finds salient from her own unique perspective.

A number of political theorists have identified similar foundational values at the heart of liberal political theory. Thomas Nagel has claimed that liberalism depends on accepting "higher-order impartiality," which "parallels the familiar problem in moral theory of integrating impartiality with moral motives."[4] Similarly, Charles Taylor and Jocelyn Maclure identify respect for conscience and the moral equality of diverse citizens as the two foundational values that liberal democratic states should appeal to when deciding how to treat religious citizens.[5] Liberal states must respect an individual's sovereign right to live in accord with her conscience and recognize that consciences will differ on matters of import. P. F. Strawson distinguishes between social morality and individual ideals.[6] Social morality includes those rules of social life that we both regard as moral constraints and that help us to coordinate our actions, whereas individual ideals are aspirations that flesh out conceptions of personal integrity. We have reason both to endorse social morality and to have individual ideals. Strawson claims that those who recognize both sources of normativity will "be most at home in a liberal society."[7]

Regarding (ii), foundational values shape the structure of justified law. Rawls's conception of the citizen as having two moral powers is an illuminating example. The citizen is conceived of as having the capacity to be both rational and reasonable.[8] A person is rational when she uses her "powers of judgment and deliberation" to seek "ends and interests peculiarly [her] own."[9] Political liberalism in this way requires that we respect persons' reasons to pursue their conceptions of the good.[10] A person is reasonable when she is "ready to propose principles and standards as fair terms of cooperation and to abide by them willingly, given the assurance that others will likewise do so" and be willing to discuss the terms she proposes.[11] Reasonable citizens must also recognize the burdens of judgment—the factors that inevitably lead citizens to affirm different but reasonable comprehensive doctrines.[12] The conception of citizens as rational and reasonable plays an enormous role in determining the structure of justified law. Political liberalism recognizes the importance of protecting the development and exercise of these powers by allowing them to shape the principles, basic rights and institutions on which coercion is based. Rawls's two moral powers thereby serve as foundational values in the second sense because they help determine what is publicly justified.

These illustrations do not fully capture the type of foundational value I am after, however, since I hope to identify foundational values that play *both* roles, values that *both* ground the Public Justification Principle and give shape to the laws to which it assigns positive justificatory status. I believe that public reason liberals are committed to two such foundational values that I shall call *respect for integrity* and *respect for reasonable pluralism*. Let's explain these values in turn.

In Chapter 2, I defined personal integrity as loyalty or fidelity to one's projects, plans and principles (Ch. 2, Sec. IV). But integrity is often a consideration used to rebut the claims of public reason liberals, so it may seem strange to cite it as a ground for the Public Justification Principle. Nonetheless, defenses of the Public Justification Principle are rooted in the recognition that living in accord with your projects and principles is something to which you have a fundamental right. Integrity for this reason has a powerful effect on the structure of legitimate law.

Integrity-based considerations help to ground the Public Justification Principle based on how the public reason liberal understands the *point* of political philosophy. For the public reason liberal, the point of political philosophy is to ensure that people can cooperate in the pursuit of diverse ends despite the fact that they disagree about what morality, justice and the good require of them. The use of coercion is worrisome in large part because it prevents persons from pursuing their own projects and plans and living in accord with their principles. When coercion is publicly justified, it no longer restrains persons' actions in ways they find objectionable. Protecting integrity thereby figures into the identification of true political principles. Respect for integrity performs the first function of a foundational value: providing a reason to endorse the Public Justification Principle.

To show that respect for integrity performs the second function of a foundational value, I should first stress that the Public Justification Principle is not directly sensitive to any form of personal integrity. Instead, it is directly sensitive to some subset of each person's *reasons*.

All coercion must be acceptable from the perspective of each person, given her various reasons for action and belief. The Public Justification Principle is in this way designed to respect each person's point of view because it makes her reasons to her pursue values and aspirations arbiters of justified law. She has a prima facie permission to pursue her own values in her own way, and this generic permission may only be hemmed in by laws that satisfy the Public Justification Principle.

Integrity enters the scene when we recognize that our life projects and principles, those bound up with our integrity, *issue* reasons, specifically core normative considerations around which our other reasons are ordered and structured. To recall a case from Chapter 2, Martin Luther's reasons for action were structured by his goal of defending the doctrine of justification by faith alone. Thus, his reasons for more minor pursuits, like writing a particular book or scheduling his day in a particular manner, were shaped by his integrity-based reasons. This means that integrity-based reasons are especially *strong* in the sense that they override a whole host of competitor reasons and hierarchically organize many others. Given the strength of these reasons, integrity-based reasons will serve as robust defeaters for a wide range of laws given the Public Justification Principle. Consequently, integrity carves out social space for each person to pursue her projects and act in concert with her principles. It therefore performs a foundational value's second role.[13]

Let me stress two more points about how integrity functions as a foundational value. First, the value of integrity requires *respect* rather than promotion. The point of the Public Justification Principle is not to maximize or promote individual liberty and integrity. Instead, it represents a deontological commitment to respect persons. Second, the value of integrity does not extend to using integrity as an excuse to coerce others for religious reasons. Diverse individuals will have defeaters for such coercion. Instead, integrity is valued by employing it to choose between interpretations of the Public Justification Principle, which will tell us what *counts as* an unjustified use of religious reasons. But whatever integrity selects, publicly unjustified coercion based on religious reasons is still prohibited.

Turning to the second value, recall from Chapter 1 (Sec. V) that to defend the Public Justification Principle, public reason liberals conjoin their conceptions of liberty, equality and respect with the recognition of reasonable pluralism. Reasonable pluralism obtains when sincere, informed persons systematically and freely disagree about what is of ultimate value. As Larmore puts it, "liberal thought is best understood as responding to an essential ingredient of our modern self-understanding. On the fundamental questions of human life, we have come to expect that reasonable people tend naturally to disagree with one another."[14] Due to a number of factors, including Rawls's burdens of judgment, we cannot reasonably hope to secure agreement on enough moral and religious matters to govern society on the basis of a single ideal or conception of the good.

To respect reasonable pluralism, then, is first to recognize that one's disagreements with her fellow citizens are not necessarily due to vice or ignorance on their part. Instead, she must be open to the fact that rational, well-informed and fair-minded persons may adhere to an ideal or philosophical doctrine entirely different from her own. To be more precise, we respect reasonable pluralism when we recognize that others' *reasons* differ from ours. With respect to the organization of political life, we must not diminish the extent of reasonable pluralism and so must be prepared to publicly justify coercion to many reasonable points of view.

The Public Justification Principle is grounded in respect for reasonable pluralism, which should be obvious by this point in the book. First, without reasonable pluralism, the call for public justification seems pointless. But if reasonable pluralism is pervasive, we rightly think that to treat others as free and equal we must ensure that coercion is justified from multiple perspectives. Second, public reason liberals think that part of the point of political philosophy is to grapple with the fact of reasonable disagreement. Gaus thinks that the core problem of political philosophy is to explain how our social morality can have authority despite the fact that we are free, equal and disagree.[15] Larmore similarly holds that political philosophy must focus on how to deal with widespread disagreement about what morality requires.[16] It should be clear then that respect for reasonable pluralism plays the first role of a foundational value: helping to ground the Public Justification Principle.

Respect for reasonable pluralism plays the second role of a foundational value as well, because the recognition of reasonable pluralism is embodied in the Public Justification Principle's sensitivity to citizens' varied reasons. While some public justification principles are sensitive only to reasons that citizens share, all versions recognize that our diverse reasons for action can restrain the reach of justified law. As we shall see (Ch. 4, Sec. V), even Rawls thought that, to be fully justified, a conception of justice derived from shared political values must prove acceptable to each reasonable comprehensive doctrine. In some sense, then, the Public Justification Principle accords a wide variety of reasons justificatory force. It also accords reasonable pluralism justificatory force because it prioritizes the formation of norms and laws that allow diverse citizens to cooperate despite their disagreements. By permitting laws and policies to form only when each person has sufficient reason to accept them, public reason liberals recognize the value of cooperation in a diverse world. The Public Justification Principle is sensitive to this valuation because it encourages cooperation on terms that a wide range of diverse individuals can accept.

Respect for integrity and reasonable pluralism are therefore excellent candidates for foundational values. This means we can use these values to order interpretations of the Public Justification Principle and, perhaps, to refute the justificatory premise. To the extent then that an interpretation of the Public Justification Principle generates respect for integrity and reasonable pluralism, it is superior to alternative interpretations. In a loose sense, the two values rank competing conceptions of public justification.

Respect for integrity will select among conceptions of public justification by determining which conceptions interfere with or restrict integrity more than others. Thus, it will judge conceptions of public justification that better protect integrity to be better than conceptions of public justification that interfere relatively more. Respect for reasonable pluralism will order conceptions of public justification by determining which conceptions recognize the reason-generating force of a greater range of projects and principles. It will rank a conception of public justification over another if the former better recognizes the validity of the pursuit of a greater range of projects and compliance with a greater range of principles. Respect for reasonable pluralism does not judge a conception of public justification to be better than another merely because it assigns *more* reasons justificatory force, but rather whether it recognizes a greater set of reasons associated with persons' core projects and principles.

III. Two Strategies for Reconciliation

Suppose that a society's laws are entirely publicly justified, in accord with an interpretation of the Public Justification Principle that adequately respects integrity and reasonable pluralism. In this society, does compliance with the law violate the integrity of reasonable and rational citizens? If so, the best public reason liberals can hope for is to *minimize* violations of the diverse integrity of citizens, as a scheme of laws that satisfies the Public Justification Principle may substantially restrict their abilities to act on their aspirations, plans and principles. Conversely, public reason liberals can try to *eliminate* these violations. They can try to realize a social order where each person is free to live an integrated life, yet is bound by the law. Some social contract liberals, such as Rousseau, attempted to harmonize conflicts between law and ideals by showing that each person has conclusive reason to accept as binding the dictates of a system of public judgment, such as a legislative assembly. If citizens' own ideals and principles commit them to recognizing the moral authority of public judgment, then putative conflicts between law and personal conviction dissolve. Thus, we might hope to identify a set of laws and policies that fully harmonize the moral demands of the law and one's personal convictions. I shall call these strategies the *modus vivendi* and *congruence* approaches to resolving such conflicts. I term the former strategy a *modus vivendi* because it accepts an agreement based on a balance of forces as a consequence of minimizing conflict rather than eliminating it. I term the latter strategy congruence because it seeks a complete, moral harmonization of citizens' reasons.

We can also understand the congruence-modus vivendi distinction in terms of whether persons have reason to *internalize* the publicly justified law or rule, or whether they simply have reason to comply with it without internalizing it. Gaus understands rule internalization in terms of acting autonomously. In Gaus's terms, "a person acts autonomously when her action is directed by her internalized *nomos* or rule, not by what she most wants or what others expect of her. An autonomous person has made the requirement hers: it is not simply a bit of "information about what is required; it is what she accepts as required."[17] The person who internalizes a moral rule will rationally feel guilt if she fails to comply, as she regards the rule as one that she herself acknowledges based on her own values. In contrast, someone might accept that she should follow a rule without giving it authority over her and internalizing it as a genuinely moral rule. A congruence approach to reconciliation assumes internalization: when we harmonize our reasons, we come to accept a publicly justified rule as one that we have most moral reason to accept. We authorize the rule. But a modus vivendi approach to reconciliation only holds that people take themselves to have sufficient reason to comply with the rule, not sufficient reason to internalize it or to make it hers. The only reason someone complies with rules under a modus vivendi is because she fears the social consequences of not doing so or because that's what she most wants—not what she takes herself to have most moral reason to do. If we take a modus vivendi approach, then we are satisfied when all laws are ones that people have sufficient reason to comply with. If we take a congruence approach, we will not be satisfied until all laws are those that people have sufficient reason to internalize, that they count as their very own rules and laws.

Our choice of strategy matters, as the modus vivendi approach endangers our entire project. If we accept that even justified law can require that citizens violate their integrity, that it is enough that people have sufficient reason to comply with laws rather than to accept them as their own, we must still choose between mainstream public reason liberals and their religious critics. Most public reason liberals side with publicly justified law over integrity: Macedo's approach is paradigmatic. Religious critics go the other way, arguing that conscience, integrity, ideals and personal principles take priority. Eberle exemplifies this approach, as he believes that public justification is worth pursuing, but only to a point. If we fail to publicly justify our proposals to others, then we can coercively impose those proposals anyway. Those who, like me, seek genuine reconciliation between the two sides cannot accept a modus vivendi approach. For this reason, I should provide further reason to reject modus vivendi approaches, assuming a congruence strategy is viable.

The standard modus vivendi strategy comes in two types, as it can prioritize the demands of the legal order or one's personal convictions, that is, stressing reasons to comply with laws rather than internalize them, or stressing that personal reasons alone are sufficient grounds to reject publicly justified law. The former approach has more prominent adherents. The early social contract theorists held that for the sake of justice and social order, law must override one's private convictions. In this way, public reason settles for a legal order characteristic of Hobbes and Locke: one that offers citizens law in exchange for freedom. Hobbes claimed that one implication of the second law of nature was "that a man be willing, when others are so too . . . to lay down this right to all things, and be contented with so much liberty against other men."[18] Locke argued that in agreeing to the social contract, man "divests himself of his natural liberty, and puts on the bonds of civil society."[19] On this modus vivendi view, then, law is sold to citizens as a bargain: good law is worth the trade-off of personal liberty and integrity.

Rousseau helps us to see the inadequacy of such normative bargains. Criticizing Hobbes and Locke, he claims that the dignity of the human person is diminished when she renounces her freedom: "To renounce liberty is to renounce one's quality as man, the rights of humanity and even its duties ... Such a renunciation is incompatible with the nature of man."[20] Persons are forced to trade off their ideals for a system of law, debasing themselves. As Gaus puts it, "Rousseau rejects such a bargain: it is exchanging liberty for chains."[21] Laws are sold at the price of citizens' integrity and their good. While the modus vivendi approach promises that the price will be low, it is a price all the same. One might reply as Gaus suggests, "Rousseau and those influenced by him simply refuse to learn the lesson of opportunity costs. In order to get something of value, we must give up something of value."[22] Perhaps the price of liberal political order is the alienation of our liberty. In this way, we may reach a rational bargain among different groups.[23] A limited peace between competing groups is a staggering achievement. How could we reasonably wish for more?

We can see why a modus vivendi is morally unattractive when it characterizes the relationship between reasons in a moral order rather than a mere political order. A political modus vivendi only bases the public justification of *laws* on relationships of power and prudence, but a *moral* modus vivendi allows *all* moral rules to be justified on the basis of power and prudence. Since moral reasons and rules pervade our lives, a moral modus vivendi permits constant impingement on our free, personal moral action. We may find ourselves constantly restrained by socially recognized rules imposed merely by the sanctions of others, sanctions we are afraid to violate but that we see as fundamentally heteronomous. Worse still, we will often impose moral restrictions on *ourselves* by acquiescing to moral demands that we cannot authorize from our own point of view. Our unity of self, as Rawls called it, will be shaken by the conflict between our irrational heteronomous guilt and self-flagellation and our conception of the good.[24]

The other interpretation of the modus vivendi approach prioritizes acting on one's convictions instead of complying with a publicly justified system of law. Some perfectionist liberals pursue this line of argument, as do religious critics like Eberle, who hold that there are no good reasons for one to restrain herself from imposing her preferred legal order on others.[25] To assess this view, let's briefly discuss a similar view defended by David McCabe. McCabe's "anti-utopian" modus vivendi liberalism "grounds political life not via its consonance with citizens' deepest moral ideals but instead as something diverse citizens can agree to as an acceptable compromise."[26] This form of modus vivendi liberalism deliberately forgoes the Rawlsian aspiration to the full public justification of coercion, or the Gausian aspiration to achieve the internalization of social morality and law. McCabe instead characterizes mutual justification in terms of more pragmatic, often nonmoral reasons. That said, McCabe endorses a loose public justification principle that he calls the "Justificatory Requirement" (JR).[27] He acknowledges important advantages for regimes that satisfy JR. However, JR can be satisfied only when two preconditions are met: parties must recognize (a) that many of their normative frameworks are illiberal and (b) that the existence of the state is either unchangeable or that it contributes to crucially important goods.[28] Liberal terms arise once competing parties accept "the value of ordered political life" and understand that their "political vision . . . cannot be achieved." In this case, the liberal state is their second-best option that they select based on a calculated risk that other citizens "will tolerate others' having broad liberties and accept that state power will not be used to advance their particular normative framework, in exchange for the assurance that their own liberties will be protected."[29] This is the best persons can reasonably expect in a diverse society. The point of liberal institutions, then, is not that the law has moral authority over you, but rather that the most reliable way to pursue your own particular values is to accept a legal order as a compromise between powerful social groups.

The standard public reason liberal concern about a modus vivendi view like McCabe's is that compromises rooted in nonmoral, merely pragmatic reasons rest on the domination of some by others. The public reason liberal ideal is to base state power on moral reason rather than brute force, and modus vivendi liberalism explicitly abandons this aspiration. While McCabe acknowledges that concerns about domination have some force, he claims that it depends on an implausibly sharp distinction between "principled reasons for compromise" and merely "pragmatic reasons." First, our deep moral judgments are "sensitive to changeable conditions."[30] Even Rawls acknowledges this point: an overlapping consensus depends on the contingent assurance that other citizens will comply with the demands of a political conception of justice. Furthermore, as McCabe points out, Rawls weakened the distinction between principled and pragmatic reasons because both *Political Liberalism* and *The Law of Peoples* recognize that public justification can be contextual and rooted in different communities' social and political history and traditions.[31] McCabe's most forceful argument against the distinction between principled and pragmatic reasons is that it depends on an implausible "Power-Independence Assumption," which holds that "one's endorsement of some policy or principle is morally grounded only if one would not support a different policy or principle under a different balance of power."[32] McCabe counters that many of our seemingly pure moral judgments are contingent on power arrangements, and that it is hard to imagine a set of laws that were not contingent in this way.

Even if the distinction between principled and pragmatic reasons is overdrawn, modus vivendi liberalism fails to recognize the full cost of conflicts between persons' reasons to follow their ideals and reasons to obey the law on the other. The costs of moral compromise include alienation from our fellow citizens and the loss of social trust. If we believe that our fellow citizens accept liberal institutions only because they cannot secure enough power to coercively impose their views on others, then it is hard to see how we can live on genuinely moral terms. The threat of intrapersonal conflict rears its head as well. Under a modus vivendi, reasons of integrity or conscience will be subverted to the demands of social order, as citizens simply comply rather than internalize legal demands. To my mind, this substantial cost is sufficient reason to aspire to something more: congruence liberalism.

The public reason liberal should therefore formulate the ideal of public reason as an attempt to harmonize the demands of public justification and the demands of living an integrated life, achieving what we might call "congruence" (Ch. 1, Sec. II). In *Theory*, Rawls described congruence as tying together "the concepts of justice and goodness."[33] Congruence plays a critical role in resolving a problem in Part III of *Theory*, namely the problem of conflicts between an individual's sense of justice and her conception of the good. Rawls thought that members of a well-ordered society might find that their sense of justice (expressed in Rawls's two principles) conflicts with the achievement of intrinsic goods (identified by Rawls's conception of the person). If such a conflict exists, then persons may find it practically irrational to comply with their sense of justice, thereby rendering justice as fairness unstable even under favorable conditions. Congruence is postulated as the resolution of the conflict, where each person endorses her sense of justice (and the principles that constitute its best expression) from within her conception of the good *apart from* the explicitly recognized good of justice. In other words, a person has a "thin theory of the good," the list of goods she endorses minus the good of complying with her sense of justice.[34] Congruence is obtained when an agent endorses the good of justice based on her thin theory of the good. Rawlsian congruence is therefore a relation of fit between two types of reasons: reasons to comply with the two principles and reasons to pursue great goods of love, friendship, excellence and the like. When congruence obtains, each person has sufficient reason to comply with her sense of justice because she includes in her list of goods the good of justice.[35]

It is true that Rawls later decided his account of congruence was unrealistic because it rested on an excessively monistic conception of the good and the person.[36] Yet Rawls's concerns about congruence extend into *Political Liberalism*, where he insisted that a political conception of justice must be "either congruent with, or supportive of, or else not in conflict with" reasonable comprehensive doctrines.[37] Rawls remained concerned to show that our reasons of right and reasons of good do not conflict. He always sought to unify practical reason by showing that our sense of justice issues demands compatible with the normative force of our conceptions of the good. Thus, Rawls thought that political liberalism must grapple with a conflict between two types of reasons, since we may have reasons of personal good to reject or override our sense of justice.[38]

By embracing the congruence standard, I commit myself to a similar resolution of the conflict between the demands of law and the demands of living an integrated life. On this view, liberal political theory is tasked with identifying and recommending laws and institutions whose social directives are compatible with each unique person's integrity and that persons can internalize as their own.

The attraction of congruence is therefore that each person *self-legislates* the law despite the fact that it coerces her.[39] Because Reba endorses a law as authoritative and regards compliance with the law as compatible with living a fully integrated life, she acts only on her own reasons. If congruence is a feasible ideal, then, it promises that citizens can retain their freedom within the bounds of public reason. From their own private perspectives, they will have sufficient reason to endorse the laws of their polity. In the same way, *religious* citizens can retain their freedom within the bounds of public reason. From their own *religious* perspectives, they will have sufficient reason to endorse the laws of their polity.

Perhaps I can make the congruence standard clearer with an example. Consider Juan, an undocumented Mexican immigrant, who has just immigrated to Tucson, Arizona to secure a higher paying job for his family. Juan considers himself a law-abiding citizen, but he cannot pass up the prospect of a ten-fold wage hike offered by many American jobs. He wants a better life for his children and supporting them is a critical part of his individual ideal. However, Juan feels guilty for working in the U.S. illegally because of the social stigma attached to disobeying the law of the country he resides in. Furthermore, he recognizes that his new friends and community members might resent him if they knew he was undocumented, which would undermine their friendship and add to his shame. Embodied in Juan's guilt and shame is his taking legal reasons prescribed by U.S. law—reasons that require him not to reside in the U.S. without legal documents—to apply to him, though not as giving him sufficient reason to internalize the norm. Juan thereby takes himself to have reason to blame himself for his actions. In this case, Juan's practical reasons are not congruent because of the conflict between his reasons of integrity ("Support my family") and his reasons rooted in public justification ("Obey the law"). The conflict remains even if Juan believes his reasons of integrity carry the day.

But now suppose that Juan is a Roman Catholic who believes the Church is a moral and theological authority. He tries to be a "good Catholic" by following Church teachings. One day, Juan discovers that his parish priest is involved in the local immigrant sanctuary movement. The priest believes that American immigration law is incompatible with Catholic social teaching on the common good and natural law. After some discussion, Juan comes to agree with his priest and thinks that his violation of immigration law is permissible, because the law is unjust. As a result, Juan's guilt dissipates because he no longer recognizes reasons to comply with U.S. immigration law, given his defeater reasons drawn from his Catholic faith. Due to his religious convictions, Juan's reasons of right and good now match. While Juan is sad that he cannot be fully forthright with his community, he feels little remorse. And in light of his new political activism, he starts to develop new friendships with others in the sanctuary movement, and so gradually builds new, more honest social bonds. His guilt and alienation are gone; he rejects the law autonomously and achieves congruence.

With a clearer understanding of congruence as a moral ideal, we should ask how settling for a modus vivendi and seeking congruence differ in practice. I assume they differ in cases where the reasons favoring a law outweigh reasons to reject the law, but that leave those subject to the law in a state of normative conflict because they cannot internalize the law in question. When Juan first arrives in the United States, he may judge that the reasons favoring present immigration law are sufficiently strong to give him reason to comply. But from the perspective of his conception of the good, he cannot endorse the law as his own. Modus vivendi liberals are only interested in whether each citizen has sufficient reason to endorse a law in the sense of having reason to comply with it, not whether individuals can internalize the laws they are subject to. Congruence liberals believe the law is morally defective because it leaves Juan with a deep moral conflict. In this way, the congruence ideal implies two "grades" of public justification, one where the balance of reasons merely favors complying with a law and one where the balance of reasons favors internalization, where each person's reasons are congruent.

Notice that when Juan reaches congruence and rejects current immigration law as unjust, the judgments of public reason liberals and their religious critics are the same. Public reason liberals regard the immigration law as publicly unjustified, and the religious critics claim that the immigration law violates Juan's integrity. If Juan is in a state of congruence, then those who emphasize the normative salience of public reason and integrity have nothing to fight about. Generalizing, the ideal of congruence aims to render all publicly justified laws compatible with the integrity of citizens, which should satisfy the demands of religious critics. Consequently, congruence liberalism breaks the impasse between public reason liberals and their religious critics by harmonizing their concerns via congruence between the reasons emphasized by both sides.

IV. When Congruence Fails

Given this description, some may find congruence an implausibly strong ideal, since I apparently claim that a regime cannot be legitimate unless all citizens' practical reasons are congruent. A few replies are in order. First, on my view, congruence is a regulative ideal—it is a state at which convergence justifications aim. As a result, publicly justified polities can be legitimate despite a failure of congruence between personal integrity and publicly justified law. These incongruous polities instead lack *full* or complete legitimacy. In other words, a publicly justified polity that falls short of congruence is morally defective, but such a social order has great value because it manifests a high (if insufficient) degree of respect for persons as free and equal.

Nonetheless, sometimes we may find ourselves in a position where a law is needed, but none can be justified. In such cases, a critic could argue that congruence prevents the imposition of much-needed law. Alternatively, we may face an overabundance of justified laws. Congruence may generate crippling indeterminacy if it cannot provide a method of deciding between them. Thus, congruence can be said to fail when it provides members of the public with too few or too many legal solutions to certain social problems.

Fortunately, public reason liberals have developed a number of mechanisms to handle such cases. I shall focus on two common examples. First, public reason liberals often appeal to *decision procedures* to resolve recalcitrant political conflicts.[40] For instance, suppose that citizens all acknowledge that some form of social safety net is publicly justified. However, they disagree about which policy is best. In this case, a democratic voting procedure might help members of the public select among proposed policies. To make a decision, they appeal to a voting rule that they all regard as fair in order to select a policy without first agreeing which option is best. Thus, if a citizen's conception of her good fails to be congruent with a particular law or policy, she might achieve congruence in virtue of her commitment to a decision procedure that selects the same law or policy in a fair manner.

Decision procedures can often dissolve disputes over the justification of laws, for as long as citizens have no conclusive reason to reject some legal solutions, they can employ a decision procedure to select a proposal of the set of undefeated laws without any member of the public having sufficient reason to reject it. Matters are less clear if all proposed laws on some issue are defeated. Of course, if citizens really do have defeaters for all laws on a particular subject, then no decision procedure can be used to justify the laws in question. But sometimes the apparent unjustifiability of a law is illusory. In many cases citizens may conclude that they have a defeater for a law or policy when in fact they merely think a competitor law or policy is superior. The fact that citizens disagree does not entail that they have defeaters for all the proposed laws in question. I shall revisit this matter in Chapter 4.

Public reason liberals also appeal to idealization to resolve failures of congruence. As we saw in Chapter 1 (Sec. IV), idealization involves altering citizens' cognitive abilities and access to information in order to determine what reasons they have, avoiding errors that arise from such limitations. In this way, idealization can resolve apparent conflicts between citizens by providing a more plausible model of their reasons. For example, idealized citizens will not object to laws simply because they are stubborn. In this way, many complaints can be set aside, as idealized citizens will make fewer erroneous claims.

Appeals to decision procedures and idealization have limitations. There may be cases where coercion is both needed and unjustified, where citizens both recognize the need for a law but some member of the public has a defeater for each alternative. I am skeptical that this problem is debilitating, however, as citizens' reasons are sensitive to their recognition that we need laws in order to have a social order at all. Consequently, it is hard to see how citizens who recognize the need for publicly justified laws would lack reason to endorse at least some law on the matter.[41]

There's no point denying that congruence failures are possible in principle. We cannot always avoid a modus vivendi. But even if congruence sometimes fails, it remains an ideal because it provides a compelling account of how to treat persons as free and equal.

V. Conclusion

By appealing to two of public reason liberalism's foundational values—respect for integrity and reasonable pluralism—we can adjudicate between competing interpretations of the Public Justification Principle. If we can vindicate an alternative to the consensus interpretation of the Public Justification Principle, we will have refuted the Master Argument by denying the justificatory premise, severing the link between public reason and restraint.

If so, we have reason to hope for reconciliation, for we can show both that public reason liberals are required by their own commitments to abandon restraint and that the religious objectors lack critical defeaters for public reason liberalism.

Notes

1. Eberle 2002, p. 68.
2. Macedo 2000b, p. 35.
3. Since for Audi restraint is only a prima facie duty, he could admit that integrity and fairness considerations sometimes override the principle of secular rationale. Audi 2011, p. 66.
4. Nagel 1987, p. 216. Other ethical theorists contrast the demands of impartiality and the existence of a personal or "agent-centered" prerogative that allows individuals to act according to their own judgment. Scheffler 1994 develops a view that hybridizes an agent-centered prerogative with the moral requirements to promote impartially good states of affairs.
5. Taylor and Maclure 2011, p. 4.
6. Strawson 2008, pp. 29–49.
7. Ibid., p. 48.
8. Rawls 2005, pp. 48–54.
9. Ibid.
10. Note here that I understand political liberalism as a version of public reason liberalism.
11. Ibid., p. 49.
12. Ibid., pp. 54–8.
13. Let me be clear that the value of integrity requires respect rather than promotion. The point of the Public Justification Principle is not to maximize or promote individual liberty and integrity. Instead, it represents a deontological commitment to respect persons.
14. Larmore 2008, p. 140.
15. Gaus 2011, p. xv.
16. Larmore 2013, p. 281.
17. Gaus 2011, p. 204.
18. Hobbes 1994, p. 80.
19. Locke 2003, p. 142.
20. Rousseau 1997, p. 5.
21. Gaus 2011, p. 48.
22. Ibid.
23. Rawls 2005, p. 147.
24. Rawls 1971, pp. 491–6.
25. Wall 1998 provides what remains perhaps the most comprehensive perfectionist attack on political liberal forms of restraint on imposing one's values on others.
26. McCabe 2010, p. 126.
27. Ibid., p. 5.
28. Ibid., p. 133.

29. Ibid., p. 133.
30. Ibid., p. 155.
31. Ibid., p. 156.
32. Ibid., p. 157.
33. Ibid., p. 498.
34. Ibid., pp. 348–9.
35. In fact, Rawls thought that the good of justice was already represented in the thin theory but under a *different description*. Weithman describes this claim in terms of an argument from a "diversity of descriptions." See Weithman 2010, p. 118.
36. Specifically, Rawls decided that the argument of Sec. 86 of *Theory* failed. For extensive discussion, see Weithman 2010, pp. 234–69.
37. Rawls 2005, p. 169.
38. Congruence can be understood in Strawsonian terms as well, as a unity of reasons of social morality and individual ideal.
39. I do not mean to understand self-legislation in its full-blown Kantian sense, as requiring autonomous endorsement of laws, but rather that an individual has sufficient moral reason to accept the law. In this way, she does impose a law on herself. I thank Robert Audi for pushing me to be more specific here.
40. See Gaus 1996, pp. 215–45 for an extensive discussion. For Rawls, public justification applies to constitutional essentials as decision procedures. Rawls 2005, p. 10.
41. A subtler issue raises its head here, namely cases where not all citizens recognize that a law is necessary when it is *in fact* necessary for some important social goal. I take it that most pressing issues should be resolved by the theory of moderate idealization I present in Ch. 5. I thank Chad Van Schoelandt for raising this point.

CHAPTER 4

Convergence
One Problem, Many Solutions

In this chapter I argue against the mainstream, consensus conception of justificatory reasons, which holds that justificatory reasons must be accessible or shareable. I then develop an alternative convergence conception of justificatory reasons, which holds that justificatory reasons need merely be *intelligible*. I show that convergence severs the connection between the restraint and the Public Justification Principle by defeating the justificatory premise of the Master Argument.

I proceed in seven sections. I first review the conceptions of public or justificatory reasons to distinguish standard conceptions from the convergence view, bringing my argumentative target into clear focus (Sec. I). Standard conceptions of reasons typically include four reasons requirements: shareability, accessibility, symmetry and sincerity. The convergence view either rejects these requirements or renders them trivial. My first critical argument refutes the accessibility requirement; I claim that either accessibility fails to realize its aims or runs afoul of our two desiderata identified in Chapter 3 (Sec. II). I then argue against the shareability requirement on the grounds that the two desiderata demonstrate that conceptions of justificatory reasons that include shareability are inferior to those that lack them. I also claim that once the accessibility and shareability requirements are defeated, that the symmetry requirement is too. Finally, I reject sincerity requirements on the grounds that they reduce to a combination of other requirements with restraint and so can be defeated by defeating their components (all in Sec. III).

By mid-chapter, I argue that convergence is the best conception of justificatory reasons on the grounds that the two desiderata vindicate it over alternatives. I shall also argue that convergence refutes the justificatory premise of the Master Argument by imposing *no* restraint on religious citizens (Sec. IV). Consequently, convergence answers the integrity, fairness and divisiveness objections. I next defend convergence against two potent objections (Sec. V–VI) and conclude that while convergence has great promise, it can nonetheless justify impositions on citizens of faith if coupled with a radical conception of idealization (Sec. VII).

I.   Conceptions of Justificatory Reasons

The mainstream, consensus conception of reasons combines accessibility or shareability with symmetry, whereas convergence only assumes intelligibility. These four requirements exhaust interpretations of justificatory reasons: (i) intelligibility, (ii) accessibility, (iii) shareability and (iv) symmetry. I explain the requirements in this section and motivate them. We can employ them to generate both principles of exclusion or principles of restraint (distinguished in Ch. 2, Sec. II). Following the literature, I focus on restraint, but given that restraint can only be defended via exclusion, I indirectly address exclusion as well.

Intelligibility, accessibility and shareability partially specify the idea of a *sufficient* reason (Ch. 1, Sec. IV). A reason is sufficient at least when it is *epistemically justified* for one or more members of the public. Specifically, a reason is sufficient for a moral agent when she affirms the reason in accord with adequate standards of inference and evidence. Accounts of epistemic justification vary, but we need only specify a conception of epistemic justification for justificatory reasons. The relevant conception of epistemic justification is a form of *access internalism*. Access internalism about beliefs holds that whenever one is entitled to believe P, one can become aware by reflection of all of one's justifiers that P.[1] Access internalism about reasons holds that whenever one is entitled to affirm reason R, one can become aware by reflection of all (or at least many of) one's justifiers for R. I believe that public reason liberals must embrace justificatory internalism about reasons. If not, we cannot plausibly claim that these reasons are rationally recognizable, as agents may lack psychological access to the relevant reasons. A reason is sufficient, therefore, only if it is epistemically justified in the internalist way. To be sufficient, a reason must also override or defeat reasons that contradict it.

Public reason liberals typically maintain that justificatory reasons must be intelligible, evaluable, comprehensible, accessible, etc., to others. I shall group these rarely distinguished properties into three degrees of stringency. The intelligibility requirement is the least stringent because it counts as justificatory any reason that can be recognized as such by members of the public. If R_x can be seen as a reason for X to act, then it can potentially play a justificatory role, so long as X is relevant, minimally moral and not overridden or undercut by another justificatory reason. That is, R_x can figure into a public justification if it is relevant and sufficient.

I take a reason R_x to be relevant just in case it counts in favor or against some proposed legislation that members of the public are presently evaluating. For example, John's reason to refine his ability to pitch a fastball does not speak to whether his country should adopt a lax or strict immigration policy. Similarly, Sarah's reason to go on a bike ride neither supports nor undermines the case for a law regulating the sale of narcotics. There are also some intuitive *moral* limits on what reasons count as relevant to a justificatory question. For example, reasons based on sadism or malice do not count as moral reasons and so are not relevant to the process of public justification. I should caution against interpreting these moral requirements too strictly, as we must still respect disagreement about what counts as a moral reason. After all, some conceptions of moral reasoning count self-interested reasons as moral reasons. If a law would improve John's well-being, then John has a reason to support it, and his reason can figure into a public justification for the law on the intelligible reasons requirement. So I shall say, perhaps too roughly, that justificatory reasons must be "minimally moral" or meet some conceptual threshold that qualifies the reason as a moral reason. Finally, as we have already noted, reasons must be sufficient in the sense that they are not rebutted or undercut by other reasons. They must be sufficient reasons to justify action and belief.

Before defining the requirements, I want to stress that a justificatory reason cannot justify coercion by itself. On some conceptions of public reasons, if a reason is public and/or justificatory, the state may permissibly act on that reason *alone* in imposing coercion. That is not my view. As I define them, justificatory reasons are ones that can *enter* the process of public justification. They are reasons that citizens and officials may use in discussion and action to advance coercive proposals. But if suitably idealized members of the public have public or justificatory reasons to reject state coercion, the coercion cannot be publicly justified even if based on a justificatory or public reason. A law is only publicly justified when each member of the public has sufficient reason to endorse the law. So a public or justificatory reason is just one that *enters the balance of reasons* in determining whether each person has sufficient reason to endorse a proposed law or policy. Genuinely private (unintelligible reasons) cannot enter the process because they lack the relevant epistemic and moral credentials. For example, on an intelligibility requirement intelligible reasons can figure into a public justification, but the state is not thereby permitted to coerce based on that reason alone in the face of countervailing intelligible reasons.

Qualifications made, I define intelligibility and the intelligibility requirement as follows:

Intelligibility: A's reason R_A is intelligible for members of the public if and only if members of the public regard R_A as epistemically justified for A according to A's evaluative standards.[2]

Intelligibility Requirement: A's reason R_A can figure into a justification for (or rejection of) a coercive law *L* only if it is intelligible to all members of the public.

Intelligibility has two elements that call out for comment: (i) the idea of regarding a reason as justified for an individual and (ii) the idea of an individual's evaluative standards. Regarding (i), we can say that John regards Sarah's reason R_S as justified for Sarah if he believes that she is epistemically rational to affirm it. Sarah makes no gross epistemic error in affirming R_S. So to regard R_S as justified is to ascribe it minimally sufficient epistemic credence. In this way, to say that R_S is justified for Sarah is to say that Sarah is either rationally entitled to affirm R_S or is rationally required to affirm R_S. The reader may find puzzling the requirement that John *regard* R_S as justified for Sarah rather than that R_S actually *be* justified for Sarah. But this epicycle of recognition is critical. A reason cannot be *public* in *any* sense if members of the public cannot see it as a reason for *anyone* from their respective points of view. A reason cannot figure into public justification unless citizens *take* the reason to be justified for the person who has it, even if the reason is *in fact* justified for the person who endorses it.

Regarding (ii), an evaluative standard is a set of norms a member of the public takes to justify her reason affirmations. Ordinary public reason views require that evaluative standards be shared. For Rawls, a political conception of justice includes shared standards of reasoning, evaluative and judgment, what he calls "guidelines of inquiry."[3] What sets the intelligibility requirement apart is that it employs *agent-relative* evaluative standards by permitting evaluative standards to differ among members of the public.[4] For a simple illustration, consider the reasons affirmed by Christian and Muslim members of the public. Christians and Muslims believe in sacred, divinely inspired texts that provide them with a great many reasons for action. As a result, they both acknowledge divine revelation as an evaluative standard, in sharp contrast with secular members of the public. Since Christians and Muslims affirm the divine inspiration of contradictory religious texts, they have distinct evaluative standards, as does the secular citizen who rejects both texts as sources of reasons. Thus, Christians, Muslims and secularists have distinct and irreconcilable evaluative standards. The intelligibility requirement allows reasons supported by one of these agent-relative evaluative standards *alone* to figure into a public justification for a law. So while a secularist will reject divine revelation as an evaluative standard, she can still count considerations derived from the Bible and the Koran as reasons for those who justifiably believe they are inspired. Thus, reasons based solely on a Christian's interpretation of the Bible (or a Muslim's interpretation of the Koran) can figure into a public justification.

What is the argument for intelligibility? I take it to be straightforward: the intelligibility requirement is *entailed* by the idea of reasoning from the standpoint of others. If I cannot see your purported reasons as reasons for you even according to *your own* evaluative standards, then I cannot reason from your standpoint by definition. That said, intelligibility might deny justificatory status to reasons based on poor inferences and bad information, as it requires that justificatory reasons possess epistemic justification. Furthermore, members of the public may decide that reasons advanced by A are unintelligible even if those reasons are *in fact* justified for A. Thus, a bona fide reason for A can fail to be intelligible because A's rational commitments differ from the commitments discernible by members of the public.

Moving forward, accessibility requires that *common* evaluative standards ratify justificatory reasons, rather than reasonable but distinct evaluative standards. While accessibility permits *reasons* to differ, it requires that they be evaluated as reasons according to evaluative standards that are shared. Thus with regard to restrictiveness, accessibility lies between intelligibility and shareability because intelligibility permits differing reasons and evaluative standards, whereas shareability permits neither. Accessibility is perhaps the most common standard in the literature, with no less than eight available interpretations.[5] Rawls embraces accessibility when he claims that public justification requires that we share "guidelines of inquiry: principles of reasoning and rules of evidence in the light of which citizens are to decide whether substantive principles properly apply and to identify laws and policies that best satisfy them."[6] Audi embraces accessibility as well.[7]

I define accessibility and the accessibility requirement as follows:

Accessibility: A's reason R_A is accessible for members of the public if and only if members of the public regard R_A as epistemically justified for A according to common evaluative standards.

Accessibility Requirement: A's reason R_A can figure into a justification for (or rejection of) a coercive law L only if it is accessible to all members of the public.

Three terms in the definition of accessibility need explanation. First, like intelligibility, accessibility requires epistemic justification. However, accessibility's distinguishing characteristic is the idea of "common" evaluative standards. Evaluative standards are "common" when they enjoy intersubjective recognition. Thus, common evaluative standards are not objective or mind-independent standards. Finally, members of the public must regard reason X as epistemically justified only "for A." According to accessibility, citizens should advance only reasons that members of the public believe are justified *for those citizens* according to recognized standards.[8] For example, the scientific method is a common evaluative standard among scientists, yet it might only justify a scientific conclusion for a subgroup of scientists given how they apply the standard to their data set.

We examined the most common argument for accessibility in Chapters 1 and 2: providing others with accessible reasons expresses respect for them by attempting to reason from their standpoint. If we care about respecting others, we will offer them reasons that they can comprehend and that can appeal to them, or that they can assess, endorse or reject. In contrast, when someone offers inaccessible reasons on behalf of her favored policies, she appears to be uninterested in respecting those who cannot be expected to endorse her reasons because they do not share her broad worldview or values.[9] Christopher Eberle thinks these arguments depend on a conception of reciprocity.[10] As Thomas Nagel says, we are supposed to "present to others the basis of [our] own beliefs, so that once [we] have done so, *they have what [we] have*, and can arrive at a judgment on the same basis."[11] If we do not regard other citizens' reasons as justified according to evaluative standards, then offering such reasons is disrespectful because they are not offered in a reciprocal spirit.

Religious reasons are often singled out as the paradigmatic inaccessible reasons. Richard Rorty claims that arguments based on religious reasons are "conversation-stoppers."[12] Abner Greene sees religious grounds as a "secret box" and Amy Gutmann and Dennis Thompson offer a similar line, claiming that the most important reason why appeals to biblical authority in support of coercive laws "must be rejected as moral reasons" and thus as an appropriate basis for coercive laws, "is that they "close off any possibility of publicly assessing or interpreting the content of the claims put forward by the authority."[13] If we do not offer others religious reasons that are accessible to them when we propose to coerce them, then we disrespect them.

Shareability is the strongest reason requirement, combining shared evaluative standards with shared reasons. Public reason liberals typically say little about what it means to share reasons. They presumably hold that reasons must be share*able*, meaning that reasonable citizens will affirm the reasons in question at the right level of idealization. To restrict justificatory reasons to those that citizens actually affirm would severely hamper political justification, as it would be tantamount to adopting a populist conception of idealization (Ch. 1, Sec. IV).[14]

Shareability identifies a reason as justificatory only if each citizen will affirm the reason *as her own* at the right level of idealization. To put it another way, for A and B to share reason X, X must be epistemically justified for both A and B. We may now define shareability and the shareability requirement as follows:

Shareability: A's reason R_A is shared with the public if and only if members of the public regard R_A as epistemically justified for each member of the public, including A.

Shareability Requirement: A's reason R_A can figure into a justification for (or rejection of) a coercive law *L* only if it is shared by all members of the public.

Here I have extended the requirement of epistemic justification to the entire public. A group shares reason R when R is justified for all of its members.

Theorists defend shareability with three different arguments. The first argument should be familiar from Chapters 1 and 2, namely that shareability is implied by a commitment to respect for persons. The argument from respect to shareability is similar to the analogous argument for accessibility. The second argument derives from the literature in deontological ethics, maintaining that a reason can only *count* as a reason if it is shareable. On this view, R is a bona fide reason for X only if it is a reason for Y in the same circumstances. Reasons are shareable by definition. Thomas Nagel has provided perhaps the most familiar statement of this argument when he asks, "How can there be a reason not to twist someone's arm which is not equally a reason to prevent his arm from being twisted by someone else?"[15] Nagel's point is that some reasons apply to persons regardless of who they are; they are shared in virtue of their agent-neutrality. Christine Korsgaard argues that the very idea of a private reason is incoherent, for reasons "are public in their very essence."[16] My moral reasons, by their nature, apply to you as well. I will reject these arguments below.[17]

The third argument is that shareability promotes the publicity of laws and policies and that publicity is valuable. Micah Schwartzman has recently argued that publicity has great value for a number of reasons. First, it may be "necessary for democratic accountability" and it may well "enhance the quality of political decisions."[18] Publicity also makes justifications for coercion publicly available so they can be evaluated and examined.[19] When citizens speak in shared terms, their interlocutors can easily evaluate their arguments because they share evaluative standards and reasons.

The symmetry requirement holds that to be justificatory, reasons must be used symmetrically across a number of contexts. Specifically, the standards we apply to reasons to propose coercive action must also be applied to defeater reasons and vice versa. We may define the symmetry requirement as follows:

Symmetry Requirement: The same evaluative standards must hold for reasons to propose law *L* as the reasons to reject law *L*.

Delineate two classes of reasons, reasons to propose laws (P) and reasons to reject or defeat laws (D). Suppose we apply a shareability requirement to P. If symmetry holds, then shareability must apply to D as well. On symmetry, *any* standard of reasons must apply symmetrically, that is, any version of intelligibility, accessibility or shareability must hold across sets of reasons P and D. If we deny symmetry, one standard could apply to P and another to D. For instance, if symmetry is rejected, set P could be shareable but D merely intelligible.

I am aware of only two works besides my own where the authors articulate the symmetry requirement and both reject it.[20] If asked, symmetry supporters may simply argue that the considerations that motivate a restriction on reasons to propose laws will motivate the restriction on reasons to reject laws, or vice versa. But so far as I can tell, no one defends it.

Public reason liberals commonly affirm accessibility, shareability and symmetry, though some reject shareability. From here forward, I will call a conception of justificatory reasons that combines shareability and symmetry a *strong symmetric consensus* conception of reasons. It is "strong" because it includes shareability and symmetric because it endorses symmetry. A *weak symmetric consensus* conception of reasons endorses accessibility rather than shareability. I shall refer to both views as *consensus* conceptions of justificatory reasons. A *convergence* conception of justificatory reasons only endorses intelligibility.

II. Against the Accessibility Requirement

Only the intelligibility requirement is manifestly entailed by a commitment to public justification. The other requirements must be inferred from additional premises. As I argued in Chapter 3, the values of respect for integrity and diversity can be used to decide between these requirements by ordering them in accord with the restrictions they place on living an integrated life and the restrictions they place on the recognition of reasonable pluralism. Consequently, a conception of justificatory reasons is superior to another if it imposes less on integrity and diversity vis-à-vis the alternative. A conception of justificatory reasons respects integrity more than another if it places fewer restrictions on the ability of citizens to live lives of integrity in accord with their own judgments. A conception of justificatory reasons respects reasonable pluralism more than another if it (i) accords justificatory force to more reasons that citizens themselves assign justificatory force at the right level of idealization and (ii) offers more opportunities to citizens to converge on common norms given their diverse reasons.

Finally, a conception of justificatory reasons should be rejected if it fails to achieve its aims. If two conceptions of justificatory reasons, A and B, count a similar set of reasons as public, but the point of A is to be somewhat restrictive vis-à-vis B, then A is inferior to B because it fails to restrict the set of justificatory reasons. Suppose we compare shareability and accessibility at a high degree of idealization. If idealization leads members of the public to affirm similar sets of reasons, then accessibility and shareability may assign justificatory force to the same set of reasons. In this case, shareability fails to identify a distinctive subset of shared reasons. Assume that shareability is supposed to restrict justificatory reasons to a shared set in order to preserve a shared justificatory perspective. By failing to constrain the set of accessible reasons, shareability fails to achieve its aim. Hence, public reason liberals should prefer accessibility at a high degree of idealization to shareability at the same degree of idealization, all else equal.

Given the above, I argue that the accessibility requirement either (a) fails to achieve its aims or (b) is excessively restrictive of integrity and diversity and so should be rejected. I begin by arguing that accessibility fails to achieve its aims. The aim of accessibility is to "separat[e] the public wheat from the private chaff" by capturing an intuitive distinction between reasons that we can all evaluate as justified and those we cannot.[21] When Greene calls religious reasons a secret box he has this distinction in mind.[22] Religious reasons are putatively inaccessible to non-adherents. I will demonstrate that the prima facie plausible distinction between accessible and inaccessible reasons cannot survive sustained criticism, such that accessibility fails to achieve its aims. My first argument for (a) is that normal interpretations of accessibility must count natural theological reasons as accessible. My second argument is that normal interpretations of accessibility must even count reasons drawn from religious testimony as accessible. Let's begin with natural theology.

Natural theology is the attempt to discern evidence for the existence or activity of the supernatural through natural reason.[23] Branches of natural theology pursue a priori argumentation for the existence of God or defenses of theological claims concerning the nature of God or God's will. Some strands of natural theology concern whether one can have good reason to believe in divine revelation or the relation God bears to the human soul.[24] Furthermore, natural theologians claim to be able to compete with secular philosophers in the realm of pure reason. Their claim is not implausible. For instance, Audi counts some natural theological claims as permissible public reasons. On his view, the reasoning of natural theologians is evidentially on par with secular reasoning.[25] And many of the great historical philosophers like Thomas Aquinas make theological arguments that can be evaluated, accepted or rejected on rational grounds alone, i.e., with no appeal to revelation (or any other evidence in a secret box).[26] A political argument based on natural theology, then, is one that either entirely or partly depends on a natural theological claim for its soundness. Thus, a natural theological argument for teaching intelligent design in the classroom might begin with the claim that natural reason can demonstrate the need for an intelligent designer much like God.

If natural theological arguments appeal to natural reason alone, their arguments can be evaluated by common evaluative standards and assigned epistemic justification on that basis. Consequently, such arguments will count as accessible, posing a challenge to accessibility's reputed stricture against religious reasons. In evaluating the accessibility of natural theological arguments, I shall therefore hold them as justified when reasonable, well-informed citizens can endorse them after a degree of reasoning appropriate for citizens engaged in public political life. Public reason liberals should not require that a citizen reason extensively about a particular argument, gathering all relevant information and processing it to the absolute best of his ability. Instead, the appropriate epistemic standard for public argument is one that we can reasonably expect our fellow citizens to live up to.[27]

Natural theological arguments, if successful, may have important political ramifications. Audi worries that if natural reason is taken to be capable of establishing theism, "then the way is open to hold that governmental establishment of at least a generic theism is justifiable independently of any particular religion."[28] If one has good reason to believe God exists, then she may think that she can discern God's will and conform her behavior—and potentially the behavior of others—to that will.[29] Consider an example. Catholic theologians often claim that there is reason to suppose that God provides a fetus with a soul at conception. Presence of the soul creates personhood in the fetus. Hence, the fetus is a person and must not to be killed. Suppose, then, that a traditional Catholic wishes to defend her vote against permitting abortions. Her argument might go as follows:

(1) The existence of God can be rationally demonstrated.[30]
(2) God gives each human body a soul that provides a human life with intrinsic worth.[31]
(3) The least arbitrary candidate for the union of soul and body is the first presence of a unique biological potentiality, i.e., conception.
(4) Thus, persons with intrinsic moral worth exist at conception.
(5) Persons must not be destroyed.
(6) Therefore, fetuses must not be destroyed.

If one can justifiably affirm this argument according to common evaluative standards, then principles of restraint based on the accessibility requirement cannot bar her from attempting to ban abortion.[32]

My claim is modest: some members of the public at the right level of idealization affirm the argument with an adequate degree of epistemic justification. I do *not* claim that the argument is ultimately sound. Unsound, false arguments can be accessible. I also do not claim that the argument is uncontroversial. Some reasonable citizens will fiercely dispute the truth of the premises, but an argument is not rendered inaccessible merely because it is contentious. Finally, an accessible argument might be inconclusive. But most arguments advanced in the public square are inconclusive.[33] We cannot rule out candidates for public justification on such grounds.[34] In sum, an argument can be accessible even if it is unsound, controversial and inconclusive. I shall now argue that some members of the public can affirm this argument with an adequate degree of epistemic justification. To support my point, I shall show that a reasonable, well-informed citizen can accept each premise.

Consider the first premise: the existence of God can be rationally demonstrated. Most reasonable persons acknowledge that positive arguments for the position cannot be immediately dismissed. There are many reputable arguments for God's existence, even if they ultimately fail. For instance, versions of the cosmological and teleological arguments are widespread, even in conversation about religious matters with ordinary citizens. Both arguments are routinely analyzed and evaluated by people with distinct views (some of whom have philosophical training). Reasonable pluralism suggests that at least some persons justifiably accept these arguments. Of course, the mere fact that a reasonable person could believe P does not show that P is accessible. My claim is rather that recognition of reasonable disagreement in this case is evidence that some people justifiably affirm these arguments for theism and so can justifiably accept the first premise.[35]

Consider the second premise: God provides human bodies with souls that give them intrinsic moral worth. Billions of humans believe in God and many more believe in at least one god; furthermore, some psychological evidence that suggests that theistic belief comes naturally to us.[36] The vast majority of humans also believe in some kind of soul as well.[37] Surely at least *some* subset of these individuals have epistemic justification for believing that God exists, creates souls and somehow attaches them to human bodies. These views may be false, and they may not be justified for radically idealized members of the public, but the views are not thereby rendered inaccessible. My claim is not that all widely held beliefs qualify as accessible, but rather that some citizens can justifiably accept these views about God and the soul.

The third premise holds that God attaches souls to bodies at conception. While the arguments for this position are complex, many pro-life theorists have defended conception as the least arbitrary point for God to attach souls to bodies. The pro-life view is at least one among a family of rational views affirmed by reflective individuals. Conception creates a new unity with a certain biological potentiality. Conception seems to be a reasonable ensoulment point as result. The fourth premise depends on the claim that persons have dignity and are inviolable, a view widely affirmed by reflective reasoners, religious or secular. If one can justifiably hold that a soul is essential to personhood, then she can justifiably hold that the presence of a soul entails the presence of a person. If fetuses are persons, then it is easy to see why they should not be killed.[38]

Since premise five is trivially true and premise six is implied by the rest, I conclude that the natural theological argument against abortion is accessible because each premise can be assigned positive epistemic credence on the basis of common evaluative standards. Consequently, the argument satisfies the accessibility requirement despite its religious content. The point can be extended to other natural theological arguments. Many argue against the moral permissibility of suicide on natural theological grounds.[39] A reasonable citizen may hold that God is the sole moral authority over life and death and conclude that suicide is impermissible. Presumably the premises of such an argument can achieve epistemic justification as well. Natural theological arguments purporting to establish substantive moral and political principles are therefore accessible given adequate standards of rationality and information appropriate for public discourse. Since accessibility is commonly used to exclude religious reasons, this is strike one against the accessibility requirement. Let us move to the challenge of religious testimony.

A stronger reason to suppose that the accessibility requirement cannot satisfy its aims is that reasons derived from religious testimony, the *paradigmatic* private reasons, are accessible. If reasons deriving from religious testimony are accessible, then accessibility fails to achieve its aims. I define religious testimony as any statement or utterance concerning the actions or communications of supernatural agents. Sacred texts that record testimonies and testimony by authorities that purport to have contact with divine beings count as accessible as well. Examples of religious testimony include the ex-cathedra infallible pronouncements of the papacy and Muhammad's link with the archangel Gabriel, the Torah and the Bible.

I shall now construct an accessible argument for a political proposal based on religious testimony. Consider Teresa, a Christian who deems homosexual practices morally impermissible. Suppose that the basis of this belief is her reading of Romans 1. In the passage, the Apostle Paul testifies that the reason God destroyed Sodom and Gomorrah was due in part to the homosexual behavior practiced and tolerated there.[40] As a result Teresa argues like so:

(i) The Bible is the central communication of God to humanity.
(ii) The Bible is therefore infallible.
(iii) The Bible teaches that homosexual practices are morally impermissible.
(iv) Therefore, homosexual practices are morally impermissible.

Due to this argument, Teresa decides to support a ban on homosexual marriage and votes against the repeal of sodomy laws in her state. Does Teresa thereby rely on a religious rationale that fails to meet the accessibility requirement?[41]

Public reason liberals will almost certainly argue that premise (i) is a paradigmatic violation of the accessibility requirement. All non-Christian citizens will reject the proposition and many will regard it as unreasonable. The standard reasons for believing (i) seem inaccessible to those who reasonably disagree. However, (i) can satisfy the accessibility requirement in two ways. First, it can be attached to reasons of natural theology. Teresa's fellow citizens might find her rationale for (i) accessible if she could situate it within an argument for God's existence and a further argument that the Bible is reliable testimony of God's will. Many great philosophers have defended arguments for God's existence.[42] Some of these philosophers of religion argue that God's existence entails His goodness.[43] Many theologians and philosophers have argued that a good God would communicate with and aid His creatures.[44] These arguments are sometimes accompanied by arguments that the best candidate for revelation is the Bible.[45] Premise (ii) seems accessible because it can be supported on the basis of the considerations that support (i). If the Bible is the central communication of God to humanity, it may well be infallible. All of these arguments proceed by deductive and inductive inferences, and the chains of reasoning contained in these works are not clearly epistemically unjustified (again, even if they are false, contentious and inconclusive).

Premise (iii) is a claim about how to interpret the Bible, even if the Bible is full of error. The case for its accessibility seems strong because even many non-Christians have engaged in such interpretative disputes with a high degree of sophistication.[46] Therefore, even many non-Christians can evaluate Biblical interpretations and assign them positive epistemic status. Premise (iv) flows naturally from premises (ii) and (iii). If God is good, has revealed His will to us in the Bible, and if the Bible says that homosexuality is wrong, then homosexuality is probably wrong. A good, honest God who tells us that homosexuality is wrong would presumably know whether it was wrong and tell us the truth about it. The argument is not deductive as it stands, but it plausibly meets the justificatory standard required to satisfy the accessibility requirement.

Reasons derived from religious testimony, such as premise (i) are also accessible because they are epistemically symmetric with reasons derived from *moral* testimony.[47] Public reason liberals raise fewer objections to relying on moral convictions than on religious convictions.[48] But this asymmetry cannot be sustained. To see why, bear in mind that moral reasoning often relies on testimony from others—from families, communities, teachers, parents, respected authorities and books. Our moral judgments seldom arise from pure reason. Instead we form many moral beliefs based on the norms those around us already accept.[49]

Yet moral beliefs based on testimony can still be epistemically justified. One reason to think such beliefs are justified is that they are formed based on the belief that the relevant testifier is *reliable*. Reliability can be understood in several ways—that testifiers are perceptive, rational, knowledgeable, cool headed, truth tracking, etc. Generally we say that testifiers are reliable when they testify based on *good reasons*, that is, their testimony is epistemically justified. Sarah can justifiably affirm a moral proposition if she believes the moral testimony of John, a man she justifiably believes is reliable.

I will assume that some moral beliefs derived from testimony are epistemically justified according to common evaluative standards. Presumably there are shared criteria we can use to judge the reliability of a moral testifier. If Reba the Testifier is honest, well informed, level headed and (at least tacitly) employs reasonable standards of evidence, Sarah probably justifiably believes that Reba is reliable; consequently, the moral beliefs Sarah forms from accepting Reba's testimony will be justified. Thus, a moral reason like, "The moral authorities in my life think X is morally wrong, so X must be wrong," is accessible because it is justifiable via common evaluative standards at the right level of idealization.[50]

Reasons derived from religious testimony are accessible on analogy. To see this, let's adopt a high standard of testifier reliability such that a generic testifier is reliable only if her testimony can be traced to a long and well-developed tradition of moral reasoning. Even this high standard of reliability will count many religious testifiers as reliable. For instance, the moral beliefs of many Catholics derive from their local priests. In seminary, these priests probably studied serious Catholic philosophers, including St. Augustine, St. Anselm and St. Thomas Aquinas. As a result, these priests may have reasonable arguments for their positions, or know someone who does. In this case, the religious testimony of Catholics traces back to a reliable source, some of the greatest moral philosophers in human history. Consequently, ordinary Roman Catholics who affirm religious reasons based on the testimony of trusted priests can do so with epistemic justification. And in this way those reasons can count as accessible.

Even reasons derived from religious testimony can satisfy the accessibility requirement. Accordingly, public reason liberals cannot use the accessibility requirement to block reasons derived from religious testimony from figuring into public justifications. Since reasons derived from religious testimony are, again, the paradigmatic private reasons, the fact that accessibility cannot exclude them deprives accessibility of its force by demonstrating that it fails to meet its aims.

The best reply to my arguments is to modify the conception of idealization used to flesh out the content of the accessibility requirement. I have implicitly assumed a moderate degree of idealization, one where each citizen reasons based on high, but not maximal, rational capacity and considerable, but not complete, information. Those who defend accessibility can therefore respond in two ways: by idealizing more or idealizing less. The goal must be to block reasons public reason liberals regard as suspect without blocking them merely because they are regarded as such.

Increasing the level of idealization seems to change little. The religious reasons in question do not require significant rational capacity or enormous amounts of information to access, evaluate or independently confirm. They only require a basic familiarity with the arguments that support them. As a result, it is unclear how additional information and rational capacity could render religious arguments inaccessible. A critic might deny this. For instance, philosophers sometimes reach a degree of understanding that shows that a purportedly justified argument is defeated for them given their arguments and evidence. Consequently, greater idealization might make some claims inaccessible. This is in principle possible, but we have little reason to think that all arguments from natural theology and religious testimony will thereby be rejected as inaccessible. The fact that so many thoughtful individuals embrace these arguments suggests that they survive a high degree of scrutiny. Consequently, it seems implausible to maintain that at high levels of idealization these arguments will lose their epistemic credence. This suggests that their arguments survive a high degree of rigor. We must also be careful not to idealize in ways that give members of the public similar beliefs. For instance, if radical idealization leads to the renunciation of arguments from natural theology and religious testimony, then it could just as easily lead to the renunciation of entire worldviews and religions. But such high degrees of idealization will thereby deny reasonable pluralism. By idealizing in this way, public reason liberals undercut one of their foundational commitments.[51]

Perhaps public reason liberals could opt for a less-than-moderate conception of idealization. One such idealization level is "populism," which implies no idealization at all.[52] But we have already discussed the inadequacies of populism (Ch. 1, Sec. IV). That means we must select a non-populist, but less-than-moderate degree of idealization. Call this a *mild* degree of idealization. It may initially seem that citizens could still have accessible religious reasons at this degree of idealization, but to buttress our case, let's assume for the sake of argument that mildly idealized citizens will decide that natural theological arguments are unjustified. I worry that mild idealization may thereby render inaccessible many forms of argument that public reason liberals wish to include in a plausible conception of idealization. Consider two examples. First, the knowledge of climatology required to form cogent global warming policy is much more complicated than the information required to evaluate arguments rooted in religious testimony. Public reason liberals will want to idealize enough to employ climatology (or reliable testimony about climatology). But mildly idealized citizens may well reject the consensus of the climatological community because they may reject the testimony of scientific experts. Second, many public reason liberals are ardent opponents of teaching intelligent design alongside evolution in public schools. But to justify excluding intelligent design, public reason liberals must show that at the right level of idealization parents and teachers will recognize that intelligent design is bad science. Yet the ability to identify good science goes beyond the ability to assess arguments based on natural theology and religious testimony, so mildly idealized citizens may endorse intelligent design.[53] Consequently, mild idealization is a dead end because it is too restrictive, in the sense that it rules out of idealization bodies of information and arguments that public reason liberals pre-theoretically assume should be included.

Accessibility seems problematic independently of our two desiderata. So we could simply reject it on this basis. But the two desiderata also speak against accessibility.[54] Any accessibility requirement that denies justificatory force to intelligible reasons is suspect, given that public reason liberals are antecedently committed to recognizing that these reasons possess justificatory force. Consider the first desideratum. Accessibility fails to respect integrity because it denies some rational and reasonable private judgments justificatory force, namely judgments that are intelligible but inaccessible. It thereby prevents citizens from offering reasons based on deeply affirmed principles and arguments, based either in religion or secular moral theory. In this way, the integrity desideratum ranks conceptions of justificatory reasons that include accessibility below conceptions that exclude accessibility, all else equal.

Now consider the second desideratum. Accessibility fails to respect reasonable pluralism because it denies justificatory force to reasons deriving from citizens' diverse, intelligible commitments. Furthermore, as a consequence, accessibility denies legitimacy to laws that all citizens affirm for merely intelligible reasons. In other words, public reason liberals both recognize that citizens have found an intelligible solution to their conflicts based on their diverse reasons and yet deny them the moral authority to do so. More troubling, laws defeated by intelligible, inaccessible reasons can acquire moral authority. Citizens must comply with laws they have intelligible, inaccessible reason to reject.

Of course, even the intelligibility requirement bars persons from acting on some of their reasons for action. But that is no objection to it. Remember that the desiderata are *comparative*—they order valid conceptions of justificatory reasons with a given, eligible range. The problem is not that reasons requirements restrict integrity or reasonable pluralism, but rather that they often do so too much, at least more so than philosophically attractive alternatives. The point is merely that public reason liberals should prefer conceptions of justificatory reasons that exclude accessibility to conceptions that include it by their own lights. In sum, then, we should reject the accessibility requirement. Accessibility fails to meet its aims and implausibly restricts integrity and diversity.

III. Shareability, Symmetry and Sincerity

Now we can criticize the shareability, symmetry and sincerity requirements. Beginning with shareability, recall that it requires that members of the public share both evaluative standards and reasons. Justificatory reasons are all and only those epistemically justified for each member of the public at the right level of idealization. Shareability is therefore highly restrictive, and will restrict integrity and diversity at every level of idealization. This is clear at near-populist levels of idealization, as people presently affirm a diversity of reasons. Thus, shareability proponents will deny justificatory status to a wide range of citizens' diverse, integrity-based reasons. But shareability remains restrictive at high degrees of idealization as well. To see this, suppose that we radically idealize members of the public by giving them near perfect information and cognitive abilities. In this case, they will either continue to disagree about reasons or not. If idealized citizens affirm only the same reasons, then adopting shareability effectively rejects reasonable pluralism.[55] To assume that citizens share all their reasons is *just to deny* reasonable pluralism. Otherwise, highly idealized individuals will disagree, which makes sense given that the burdens of judgment presumably still apply to them.[56] And if highly idealized citizens disagree, then shareability will deny justificatory status not only to their intelligible reasons but to their accessible reasons as well.

Give shareability's restrictiveness, the two desiderata rank conceptions of justificatory reasons with a shareability requirement below conceptions of justificatory reasons that lack one. We have already established that accessibility-based conceptions rank below convergence conceptions. Since shareability conceptions are more restrictive than accessibility conceptions, they rank below both accessibility and convergence conceptions. According to the first desideratum, shareability rules out appeals to a vast array of intelligible reasons, including all accessible, unshareable reasons. It significantly restricts the freedom of individuals to live integrated lives according to their individual ideals. Consequently, shareability poorly expresses respect for integrity. According to the second desideratum, shareability will both ratify laws that citizens have accessible reason to reject and bar the imposition of laws that citizens have accessible, but not shareable, reason to accept. In this way shareability poorly expresses respect for public judgment or reasonable pluralism.

To complete the case against shareability, let's briefly reassess the three arguments for shareability discussed in Section I. The first argument claims that shareability is conceptually entailed by a commitment to respect for persons: to treat others with respect, we may only offer them shared reasons. But we saw in Chapter 2 (Sec. II) that this conceptual argument for restraint depends on already accepting a shareability requirement. The second argument for shareability holds that reasons are by definition shareable: a consideration counts as a reason for X only if it counts as a reason for any person in identical circumstances. From the perspective of public reason, the essential shareability of reasons view is either trivial or false, depending on the meaning of "in identical circumstances." If "in identical circumstances" means "with identical beliefs and values," then the claim is trivial. Of course two people with identical beliefs and values will have identical reasons. Since people do not have identical beliefs and values, they will still have distinct reasons. But if "in identical circumstances" is understood more loosely, then the shareability requirement denies reasonable pluralism, as public reason liberalism presumes that citizens' reasons can differ across a broad range of circumstances.

The third argument holds that publicity requires shareability. A society's laws and institutions satisfy a publicity conditions when its members regard these laws and institutions as justified and are aware that others do the same. One could argue that limiting public justification to shared reasons makes publicity easier to achieve, given that there will be less noise and drift in the development and maintenance of stable political institutions (Ch. 1, Sec. VI). But we have already seen that principles of restraint cannot perform this stabilizing function in our discussion of the argument from divisiveness. And even if they could, the importance of stability may not outweigh the disadvantages of shareability requirements. In particular, stability-based considerations will likely be insufficient to justify the relevant restrictions on integrity and diversity. Given that shareability significantly restricts integrity and diversity, public reason liberals should reject it on their own terms.

Turning to symmetry, this requirement applies the restrictions on reasons to propose laws to reasons to reject laws, and vice versa. For instance, if shareability holds for reasons to propose laws, then symmetry imposes a shareability requirement on reasons to reject laws. One might wonder whether symmetry has any benefits. There is little to say, since no such benefits have been advanced.[57] But even if symmetry had benefits, we render it inert if we reject accessibility and shareability. Intelligibility is *automatically* symmetrical because it is required by the very idea of public justification. Consequently, symmetry fails to do any work. Since the symmetry requirement is presumed to do *something*, it fails to achieve its aim. We can conclude, therefore, that symmetry should be rejected.

Finally we turn to sincerity. Public reason liberals often hold that justificatory reasons must be offered in a sincere fashion.[58] I believe the case for sincerity requirements derives entirely from other reasons requirements.[59] We derive them by applying reasons requirements (shareability, accessibility or intelligibility) to a principle of restraint governing what reasons may be advanced and acted upon in the public square. If shareability is the only relevant standard, then a sincerity principle requires only offering shareable reasons in public political argument. Consider a similar sincerity requirement defended by Jonathan Quong:

A may only endorse X if the following are true (and vice versa for B): (1) A reasonably believes he is justified in endorsing X, (2) A reasonably believes that B is justified in endorsing X and thus (3) A may only (in the political domain) offer arguments in favor of X to B that he reasonably believes B would be justified in accepting.[60]

Quong's principle seems to combine shareability and restraint.[61] A can only advance X as law if he believes that both A and B are justified in accepting X. Otherwise, A asks B to accept a poor reason, and so A attempts to deceive or manipulate B.

To see why we should suppose that most sincerity requirements decompose into a reasons requirement, let's ask why anyone should care about being sincere. The common answer is that sincerity is required by respect for persons. If we believe that coercion must be publicly justified out of respect for others, but we ask others to accept coercion for bad reasons, we disrespect them on their own terms. Instead, we should offer others what we think are *good* reasons for our proposals. The problem with the common answer is that the Public Justification Principle is ambiguous between conceptions of the evaluative standards required to *count* something as a good reason. For instance, accessibility requires that we share evaluative standards, whereas intelligibility does not. If accessibility holds, then *what it means* to be sincere will be to offer arguments for proposals that one believes are justified according to common evaluative standards. Similarly, if only intelligibility holds, then *what it means* to be sincere is to offer arguments for proposals that one believes are justified according to the evaluative standards of one's discussant and one's own evaluative standards. For this reason sincerity discussions do not mark off a distinct domain of normative concern.[62] Whether a principle of sincerity holds depends on (i) a conception of justificatory reasons combined with (ii) a principle of restraint. Since we can deal with (i) and (ii) directly, and the treatment of sincerity falls out of an approach to (i) and (ii), let's set it aside.

IV. The Promise of Convergence

We should reject accessibility, shareability, symmetry and sincerity requirements, and so we should reject the consensus view. Convergence is the superior conception of justificatory reasons given public reason liberalism's foundational values. It follows, therefore, that the justificatory premise is false: the Public Justification Principle does not entail accessibility or shareability requirements, and so does not entail restraint. But one might still worry that convergence raises the integrity and fairness objections, so let us see if I can quiet these concerns.

I should first point out that given the recognition of reasonable pluralism about reasons *and* evaluative standards, it might initially appear that the vast majority of religious reasons are intelligible. If so, convergence is friendly to religious reasons because all intelligible reasons can figure into public justifications. But one might doubt this claim. Consider an ardent secularist member of the public, such as Richard Dawkins, the famous biologist who has argued that theistic belief is irrational.[63] As a member of the public in good standing, whose reasoning approaches a high degree of idealization, he denies that religious beliefs have rational justification, and so reasons derived from those beliefs are unintelligible in the sense I have specified previously (Sec. I). The convergence theorist might reply that while religious reasons may be unjustifiable based on common evaluative standards (and so inaccessible), they may still be justified based on reasonable evaluative standards employed by religious persons. But Dawkins denies that religious persons have reasonable evaluative standards, because religious systems include faith as a path to knowledge. Dawkins could acknowledge that religious reasons are justified given religious citizens' evaluative standards but deny that these standards are reasonable.

While Dawkins may be entitled to hold that sound and well-informed reasoning will vindicate atheism, public reason liberals must deny his further claim that all religious citizens are epistemically derelict in believing as they do. Many religious reasons are intelligible, and so convergence is friendly to religious reasoning. To deny this is to claim, in effect, that reasonable pluralism does not extend to religion at all. If those who agree with Dawkins wish to be public reason liberals, they do best to accept that the appropriate standard of *justificatory* reasons is modest enough to assign religious reasons justificatory force.

Turning to the integrity objection, we can now see that many religious reasons are intelligible and can thereby figure into public justifications. It seems therefore that religious citizens should be happy, right? Perhaps not. Convergence will still restrict the free action of many religious citizens by preventing them from imposing their preferred laws on others. Consequently, religious objectors might claim that the integrity of citizens must be preserved to a greater degree than the Public Justification Principle allows.[64] If they are correct, the integrity objection applies to convergence liberalism as well, even if convergence is superior to consensus on integrity-based grounds. To vindicate my thesis, I must show that the integrity costs of convergence are sufficiently low so that citizens of faith have reason to impose these costs on themselves, thereby unifying the moral demands of public reason liberalism with personal integrity.[65]

Fortunately, this is an easy task, for convergence imposes fewer restrictions on integrity than religious critics' own principles of restraint. The religious critics therefore cannot raise integrity objections against convergence on pain of inconsistency. To show this, contrast convergence with religious critic Christopher Eberle's principle of restraint, "The Ideal of Conscientious Engagement."[66] If convergence imposes fewer integrity costs than the Ideal of Conscientious Engagement, we can safely conclude that even the religious critics can accept the convergence-based restrictions on integrity. They will have no objection to my core claim that religious citizens can *self-legislate* the restrictions imposed by convergence on their actions.

Someone who pursues Eberle's ideal acts as follows:

(1) She will pursue a high degree of rational justification for the claim that a favored coercive policy is morally appropriate.
(2) She will withhold support from a given coercive policy if she can't acquire a sufficiently high degree of rational justification for the claim that that policy is morally appropriate.
(3) She will attempt to communicate to her compatriots her reasons for coercing them.
(4) She will pursue public justification for her favored coercive policies.
(5) She will listen to her compatriots' evaluation of her reasons for her favored coercive policies with the intention of learning from them about the moral (im)propriety of those policies.
(6) She will not support any policy on the basis of a rationale that denies the dignity of her compatriots.[67]

Living up to Eberle's ideal might be quite onerous. First, a citizen who fails to live up to the ideal can be properly criticized for failing to do so, since Eberle claims that a citizen "who fails to satisfy that ideal is, ceteris paribus, the object of reasonable moral criticism."[68] In this way, if citizens do not conscientiously engage others, they face alienation from their communities. Recall Paul Weithman's complaint against the

Rawlsian duty of civility.[69] Weithman worries that the duty of civility requires citizens to develop significant critical capacities in order to permissibly engage in public political action (Ch. 2, Sec. III). Eberle's ideal is vulnerable to the same concern. To discharge their public duties, citizens must reason at a high degree of sophistication and effectively gather evidence. Further, they must develop sufficient communication skills and moral virtue to refrain from supporting policies that violate the dignity of their compatriots. If citizens do not expend the costs required to acquire these abilities and act on them, they can be ostracized. The ideal of conscientious engagement may become an obstacle to citizens seeking to live an integrated life.

Religious critics might reply by rejecting the ideal of conscientious engagement *and* the intelligibility requirement on the grounds that both bar citizens of faith from using coercion to advance their religious ends. Consider same-sex marriage: many citizens of faith would like to ban same-sex marriage on the grounds that it violates God's will that marriage can only occur between a man and a woman.[70] Such persons will dislike convergence because it bars them from banning same-sex marriage, given that advocates of same-sex marriage arguably have intelligible defeaters for such legislation.

I will argue in more detail in Chapter 6 that restraint does not apply to citizens in their capacity as voters. So the religious objector need not be concerned about the vast majority of citizens. That said, I claim that convergence restricts the behavior of legislators and judges. Political officials are not permitted to use coercion to further their sectarian, religious ends in the face of defeater reasons affirmed by members of the public. Surely there are religious citizens who will resent the restriction. I am not sure whether that resentment amounts to a valid objection, but I *am* sure that the resentment does not amount to an *integrity or fairness* objection. Convergence-based restraint does not violate the integrity of religious officials by requiring that they not coercively ban same-sex marriage. Few object to restrictions on their ability to impose their will on others on grounds of *conscience* or *integrity*, but instead complain that some other good is lost. What's more, our intuitions about integrity change somewhat when people take positions of power. For instance, we typically don't think integrity concerns apply to judges: the idea that a judge could complain that her integrity is violated by convergence-based restraint is not credible. The judge willingly took on the job—she was not coerced into it. What's more, she is still free to exercise her integrity in politics in all sorts of ways besides her office as judge. The fairness objection also does not apply here, as the relevant restraint on officials applies to anyone attempting to advance sectarian ends.[71]

An interesting further objection could be raised here, namely that whether convergence raises the integrity objection seems to depend on whether we adopt an indirect or direct approach to public justification (Ch. 2, Sec. II). To recap, a direct approach to restraint requires that citizens themselves restrain their activities, whereas an indirect approach relies more on institutional design to prevent private reasons from generating publicly unjustified law. The objection is that an indirect approach will not apply restraint to citizens *even on consensus views*. But if we take a direct approach, citizens will be required to deliberately exclude unintelligible reasons, which could require them to forgo advocating publicly unjustified laws. Citizens must not merely offer intelligible reasons, they must do what they can to ensure that publicly unjustified legislation is not passed. In that case, restrictions on religious advocacy will be severe. The worry, then, is that convergence is not doing the work in preserving the integrity of religious citizens. Rather, the adoption of the indirect approach is doing the work, and we might adopt an indirect approach on the consensus view.

In response, note that one reason I went after the justificatory premise is because in so doing I can sidestep downstream issues like settling on a direct or indirect approach to restraint. If the justificatory premise is false, then we refute the case for restraint without endorsing either the indirect or direct approach to public justification. So convergence is doing work by enabling us to set the direct approach aside.

Having said that, in Chapter 6 I defend a "New Master Argument" that imposes a principle of restraint on legislators and judicial officials. In this way, I take an indirect approach to citizens after rejecting the justificatory premise. But the grounds on which I defend restraint, namely that compliance with principles of restraint will help bar the imposition of publicly unjustified laws, could undermine the restrictiveness of restraint on a consensus view as well. Consensus citizens would also have no duty to engage in integrity-violating political conduct. This means that, contrary to what I claim, I avoid the integrity objection merely by taking an indirect approach to public justification, *regardless* of whether we adopt a consensus or convergence conception of justificatory reasons. So it may still appear that the convergence view does not seem to be doing the real work. The indirect approach is doing the work instead.

I reply that the convergence view avoids the integrity objection even on a direct approach, since all a convergence-based principle of restraint could require is that citizens not use unintelligible reasons in discourse and debate. Given that intelligibility is extremely permissive, direct convergence-based restraint still places few significant restrictions on the public use of religious reasoning. The insistent critic will complain that if we take a direct approach, we must require that citizens also act to bar the imposition of publicly unjustified coercion. But this requirement is too strong, given that no public reason liberal comes close to imposing such a demanding principle of restraint on citizens. In a free society, we can only require so much of citizens, even on the direct view. Everyone is willing to leave some of the process of public justification to institutional design and the regulation of the behavior of officials. In sum, then, while the indirect approach certainly helps avoid the integrity objection, convergence can do the necessary work all by itself.

So it is fair to conclude that convergence imposes considerably fewer restrictions on religious advocacy and activity than consensus. While convergence entails a principle of exclusion (Ch. 6, Sec. I), it merely requires that officeholders refrain from supporting laws that they believe are unjustified in a limited range of cases. Religious critics of public reason should have no objection to such restrictions on integrity grounds.[72] Let me drive this point home: *integrity concerns do not apply to convergence liberalism.* Convergence *silences* the integrity objection.

Turning to the fairness objection, which holds that restraint imposes unequal burdens on religious citizens, we need merely observe that convergence assigns huge numbers of religious reasons, values, projects and principles justificatory force. Since many religions affirm the veracity of religious experience, even the deliverances of *religious visions* can generate reasons for action that can be employed both in dialogue and political activism.[73] Again, we shall see that greater restrictions apply to those who hold political office, but beyond this public reason liberals should place no restriction on the employment of religious reasoning. Similarly, they should impose no restriction on the employment of secular reasoning. Convergence therefore places religious reasoning *on an epistemic par* with secular reasoning. Convergence is fair.

Note that some of public reason's critics argue that, with respect to many political questions, public reason is "incomplete."[74] As Micah Schwartzman puts it, these critics argue "that public reason cannot resolve fundamental moral and political issues because it excludes too many considerations from the political domain."[75] For example, political liberals construct a political conception of justice independently of comprehensive doctrines in order to provide a shared legal and ethical framework for solving our common problems despite our differences. But if public reason is incomplete, then the political conception cannot serve this function. Public reason cannot solve the task it sets itself. Fortunately, we need not weigh in on these debates. Convergence has an added bonus: by allowing all intelligible reasons to play both a justificatory and deliberative role, convergence dramatically expands the range of reasons permitted into discourse and decision making. Steven Smith has complained that restraint pushes our deep disagreements into the shadows. But given that our surface disagreements rest on complex ideas of the human good and life's final end, we cannot help but appeal to comprehensive considerations within the bounds of public reason. As a result, our discourse becomes dishonest because we must "smuggle" comprehensive reasons into public life.[76] This problem evaporates on convergence.[77] When it comes to comprehensive reasons, convergence says: "let 'er rip."

V. Stuffed and Empty Sets

To fully vindicate convergence, I should address two related objections: convergence either allows an unmanageably large number of laws to be justified or a dysfunctionally small number of laws to be justified. That is, either convergence is too permissive or too restrictive; the sets of eligible laws are either *stuffed* or *empty*.

We can develop the stuffed set objection by appealing to Rawls's consensus-convergence hybrid view of public reason.[78] To understand why Rawls has a hybrid view, recall the two-step structure of political justification in *Political Liberalism*.[79] (1) The first stage, the original position, generates a political conception of justice understood as a module that can fit within the comprehensive doctrines of all reasonable persons. In this stage of justification, the parties to the original position reason identically due to the stringent restrictions on information and reasoning behind the veil of ignorance, for "the veil of ignorance makes possible a unanimous choice of a particular conception of justice."[80] The parties' reasoning does not draw on their comprehensive doctrines. We can characterize this "pro tanto" stage of justification as an extreme consensus views, since parties reason on precisely the same basis.

(2) The second stage, full justification, has citizens of a well-ordered society test the political conception to see if it can fit within each reasonable comprehensive doctrine. Citizens must complete full justification themselves, given their own private reasons, as full justification leaves "to each citizen . . . to say how the claims of political justification are to be ordered, or weighed, against nonpolitical values."[81] Full justification is a convergence conception.

While Rawls thinks that the first two stages of political justification are necessary to publicly justify a political conception of justice, the convergence theorist disagrees. She maintains that full justification—convergence—is the only normatively significant stage of political justification. Political institutions are justified to each person solely on the basis of her own reasons. Pro tanto justification is merely a heuristic for locating a set of potentially justified principles. Rawls might reply that the consensus stage of justification is required to avoid indeterminacy in determining a conception of justice. As Rawls notes, "Without these limitations on knowledge the bargaining problem of the original position would be *hopelessly* complicated," such that we could not determine whether a solution existed even if it did in fact exist.[82] Rawls assumes that without the substantive constraints of the original position, philosophers could not rationally select a member of the set of justifiable political principles, as it would be unmanageably large. Members of the public wish to secure the gains from social cooperation, but many principles allow them to do so. Rawls hopes to identify which of these principles are best, and convergence is little help.

As we have seen, convergence theorists can employ a publicly justified decision procedure to select principles from an eligible set (Ch. 3, Sec. V). They can do so in two steps. First, members of the public list undefeated but eligible principles. Second, they select a decision procedure to choose a proposal from the set. For the convergence theorist, as long as citizens have some conclusive reason of their own to regard a decision procedure as justified, the problems Rawls could raise for convergence liberals can be solved.[83] This two-step strategy should be familiar from the classical social-contract theorists. On their view, governmental institutions are justified to the extent that they can resolve disputes about rankings. Hobbes pursues this strategy by defending the use of a sovereign power, and it is on this basis that Locke and Rousseau recommend democracy.[84] Thus, the problem of stuffed sets seems manageable.

We can illustrate the empty set objection by drawing on Eberle's arguments to this effect.[85] Eberle rightly recognizes that convergence gives religious reasons a "potentially decisive defeating role" such that "state coercion will be that much more difficult to justify."[86] Secular citizens can defeat coercion in the same way. As a result, convergence may enable secular and religious citizens to jointly defeat *all* reasonable proposals with respect to some key issue. Convergence is therefore too demanding because "[i]n a pluralistic liberal policy, there will always be sensible, epistemically competent, and morally serious citizens who have conclusive reason to reject any significant state policy."[87] Even the coercion required for liberal democracy may not be justified. And so, Eberle concludes, "we should therefore reject that stringent conception" of justificatory reasons.[88]

We can illustrate Eberle's point with an example.[89] Consider the role that an "Agapic Pacifist" plays within public reasoning about national foreign policy. An Agapic Pacifist is one who thinks that Jesus's command to "love thy neighbor" bars the lethal use of violence; on Christian grounds, she opposes war. The Agapic Pacifist takes herself to have compelling theological reasons to reject the coercion required to protect rights. Let us assume for the sake of discussion that the Agapic Pacifist is rational and reasonable: she has coherent and sound epistemic commitments and is generally willing to compromise with others (although not in this case, given what is at stake). On convergence, then, the Agapic Pacifist can threaten the legitimacy of almost any war because her reasons can defeat the justification for war. And if public reason liberalism cannot justify defending a liberal social order from violent attack, that is a strong mark against it.

Perhaps the convergence theorist could exempt the Agapic Pacifist from financing war. Eberle could counter that this reply fails to give due weight to the Agapic Pacifist's concerns. The Agapic Pacifist objects not only to financing the war effort, but also to her government killing at all. Her government, after all, must represent her, and she believes that killing is always evil. Furthermore, she objects to nontrivial policy, policy that might massively affect her life. Thus, no matter the accommodation, the liberal state's employment of lethal violence will unavoidably and powerfully affect the Agapic Pacifist's well-being.

We can take this reply in two ways, depending upon the reasons we have to worry that the Agapic Pacifist's well-being is affected. (1) On one interpretation, publicly justifying war to the Agapic Pacifist may be required simply because her well-being is affected. (2) Alternatively, publicly justifying war could be required because some principle of concern for well-being is already publicly justified to the Agapic Pacifist and her political community. The first interpretation holds that the fact that the Agapic Pacifist's well-being is affected is a sufficient reason to require that a rule be publicly justified to her. The second interpretation holds that justification is owed to the Agapic Pacifist on the basis of already publicly justified rules against diminishing the well-being of others.

The two objections are importantly distinct. The first objection seems to fail, for a complaint of a loss of well-being is insufficient to trigger the requirement of public justification. Public reason liberalism is rooted in a presumption in favor of liberty that can only be met by a public justification, so we can set this challenge aside. Instead, let us consider whether publicly justifying war to the Agapic Pacifist (even after exemptions are granted to her) is required by a publicly justified principle of concern for well-being. If such a principle is publicly justified in the Agapic Pacifist's society, she has *some* complaint against her government. But it is hard to see how her concerns about compensation are strong enough to defeat the public justification of war for her entire society. The state could pay to relocate her to another country for the duration of the war or provide her with funds that could aid her in fighting the war effort, to provide two examples. The Agapic Pacifist does not have a defeater for state action from which she can entirely dissociate. Convergence liberalism need not allow defeater reasons *that* much power.

I will address accommodation in detail in Chapter 6, but I should speak to the question of when the Public Justification Principle requires accommodation and when it requires repealing a law. To handle the Agapic Pacifist, I suppose that her defeater reasons do not amount to a defeater for the law, but do amount to a defeater for applying the law to her (or at least requires compensating her for the special burden the law imposes on her). So how do we determine which course of action—repeal or exemption—to take? At least two factors are relevant: (i) the ease of accommodation, based on the number of objectors and the intensity of their objections and (ii) the importance that non-objectors place on the law. Regarding (i), if a great many citizens intensely object to a law, accommodation is much less feasible, as accommodations require procedures for identifying sincere objectors. What's more, given a large number of objectors, those who bear the burden of the law are likely to feel that they are being treated unfairly. In contrast, if a small number of citizens have a very strong objection, accommodation is more feasible and less likely to breed resentment. Regarding (ii), accommodation becomes relevant when most members of the public at the right level of idealization believe the law provides substantial benefits from their own points of view. In that case, it is important to keep the law in force to achieve the benefit for the large number of people who support it. In light of (i) and (ii), it is clear that the proper remedy for the Agapic Pacifist is an exemption. Few people are pacifists and exemption will probably not breed resentment among the general public. Furthermore, the vast majority of people hold that national defense and violent foreign policy is critical to their well-being, such that they should enjoy the benefits of the law, even if a handful of people object (also see Ch. 6, Sec. IV).

Eberle's criticism is that convergence is so hostile to coercion that it may prevent a society from morally performing its most basic functions. But the case of the Agapic Pacifist does not demonstrate his conclusion. The eligible set of foreign policy actions is not null in the Agapic Pacifist's country. Eberle is right that convergence will often reduce opportunities for justified coercion. But that alone does not make it problematic. What's more, for all we know, convergence may sometimes add proposals to the eligible set, as we saw previously. So it is unclear in the abstract whether convergence will tend to generate problematically empty, eligible sets of justified law. In sum, then, convergence can survive the empty set objection as well.

VI. The Benefits of Shared Community

The attraction of the convergence conception of justificatory reasons is that it respects individual integrity and diversity. But one might argue that it does so to the disadvantage of other important values that public reason liberals affirm. One of these ideals might be that public reason liberalism produces a sense of public fraternity, a sense of shared community concerned with justice that in turn generates a number of positive externalities. Thus, a potent objection to convergence would be that it abandons public reason's traditional ideal of a shared commitment to justice. Stephen Macedo has recently provided a detailed argument of this sort that we should address.

Macedo argues that consensus views have six benefits:

(1) Promoting mutual assurance of our joint commitment to fair cooperation as a matter of common knowledge.
(2) Helping us interpret and apply law and extend it to new circumstances.
(3) Helping the community to fairly integrate new groups.
(4) Helping the community to fairly integrate new generations.
(5) Facilitating the accomplishment of the public agenda.
(6) Doing all this most especially for the sake of the least well-off.[90]

I will address Macedo's claims that convergence forgoes benefits (1) and (6). The others can be addressed indirectly.

Macedo's first concern is that support for shared principles of justice provides a number of social or community benefits that are otherwise threatened by conflicts and disagreements between citizens' ethical and religious doctrines.[91] The problem with evaluative diversity is that individuals might simply reason from their own point of view. As Macedo notes, "from the standpoint of individual rationality, I might prefer that the law conform to my own comprehensive conception of meaning and value."[92] Thus if I act on my own comprehensive reasons, I can threaten social stability. For Macedo, public reasons must be shared in order to properly assure citizens that they support one another.[93] In contrast, convergence permits our common agreement on principles of justice to be based on "systems of ideals that I may find baffling" or that they may be subject to revision based only on "logics that are opaque or alien to me." If so, Macedo wonders how he can be confident that his fellows are committed to fair cooperation since their "reasons and grounds for supporting shared principles are not only various but (as will seem to me) dubious?"[94] Convergence, in other words, lets public justification proceed in terms that all cannot comprehend. As a result, no one can be sure that others affirm shared principles of justice for good reasons. Contractual agreements to common principles that are not based on shared reasons are "inherently non-robust, representing a thin form of mutual intelligibility and a weak form of mutual assurance."[95] Assurance is easier when rooted in a shared, independent logic. When citizens speak in shared terms, their interlocutors can more easily evaluate their arguments because all parties share evaluative standards and reasons. Convergence, in contrast, enervates the public sphere's ability to generate common knowledge. Mutually intelligible shared commitments provide benefits that convergence-based societies fail to generate in adequate supply—specifically benefits (2)–(6). For Macedo, shared commitments are similar to public goods. Without a civic guarantee that reasoning will occur on the basis of shared commitments, citizens will go their own private way, and good norms will evaporate.

Macedo's most forceful example of a shared commitment threatened by convergence concerns the protection of vulnerable minorities. If shared norms disappear, the relatively powerful will have the resources and wealth necessary to protect themselves. The relatively weak and vulnerable, in contrast, "most depend upon and benefit from a shared commitment to fair and shared terms of social cooperation."[96] To put it another way, norms are upheld by shared beliefs and practices about what is right and good. If the powerful do not follow these norms in order to secure advantages for themselves, they undermine the joint basis of enforcement of these norms.

What should we think about Macedo's claim that convergence creates problems for common knowledge? It is not clear. Convergence does not rule our common reasoning; it simply allows diverse reasoning. To refute convergence, Macedo must argue that broadening permissible justifications leads to a paucity of shared norms needed to protect potentially marginalized citizens, but Macedo makes no such argument. For all we know, convergence reasoning may increase the opportunities to develop shared commitments and values. Convergence permits points of overlapping justifications that citizens could not form under consensus views. Because convergence is less restrictive, citizens can converge on common proposals and norms through a wider range of mechanisms and reasoning systems. With more reasons on the table, citizens become aware of a broader range of considerations and have more resources from which to work out shared political principles and institutions. On the whole, convergence increases the amount of information available to the public. Unless the increase in information creates some sort of noise effect, where opportunities for public justification are obscured, it is hard to see why convergence should pose a problem for creating common commitments.

But suppose convergence did reduce the number of potentially justified laws. That in itself is not a problem, for without the ability to defeat unjustified coercion, laws and policies passed will often be unjust. On the convergence view, sufficient intelligible reasons can defeat the law or proposal on the table. Consensus denies intelligible reasons justificatory status. To create justifiably coercive institutions, citizens must be rationally committed to the coercion imposed on them, not merely by the "public" subset of their reasons but by their *entire rational will*.[97] Mainstream public reason liberals miss the fact that restricting the set of justificatory reasons obscures the full set of an individual's reasons, reasons that must have justificatory force if laws are to preserve her dignity as a free and rational being (Ch. 3, Sec. IV).

The obvious reply is that the convergence view is simply too libertarian, especially when combined with a moderate conception of idealization (such as the one I defend in Ch. 5). Separatist political liberals and religious conservatives concerned with the common good are *both* likely to resist the convergence view because it defeats too many laws required to realize social justice and promote the common good.[98] Convergence threatens attempts to realize just laws for helping the least advantaged. In a moment, I will argue that convergence provides protections for the marginalized that consensus cannot, but it is important to stress that convergence counts non-libertarians as reasonable, such that their objections to strong libertarian protections for property rights against redistribution will often *be defeated*. Libertarians, generally speaking, endorse the coercion necessary to enforce property rights against redistributive proposals, and that coercion must be publicly justified. If non-libertarian members of the public have genuine objections to such coercion, then they may well have defeaters for libertarian property arrangements. If so, convergence may allow for defeaters for libertarian arrangements that consensus will not. I do not have the space to address the worry here, save to point to work that tries to substantiate this conclusion.[99]

However, what I will stress is that even orthodox Rawlsians reject political conceptions that cannot achieve an overlapping consensus. A political conception is only justified if it is fully justified or shown to fit within all reasonable comprehensive doctrines in a society. Consequently, the Rawlsian view *cannot possibly* generate a thicker conception of politics—that is, one with more shared norms—than a mere convergence view. The set of publicly justified principles on mere convergence is a superset of the principles recognized by Rawlsians and consensus theorists. Now it bears mentioning that some Rawlsians, say those who follow Jonathan Quong, may alter the role of the overlapping consensus, such that shared reasoning is much harder, if not impossible, to override with diverse reasons.[100] But this reaction to diverse reasoning is much too strong, as it will permit coercion even when people have extremely strong unshared reason to object. Furthermore, it's a position that few Rawlsians would adopt, including Macedo.

The only way for convergence to generate more opportunities for defeat is if it is combined with a fine-grained individuation of coercive actions. If convergence requires that each law be publicly justified, then perhaps more opportunities for defeat will present themselves.[101] But this objection to convergence fails. The individuation of coercive actions is an independent matter. If we have good reason to finely individuate coercive actions, we have reason to do so on consensus or convergence.

Finally, convergence protects the poor and marginalized. By allowing private reasons into public justification, convergence permits considerations to enter public discourse developed exclusively by poor and marginalized communities. Consider the African American community in the United States. Due to their shared historical experience, blacks developed several languages of empowerment that many whites have trouble understanding. From linguistic convergence to shared historical documents and interpretations of common values, black communities have created forms of reasoning more appropriately understood as private. This is true of the Black Power movement, which latched onto a necessarily private value in order to empower African Americans. It is hard to square black communities' use of private reasoning with a strong commitment to consensus reasoning. I submit that the same holds for the feminist community. Some feminists have argued that women tend to appeal to different ethical concepts than men do and so speak their own language of "the ethics of care."[102] While care ethics need not be restricted to women, a convergence theorist can argue that as a matter of historical fact, care ethics has provided women with a source of reasoning of particular import and has thereby acquired a nonpublic dimension.[103] Consensus approaches threaten to close off unique, nonpublic paths to the genuine protection of minority interests. Convergence *empowers* because it ratifies the private reasoning of marginalized groups.

Macedo knows that convergence theorists complain that consensus views pay little attention to the unique voices of those who have been marginalized and oppressed, especially those who are unable to engage in ideal deliberation. And he admits that we "owe it to minorities, including new groups, to attend carefully to complaints rooted in their distinctive beliefs."[104] Macedo maintains that consensus can take on these concerns if we relax its restrictiveness. He claims that consensus views require citizens to be open and flexible regarding alternative forms of arguments, for consensus "is a gold standard for public justification which allows that we sometimes do better to settle for silver or bronze, fostering support for just laws by other means."[105]

If consensus is merely "gold" to convergence's "silver," then Macedo allows that convergence justifications are not only permitted but *good*. This entails a weakening of the priority of consensus reasoning. I submit that such reasoning leaves Macedo with a dilemma. If the priority of consensus over convergence is strong, in that sometimes only consensus justifications will do, then to that extent consensus cannot account for the benefits of convergence. Conversely, if the priority is weak, Macedo runs into two problems. First, the consensus view loses its putative benefits. For example, it is hard to see how a weak priority view can avoid the common knowledge problems Macedo raises against the convergence view. Second, permitting appeal to private reasons is part of *what it means* to embrace a convergence view. If we can go for silver whenever we like, how have we adopted a gold standard? By accommodating convergence, Macedo deprives consensus views either of their putative advantages or their distinctive character.

It is much harder to show that convergence cannot provide many of the community-based benefits of consensus, given convergence's emphasis on protecting integrity and diversity. So we should not reject convergence because it abandons other foundational values of public reason.

VII. Conclusion

Convergence is superior to the mainstream consensus view *from the perspective of public reason itself.* The foundational values of public reason liberalism, respect for integrity and reasonable pluralism, provide decisive reason to prefer convergence to consensus. If public reason liberals seek congruence, they can only impose laws that are congruent with each citizen's entire set of intelligible reasons for action, that is, with her entire rational will. And even when congruence is beyond our grasp, convergence is the measure of legitimacy.

But despite these benefits, convergence cannot perform the work of reconciliation alone. For convergence's fortune depends upon how we idealize citizens, that is, how we specify the members of the public P variable in the PJP. A problem arises if we follow standard practice and idealize radically. Radical idealization assigns justificatory force only to those reasons that would be affirmed by an agent's fully rational and fully informed counterpart. But our radically idealized counterparts may adopt different principles and affirm different values. Accordingly, the reasons they endorse may substantially differ from our own. In this way, laws may be imposed upon citizens for reasons that seem entirely alien to them. The resulting scheme of justified laws can frustrate or undercut the liberty and integrity of real citizens. Radical idealization, then, might permit the legal obliteration of a citizen's present projects and plans.

If public reason liberals combine convergence and radical idealization, they may be able to resurrect the case for restraint. If religious reasons cannot survive the idealization process, then even convergence could require that religious citizens not offer or act upon religious reasons in public life. Consequently, to vindicate the thesis of the book, I must provide reason to resist radical idealization while avoiding the errors of justificatory populism (Ch. 1, Sec. IV). Chapter 5 rejects radical idealization and develops an alternative, *moderate* conception of idealization that, when coupled with convergence, shows that public reason liberalism does not require restraint.

Notes

1. Roderick Chisholm puts the view as follows: "We presuppose, second, that the things we know are justified for us in the following sense: we can know what it is, on any occasion, that constitutes our grounds, or reason, or evidence for thinking we know." See Chisholm 1989, p. 17. Also see Pappas 2005 for other forms of justification internalism.
2. I draw this formulation from D'Agostino and Vallier 2013. Note that "members of the public" has the right level of idealization built into it. So it refers to what citizens would under proper reflection regard as epistemically justified.
3. Rawls 2005, p. 24.
4. Note that reasons as such may still be essentially agent-neutral; even if to be justificatory, they must be epistemic commitments of specific members of the public, and so agent-relative in another sense.
5. Christopher Eberle has already outlined them in one place. See Eberle 2002, pp. 252–86. I review these standards in some detail in Vallier 2012. See Audi 2011, p. 91, for the most recent defense of an accessibility requirement.
6. Rawls 2005, p. 224. Though in other places in *Political Liberalism*, Rawls seems to endorse a shareability standard, as the duty of civility requires that we reason in terms of shared, political values.

7. Audi 2011, p. 70.
8. Here I speak of the requirement that imposes constraints on what reasons citizens may advance, which implicitly assumes that accessibility is applied to restraint. The standard is usually taken to apply to both exclusion and restraint.
9. Notice that arguments for accessibility are often made with respect to restraint rather than exclusion; this fact illustrates the confusion in the literature.
10. Eberle 2002, pp. 109–51. We have already covered Gaus's argument for the connection in another context. See Ch. 3, Sec. II.
11. Nagel 1987, p. 232. Emphasis mine.
12. Rorty 2009.
13. Gutmann and Thompson 1996, p. 70. Also see Greene 1994, p. 659, and Fish 1996, p. 22.
14. Nonetheless, two recent articles defend an *actually* shared reasons standard. See Bohman and Richardson 2010, Schwartzman 2011.
15. Nagel 1986, p. 178. Also see Scanlon 1998, p. 73.
16. Korsgaard 1996, p. 135.
17. Importantly, these arguments are not meant to vindicate a shareability requirement within public reason but rather arguments about a particular view about the grammar of reasons; but if all reasons are shareable by definition, that would certainly vindicate a shareability requirement.
18. Schwartzman 2011, p. 381.
19. Ibid., p. 382.
20. For my contribution, see Gaus and Vallier 2009, pp. 62–4. For the others, see Audi 2011, p. 68, and Lister 2010, pp. 165–6. Lister discusses symmetry but does not defend the symmetry requirement as I have understood it here. Lister does point out that statements of the symmetry requirements are ambiguous between reasons to reject a law for an entire public or just a particular subgroup. I think the application of symmetry will vary depending on the context, as I point out in Ch. 6, Sec. IV.
21. Eberle 2002, p. 14.
22. Greene 1994.
23. George Howard Joyce, S.J., describes natural theology as "that branch of philosophy which investigates what human reason unaided by revelation can tell us concerning God." Joyce 1922, p. 1.
24. See Swinburne 1997 and Swinburne 2007.
25. For some caveats, see Audi 2009a, p. 165.
26. I do not mean to imply that faith is irrational; I merely mean that natural theology does not rely on supernatural testimony, i.e., revelation. On this, see ibid., p. 167.
27. I pursue this matter further in Ch. 5, Sec. V. For a similar standard of a "respectable" amount of reasoning, see Gaus 2011, pp. 254–60.
28. Audi 2009a, p. 166.
29. Audi argues that natural theology cannot establish any "specific moral and political standards" without appealing to a religious tradition. Ibid., p. 168.
30. The Catholic Church has maintained for centuries that the existence of God can be demonstrated by an appeal to natural reason. Boniface VIII 1302. One classic argument can be found in Aquinas [1268] 1975, pp. 139–41.
31. Several theistic philosophers have maintained that the ensoulment hypothesis is one of the best ways to explain the "fact" that we have souls. Swinburne 1997, pp. 174–99.
32. Of course, she may face other restrictions on doing so.

33. Gerald Gaus argues this point persuasively. See Gaus 1996, pp. 152–3.
34. The arguments might also be *defeated* within the belief systems of those advancing the argument. If all religious rationales were so defeated, then they would not be admissible into public reason. I presume that not all of them will be, given the public reason liberal commitment to reasonable pluralism.
35. I thank Chad Van Schoelandt for this point.
36. See Barrett 2004 for an attempt to show that theistic belief is cognitively natural for humans.
37. See Bloom 2005 for an argument that belief in the soul comes naturally to humans.
38. Of course, philosophers like Judith Jarvis Thomson argue that even if fetuses are persons, that abortion should still be permitted. But I assume that many reasonable persons will reject Thomson's argument. See Thomson 1971. Also see Rawls's somewhat notorious abortion footnote in Rawls 2005, pp. liii–liv.
39. John Locke makes one such argument, that an individual "has not liberty to destroy himself" because God has not authorized him to take such an action. Locke 2003, p. 102.
40. This is a matter of some controversy among Biblical scholars. See Boswell 1981 and Gagnon 2004.
41. I should state here that merely because these reasons are accessible does not mean that, on my account, banning sodomy could be publicly justified.
42. Many philosophers do to this day. See Moreland 2009, Plantinga 1990, and Swinburne 2004 for some recent attempts.
43. Again, see Aquinas [1268] 1975, pp. 139–41. For a sympathetic analysis of the argument, see Kretzmann 1997.
44. Swinburne 2007, pp. 79–106.
45. Ibid., pp. 239–88.
46. For a study of arguments about interpretative disputes, see Mize 1996.
47. Christopher Eberle makes such an argument, drawing an analogy between justifications derived from morality and those derived from religious experience. He claims that neither moral nor religious rationales are subject to independent confirmation and that there is no noncircular argument on behalf of the reliability of religious experiences or moral rationales. See Eberle 2002, p. 245.
48. As Thomas Nagel has claimed: "conflicts of religious faith fail this test [of common critical rationality], and more empirical and many moral disagreements do not." Nagel 1987, p. 270.
49. For more on trusting the testimony of our communities, see Reid 1983, pp. 281–2.
50. A critic might argue that testimonial beliefs are redundant at the right level of idealization because agents will already have direct access to all the information they would learn from testimony. I reject this more radical conception of idealization in Ch. 5, Sec. II–IV.
51. For more detailed arguments to this effect, see Ch. 5, Sec. III–IV.
52. Gaus 1996, pp. 130–6.
53. I think that moderately (and thus appropriately) idealized members of the public can affirm intelligent design. See Ch. 7, Sec. III.
54. At least against nontrivial versions of accessibility.
55. See Rawls 1971, pp. 15–19. In Ch. 7, we will examine how and why Rawls's theory of public justification lacks a shareability requirement despite his conception of idealization.

56. See Rawls 2005, pp. 54–8, for a discussion of the burdens of judgment and their relationship to reasonable pluralism. I shall revisit the issue of disagreement at high degrees of idealization in Ch. 5, Sec. IV.
57. Audi 2011 argues against symmetry as well. See esp. pp. 400–3.
58. Schwartzman 2011 provides one recent example.
59. Though such requirements sometimes make clearer than most principles of restraint that one should offer the reasons in the right spirit. I thank Robert Audi for this point.
60. Quong 2011, p. 266.
61. Quong clearly intends for sincerity to apply to restraint, given his claim that "A may only (in the political domain) *offer arguments* in favor of X to be that he reasonably believe B would be justified in accepting." Ibid., p. 266. Emphasis mine.
62. Of course, there are ways of being "insincere" by using justificatory reasons in a misleading manner, but that's not the specific sense of sincerity public reason liberals are worried about.
63. See Dawkins 2006 for his arguments against God's existence.
64. Lister 2011 argues that convergence will not satisfy religious reasoners.
65. In the sense specified in Ch. 3, Sec. IV.
66. Eberle 2002, p. 104.
67. Ibid., p. 104.
68. Ibid., p. 105.
69. That is, in Weithman's 2002 incarnation. After Weithman 2010, it is no longer clear whether he still affirms his criticisms in Weithman 2002.
70. On this matter, one may naturally raise abortion as the most pressing case of religious citizens being unhappy with convergence. It appears, at least prima facie, that a convergence view prevents the public justification of abortion restrictions, given reasonable pro-choice members of the populace. The reason I don't address abortion is because I don't think this prima facie appearance can withstand examination. Public reason liberalism requires that coercion be justified for all members of the public—but this requirement leaves open who counts as a member of the public, that is, whether fetuses count as persons. If fetuses count as persons, then abortion restrictions could probably be publicly justified with some ease, given that fetuses presumably have or will have defeaters for laws that permit them to be killed at will by their parents and abortion providers. This is just to say that how public reason treats abortion depends on settling a point of controversy in the abortion debate—about whether fetuses are persons and so members of the public. In sum, abortion raises too many side issues to safely employ it as an example.
71. Obviously the divisiveness objection is not relevant either.
72. Of course, they may have *other* objections to the Public Justification Principle, but those objections are not germane here.
73. Alston 1991 provides what is perhaps the most extensive defense of an epistemology of religious experience.
74. Greenawalt 1988, Ch. 6–8, is one of the first cases of such an objection. Also see Quinn 1997, Reidy 2000 and Smith 2010. I set this objection aside in Sec. I.
75. Schwartzman 2004, p. 192.
76. Smith 2010, esp. pp. 26–41.
77. Convergence may face a related problem by providing defeaters for much-needed coercion. I have already addressed this objection in Ch. 3, Sec. V.

78. For the remainder of this section, I shall focus on the public justification of principles of justice, as Rawls does, but the arguments I give should hold for laws, the object of public justification mentioned in Ch. 1.
79. Rawls actually has three steps, the final being "public justification." See Rawls 2005, pp. 385–94.
80. Rawls 1971, p. 121.
81. Rawls 2005, p. 386.
82. Rawls 1971, p. 21. Emphasis in original.
83. We will cover a range of decision procedures as solutions to indeterminacy in idealization in Ch. 5.
84. Hobbes 1994, pp. 66–7; Locke 2003, p. 160; Rousseau 1997, pp. 90–2.
85. I addressed this objection in Ch. 3, Sec. V.
86. Eberle 2012, p. 291. Emphasis in original.
87. Ibid., p. 301.
88. Ibid.
89. I owe this case to Eberle in discussion.
90. Macedo 2014, p. 5. (20, 33)
91. Ibid., p. 17.
92. Ibid., p. 17.
93. Ibid., p. 18.
94. Ibid., pp. 20–1.
95. Ibid., p. 20.
96. Ibid., p. 33.
97. For the original articulation of this ideal, see Rousseau 1997, p. 50.
98. Both Gaus 2010b and Lister 2010 suggest that a convergence-based public reason at least "tilts" in a libertarian direction.
99. Gaus 2011, pp. 506–8 uses a convergence view to critique the "small state." See Vallier 2014b for discussion.
100. Quong 2011, pp. 161–91. For a criticism of Quong, see Vallier 2014a.
101. This may be part of the reason that Rawls thought only constitutional essentials must be publicly justified. Rawls 2005, p. 224.
102. For one example of such a view, see Noddings 2003.
103. Rawls 2005, p. 37.
104. Macedo 2014, p. 26.
105. Ibid., p. 5.

Moderate Idealization
Preserving Diversity

To save convergence, we must supplement it with a *moderate* conception of idealization. Chapter 5 provides such an account by specifying a value for the members of the public P variable in the Public Justification Principle, which holds,

> *The Public Justification Principle (PJP)*: A coercive law L is justified only if each member I of the public P has some sufficient reason(s) R_i to endorse L.

I develop this account in three steps via eight sections: first, I describe the standard conception of idealization (Sec. I), second, I provide reason to reject the standard conception (Sec. II–IV) and finally, I develop (Sec. V–VI) and defend (Sec. VII–VIII) an alternative, moderate conception of idealization.

The standard conception of idealization has two dimensions: a rationality dimension that specifies how much inferential ability our idealized models possess and an informational dimension that specifies how much information our idealized models possess.[1] The standard conception of idealization is radical—it pushes the rationality and informational dimensions to their upper bounds. Radical *idealizers* defend their views on two grounds: radical idealization generates coherent, determinate recommendations and bases citizens' reasons on flawless information and reasoning. I argue against the standard view by claiming (i) that it is indeterminate and perhaps even incoherent, and (ii) that our two desiderata rank it below a moderate conception of idealization. That is, radical idealization fails to sufficiently respect integrity and reasonable pluralism. I then develop what I shall call a "Pollock-Harman" conception of moderate idealization and show how moderately idealized agents converge on common norms. I next explain how we can uncover these agents' endorsements. By this chapter's end, then, we should have an adequate supplement to convergence, rendering it immune to religious objections and amputating restraint from public justification.

I. The Standard Conception of Idealization

Recall from Chapter 4 that the three major reason requirements—shareability, accessibility and intelligibility—refer to members of the public. Idealization specifies not merely who these agents are but their reasoning capacities and information sets.[2] In doing so, a conception of idealization specifies the conception of epistemic justification at work in the relevant requirement. For example, the intelligibility requirement holds that R is a reason for A if each member of the public can see R as epistemically justified for A given A's evaluative standards. A conception of idealization explains which reasons are epistemically justified by specifying how members of the public make inferences and thus what they will take to be justified for A. Idealization nearly always involves upgrading the rational capacities and informational sets of members of the public such that they will make higher-quality inferences than they otherwise would. When combined with a reasons requirement, therefore, idealization provides a full account of citizens' justificatory reasons.

To determine citizens' reasons, public reason liberals construct an idealized model of citizens. This model signifies the reasons that are justified for each person. For instance, if an agent model is perfectly rational, then it ascribes reasons to agents based on perfect reasoning. In this way, the model provides an interpretation of proper inference that frames a reasons requirement. Rawls's parties to the original position, to give one prominent example, provide an account of valid inference, demonstrating that persons' reasons are properly described by what the parties endorse.

The function of idealization is often misunderstood; so let me forestall confusion with two caveats. First, idealization does not model citizens' moral psychology.[3] Instead, it is an explanation and interpretation of their reasons. Idealization abstracts from citizens' present belief-value sets to determine the reasons to which they are plausibly committed. Second, idealized agents in *my* sense do not "choose" principles or laws for their real-world counterparts. Rather, idealized models simply *represent* the updated and corrected belief-value sets of citizens.

All models of idealization employ a conception of *reasonableness*. Reasonableness is a distinct element of idealization because it attributes motives and beliefs to models that cannot be captured by informational and inferential upgrades. To give one example, Rawls's conception of the reasonable plays two roles in his theory of justice. While the veil of ignorance models reasonableness, citizens of the well-ordered society are reasonable because they possess the following five dispositions:

(i) A disposition to engage in public justification, or to offer justifications for her principles and abide by the justified principles of others.

(ii) A disposition to recognize the "burdens of judgment." The burdens of judgment are properties of cognition and discussion that will lead reasonable people to disagree. These properties include difficulties assessing how evidence weighs in favor of one position or another, how to weight different, relevant factors, how to resolve conceptual vagueness, how their social status affects their weighing of evidence and values, how to balance difference sides of an issue and how to resolve or accept value conflicts.

(iii) A disposition to reject the repression of other reasonable points of view.

(iv) A disposition to reason rationally, or to largely avoid common errors in reasoning.

(v) A disposition to rely on methods of reasoning that others can share or access.[4]

Citizens' reasons are partially delineated by idealization models that possess these five dispositions, dispositions that would not otherwise have been assigned to them by standards of rationality and information.

The standard conception of reasonableness closely resembles the Rawlsian view. Public reason liberalism is rooted in the recognition of reasonable pluralism and the burdens of judgment, so disposition (ii) is a feature of the standard conception of idealization. Disposition (i) is part of the standard conception because all parties recognize that political morality requires public justification. Disposition (iii) seems to follow from (i) and (ii), as individuals will judge that morality requires public justification and that the burdens of judgment require recognizing reasonable pluralism. Consequently, they will resist repressing others' actions in publicly unjustified ways.[5] Disposition (iv) is superfluous to the standard conception, as it is represented by the rationality dimension. As we saw above (Ch. 4, Sec. I), disposition (v) is part of the standard conception of justificatory reasons, and so not essential to conceptions of idealization. In this way, dispositions (i)–(iii) characterize the standard conception of reasonableness.

I believe that dispositions (i)–(iii) are rightly assigned to idealized agents. Since public reason liberalism *per se* requires the recognition of reasonable pluralism, and the Public Justification Principle blocks coercion that lacks a public justification, dispositions (i)–(iii) seem to accompany a general commitment to public justification. For this reason, I will set a discussion of reasonableness aside, as I accept something approaching the standard view. I grant that public reason liberals have abused the notion of the reasonable. But we do not need to catalogue and correct these abuses here. In my view, once we flesh out convergence and moderate idealization, reasonableness will become innocuous.

Note that these are only conditions for the reasonableness parameter of idealization, not for idealization generally. So we now turn to the rationality and information dimensions, beginning by outlining the rationality dimension and the rationale for ascribing perfect rationality to model citizens.

The rationality dimension determines how and how well citizens reason. It contains various conceptions of proper reasoning that we can divide into three dichotomies: individual vs. collective rationality, interactive vs. noninteractive rationality, and full vs. bounded rationality. The standard conception of rationality is usually individual, noninteractive and full, though there are exceptions.

Individual rationality concerns individual choice, whereas collective rationality concerns choice from a collective or "we" perspective. On a maximizing conception, individual rationality requires that persons maximize value for themselves, whereas collective rationality requires that persons maximize value as a group.[6] Collective rationality, I should stress, does not require that an individual maximize value for her group; instead, assessments are made from the perspective of the group. The distinction between interactive and noninteractive reasoning depends upon whether a model of reasoning involves "interaction between the parties" or not.[7] Rawls's theory is typical of noninteractive theories, as there is no true interaction between parties to the original position. In Habermas's model, in contrast, idealized parties interact via deliberation to produce an account of citizens' reasons.[8] These two dichotomies are not central to our concerns because accounts of citizens' reasons in the role of religion debate are constructed based on an individual and noninteractive basis. While some deliberative democrats, following Habermas, may worry that religious contributions to the public sphere are not sufficiently susceptible to dialogical challenge, these concerns need not lead us to adopt an interactive model of reasoning. And to my knowledge, no prominent public reason liberal idealizes rationality into a collective form. Let us therefore set these two distinctions aside.

The full/bounded rationality distinction is the one that matters. Fully rational and boundedly rational agents, as we shall see, identify distinct sets of reasons by combining a person's present belief-value set with significantly different standards of reasoning. Both standards idealize based on an individual's present belief-value set and on her projects and plans.

Full or perfect rationality provides ideal agents with flawless cognitive power.[9] Gaus holds that a fully rational agent "follows impeccable epistemic norms . . . changes his beliefs by making all the inferences from his current set of fully affirmed beliefs, and . . . employs the fullest possible information set."[10] I have separated out the information condition, but the rest of Gaus's description holds. The fully rational agent reasons according to the standard axioms of decision theory (completeness, asymmetry, transitivity, etc.) and make perfect inferences based on her beliefs and values. Bounded rationality relaxes these requirements.[11] Accounts of bounded rationality model reasoning based on the constraints faced by real-world agents, such as limited processing power and high information collection costs.

For public reason liberals, full rationality has great appeal. They wish to determine the true justificatory reasons of citizens—surely a perfectly rational agent identifies those reasons. Abandoning full rationality thereby permits at least some of the defects of justificatory populism into public justification. Reasons attributed to citizens on bounded rationality will be based on partially flawed reasoning. Second, full rationality is often thought to guarantee agreement. Many tacitly assume that suitably idealized, rational and reasonable individuals will agree about which principles or laws are justified. Rawls explicitly builds his model of reasoning on this assumption; he makes his parties to the original position fully rational to induce agreement; were the parties less than fully rational, they might reach different conclusions.[12]

It is clear that Rawls appeals to a full conception of rationality, but do other public justification models idealize similarly? It is surely the case for contractarian conceptions of public justification. In *Morals by Agreement*, David Gauthier holds that rational individuals "maximize their own utility," meaning that agents in his bargaining system follow the standard axioms of decision theory.[13] Gauthier explicitly claims that the ideal actor is "fully rational."[14] Deliberative democrats have similar, albeit less precise commitments. Their conception of rationality is distinct because it is interactive, such that rational outcomes are the result of discussion, deliberation, correction and revision of different views. But presumably the point of interaction under idealized conditions is not merely to reach agreement but to reach agreement based on flawless reasoning. Thus, while Habermas does not explicitly embrace radical idealization of rationality, the process of "will formation" probably generates an equivalent outcome, as ideal deliberators continually challenge and correct one another's errors.[15]

The information dimension determines the *informational set* of idealized agents, an agent's total evidential base. Informational idealization ranges between a full information standard and a weaker, adequate information standard. Full information includes all information relevant to decision making, whereas adequate information does not. Standard informational idealization is not exactly full, however, as public reason liberals both add and *subtract* information from the belief-value sets of ordinary citizens. They add information to avoid holding public justification captive to ignorance, but they often subtract information to avoid attributing partial reasons to citizens that could bias public justification. Rawls, Gauthier and Habermas all pursue this strategy. Rawls's parties, for instance, know the general laws of economics and psychology, but he denies citizens knowledge of their conceptions of the good and contingent characteristics. Similarly, Gauthier's members of the public are "fully informed," though not "about [their] own particular capacities and preferences, but about human capacities, preferences, and circumstances."[16] Thus the ideal agent has an "internally rational system" of preferences and beliefs. Habermas's theory assumes a similar attribution of massive amounts of information. While he does not ide-alize individual preferences, he still gauges the justification of norms apart from citizens' contingencies and "empirical" features. For other-wise, norms cannot be binding: ". . . [I]f only empirical motives (such as inclinations, interests, and fear of sanctions) sustain the agreement [to accept a norm], it is impossible to see why a party to the contract should continue to feel bound to the norms when his original motives change."[17] Thus, discourse must proceed in an idealized situation "removed from contexts of experience and action" and divorced from "all motives except that of the cooperative search for truth."[18] Idealized deliberators must set aside their conception of the good life, because they will obscure our attempts to set "before us an abstract 'ought.'"[19] As we isolate the moral questions concerning justice, we achieve a moral point of view "dissociated from the local conventions and historical col-oration of a particular form of life."[20] In general, then, public reason liberals *remove* partializing information and *add* general information. I shall call this standard conception of information a *full, general* infor-mation standard, or *full* information for short.

Much like full rationality, full information standards are attractive because they (a) avoid attributing reasons to citizens based on falsehoods and (b) generate determinacy. First, full information accounts attribute reasons to citizens based on many true propositions and no false ones, whereas an adequate information account might not. Furthermore, full information could aid the process of generating determinate recom-mendations. If agents have all of the same, accurate information, they may be more likely to converge on similar conclusions.[21] Rawls's model illustrates both purported advantages. The parties select determinate principles based on general and complete information.

For the remainder of the book, let us call a conception of ideal-ization that combines full rationality and full information a *radical* conception and one that combines bounded rationality with adequate information a *moderate* conception.

II. An Argument from Incoherence

The case for radical idealization depends on its capacity to reduce errors in reasoning. But I contend that idealizing in the standard way will not reliably decrease errors in decision making. What's worse, radically ide-alized agents provide such odd recommendations that they may fail to *count* as an idealization of real-world agents. Consequently, radical idealization is incoherent.

Radical idealization appeals to assumptions in classical decision theory because classical decision theory applies to fully informed and rational choices. For this reason, we can employ arguments against classical decision theory to our case against the standard conception. John Pollock argues that classical decision theory rarely applies to the decision making of real-world agents, which provides evidence of a gulf between the cognition of real-world agents and their idealized counterparts. If we can show that this gulf exists, we can decouple the reasoning of idealized agents from the reasons of real-world agents.

Classical decision theory holds that a rational agent is one who always makes an optimal choice or chooses an action with the highest expected utility.[22] Given that agents idealized in the standard way have perfect reasoning power and full information, they cannot help but make optimal choices. But unidealized agents fail to make optimal choices, so why should they care about the recommendations provided by the optimality prescription? One reason is that ideally rational agents represent the reasoning power of a real agent pushed to the limit.[23] On this view, ideal agents always make *warranted* choices, choices that are justified after an agent completes all possible relevant reasoning. Warranted choices look normative for real-world agents because they are made on the basis of better reasoning.

Pollock maintains that real agents cannot and should not always aim to make warranted choices. One reason for this is that reasoning for cognitively sophisticated agents like human beings is "non-terminating."[24] Because agents must act, they seldom complete all relevant reasoning to solve nontrivial problems.[25] Further, real agents must reason "defeasibly," meaning that the future acquisition of additional information or the performance of additional reasoning may rationally necessitate the agent's changing her mind.[26] Perfectly idealized agents do not reason defeasibly because they can complete all relevant reasoning given relevant information. Since real-world agents are constrained by time, we can only require that they perform a "respectable amount" of reasoning before they act.[27] Thus the recommendations of idealized agents will be rooted in reasoning and information that real-world agents are too constrained to utilize. As a result, real-world agents would often be *irrational* to make warranted choices because they would not be able to apply the relevant information in ways that make sense to them.

To illustrate, consider the case of Superman. Superman is in fact Clark Kent, but throughout most Superman comics, few people are aware of this and could not become aware of it easily. So suppose that a real agent, John, does not know that Clark Kent is Superman given his present reasoning. In this case, while John would be warranted in holding that Clark Kent is Superman, he would not be justified in so assuming. Consequently, if John were thankful to Superman for saving his wife from drowning, he would not be justified in thanking Clark Kent, though he would be warranted in doing so. An idealized agent would know that Clark Kent is Superman and so would express gratitude to Clark Kent, but John, given his present reasoning, does not know this and so would presumably be irrational to thank Clark Kent for saving his wife. Therefore, the rational choices of real agents and ideal agents sometimes diverge. While many believe that the rationality of real agents or "real rationality" should approximate ideal rationality, a theory of rational choice for a real agent is only correct if it describes how a real rational agent should act. Thus, given that agents should rely on justified choices, further reasoning might always overrule a justified choice or belief. Consequently, the reasoning and beliefs of agents are "defeasible" in that they can be held until they are faced with a defeater.

Second, the cognitive limitations of real agents require that we make choices about plans, rather than actions. We often imagine that our regular decision making ranges over acts, but Pollock denies this. In many cases, we choose a plan without filling in the details about the acts required to implement the plan. We do this in part because we are often unaware of the conditions we will face when we implement the plan. Consider for example John's typical drive home from work. John knows a number of ways home and usually selects a route based on how much traffic he encounters early on in his drive. So when John plans to drive home, he does not decide which specific route to take. Instead, he makes those decisions on the fly, given his present reasoning. Plans in this way are "somewhat schematic."[28] Furthermore, agents may be required to choose before they can figure out the details of the plan. For instance, John may commit himself to being the best man in his friend's wedding before he knows his travel plans. When John's friend Aaron asks him to be his best man, John commits then and there to going, making a fast decision despite having no idea how he will get there. John therefore chooses to work out the details later when he has both "more time and a lighter cognitive load."[29] For this reason, real agents should adopt plans and fill out the details later, but ideal agents can immediately complete the relevant cognitive task and so choose optimal acts. Real agents choose good plans, and ideal agents select optimal acts.

Real-world agents differ dramatically from the ideal agents generated by the standard conception. As such, they will often be irrational to follow the recommendations of an ideal agent given their current knowledge. Furthermore, the ideal agent will make choices over actions rather than plans and so provide recommendations that range over excessively fine-grained actions. The standard conception risks incoherence because an ideal agent's choice context substantially differs from those of the real agent.

A critic could reply to these arguments by advancing an ideal *advisor* account of reason attribution. The ideal advisor possesses all the features of the standard ideal agent, but instead of representing citizens, she simply *advises* them about what their reasons for action are. The ideal adviser generates an agent's reasons by asking what she would do in her circumstances. She therefore optimizes the set of rules or norms that nonideal or nonoptimizing agents should live under. My critic could maintain that the ideal adviser can in this way account for the Pollockian problems I have raised.

I do not think this reply succeeds. To see why, let's examine a prominent ideal adviser account of reasons defended by Peter Railton. For Railton, reasons are rooted in "objectified subjective interests," interests articulated by an agent idealized in the standard way; call this agent A+, an adviser to unidealized agent A. The objectified subjective interest is "not what *he* [A+] currently wants, but what he would want his nonidealized self A to want—or, more generally, to seek—were he to find himself in the actual condition and circumstances of A."[30] One might wonder why we cannot ask an idealized A what *he* wants. In short, who cares about A+? The problem is that if we idealize A, the interests he endorses "might be quite different owing to the changes in idealization."[31]

But A+ might have similar problems advising A, since A+ may not be able to set aside his present desires about himself in the relevant cases. In other words, his present interests and wants may "perturb his psychology" such that the phenomenon his observes is altered.[32] Railton seems to sense Pollockian concerns, but denies that they are "sufficient ground for skepticism."[33] But I submit that the perturbation theory will either make A+ a spare wheel or make his recommendations similar to that of a moderately idealized A. If A+'s recommendations are the same as A's, then he is by definition a spare wheel. However, if his recommendations differ, they will not be radical. A+'s recommendations will depend on A's cognitive and environmental circumstances. Furthermore, he will make recommendations about which *defeasible plan* to select rather than optimal acts. In this case, I suggest that A+'s recommendations will be based on idealization subject to A's cognitive and environmental constraints. This form of idealization will likely be moderate.

III. The Integrity-Based Critique of the Standard Conception

Our first desideratum, respect for integrity, provides reason to reject the standard conception on both the rationality and informational dimensions. However, it may initially seem odd to claim that idealization can restrict integrity because it does not bar action on its own. Instead, it simply specifies what reasons citizens have, a determination that seems conceptually prior to deciding whether they may act on those reasons. To the contrary, I argue that idealization imposes integrity costs to the extent that it *revises* an agent's belief-value set.[34] The point of idealizing is to provide an accurate account of citizens' reasons so as to treat them in accord with their deepest commitments. However, because idealization alters citizens' beliefs and values by definition, it must always somewhat deviate from their present concerns. But if idealization abstracts from citizens' present concerns and commitments, it may permit them to be coerced on the basis of considerations they may not identify with. In this way, idealization imposes integrity costs. While idealization may extend an agent's capacity to live a life of integrity on net, it should still be understood as imposing integrity costs because it authorizes coercion, that is, restrictions on citizens' freedom to act in accord with their commitments.

To expand this idea, let's develop some principles of practical reasoning that will help us to count the costs. I follow Gilbert Harman in supposing that there is a presumption against revising one's belief-value set in determining agents' reasons for action.[35] Harman suggests the following related principles of belief revision:

Clutter Avoidance: One should not clutter one's mind with trivialities.

Interest Condition: One is to add a new proposition P to one's beliefs only if one is interested in whether P is true (and it is otherwise reasonable for one to believe P).[36]

The presumption against belief formation is rooted in the fact that real agents "can handle only a limited amount of . . . tentative acceptance since one can engage in only a limited amount of inquiry at one time."[37] Real agents should economize on cognition costs. The interest condition is too strong for our purposes, as we do not need to add beliefs *only* if one is interested in whether a claim is true, as one might store information that may turn out to be relevant later. But in general, a moderately idealized agent primarily forms belief in response to challenges to its interests. Let's tentatively define an interest as a curiosity motivated by reasons to meet goals. If so, we can be ascribed an Interest in Facilitating Practical Reasoning, which holds that "[i]f one desires E and believes M's being true would facilitate or hinder E, one has a reason to be interested in whether M is true."[38] What justifies developing, altering and extending our beliefs is that it helps to achieve our goals. Otherwise, we waste scarce cognitive resources.

To apply Harman's principles to our subject matter, we must identify an interest in belief and value revision possessed by ordinary agents. Based on previous discussions, I claim that citizens have an interest in extending their effective power to act with integrity, to live consistently with their ultimate projects and plans. If so, they have an interest in reforming inconsistent beliefs and values. In this way, their interest in living with integrity justifies idealization because it furthers their interest in living according to their ideals. However, the same interest also provides a justification for constraining idealization. While we might idealize radically to avoid error, we must be sure that agents have an interest in correcting such errors given their cognitive limitations. They might lack such an interest if the reasons identified by a radically idealized model seem alien to them. A radically idealized model may so dramatically revise a citizen's commitments that she will regard its recommendations as *antithetical* to advancing her interests.[39] Idealization models become less plausible as they determine citizens' reasons based on considerations that increasingly deviate from the citizens' own reasons. Consequently, Harman's principles and citizens' integrity-preserving interests restrict how much we can idealize. For this reason public reason liberals should only support the minimal amount of idealization required to extend integrity with respect to integrity costs.

If we follow the Harman model, the integrity costs of idealization increase as we increasingly revise beliefs in response to challenges to our interests. However, the benefits of idealization have diminishing returns and eventually disappear. To see why, imagine our system of beliefs and values linked in a Quinean web, with core beliefs and values at the center, and other beliefs and values located at the periphery. Idealization begins revision at the periphery, first emending beliefs and values that are of less importance. But as the harmonization of one's belief-value set increases, revision moves towards the core of the web and may begin to disrupt beliefs constitutive of citizens' projects, plans and ideals. Perhaps at high degrees of idealization, some individuals will realize that their religion is based on faulty evidence. A conception of idealization radical enough to undermine one's religious faith would thus attribute reasons to citizens that would directly contradict their real-world values and principles. In this case, the integrity-based benefits of idealization evaporate.

Thus the integrity desideratum employs two elements to evaluate forms of idealization. As idealization increases, integrity costs increase to a point, and then begin to decrease. We can represent these two elements as cost and benefit curves.

Figure 5.1 displays two curves. Curve A is the integrity cost curve. It represents revision costs as a function of the degree of idealization. At populist levels of idealization, there is a slow uptick of revision costs as peripheral beliefs and values are revised. But as revision mechanisms work their way into citizens' core beliefs and values, costs skyrocket. Curve B is the integrity benefit curve. The benefits are those that extend citizens' reasoning as a function of idealization. As idealization

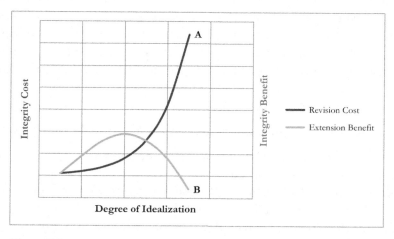

Figure 5.1

increases, reasons at the periphery of an agent's belief-value set are revised, making them more consistent with her core values and principles, a benefit. However, beyond moderate levels of idealization, core beliefs and values are revised. Consequently, the benefits of idealization sharply diminish.

I assume that the marginal benefits of idealization first increase and then decrease, whereas the marginal costs of revision consistently increase. Figure 5.1 shows that the cost and benefit curves intersect where one additional unit of benefit achieved from idealization is no longer worth the additional unit of cost—the marginal benefits of idealization equal the marginal costs. The intersection point arguably lies substantially to the left of the standard, radical conception of idealization, as it possesses high revision costs and few, if any, extension benefits. Nonetheless, the benefits of extension push right from populism, moving the intersection point towards the standard conception. Optimizing the benefits of idealization relative to the costs demonstrates that a moderate conception of idealization is superior to both populism and radical idealization. I will explain further what moderate idealization involves later on, but for now we can see why we should reject the standard conception. It imposes more costs on integrity vis-à-vis a more moderate conception of idealization.

Let me be clear that my argumentative strategy is not merely that there are two sets of considerations, one of which favors moderate idealization over radical idealization, the other of which favors moderate idealization over populism. A critic could raise the worry that I have illicitly assumed that the two sets of considerations are not somehow in tension. But the argumentative strategy based on the extension of integrity shows that moderate idealization is superior to *both* populism and radical idealization based on *one* consideration. So integrity allows us to resist both alternatives for the same reason.[40]

IV.   The Diversity-Based Critique of the Standard Conception

We can use the diversity desideratum to decide between radical and moderate conceptions of idealization if we recall that part of the *point* of radical idealization is to generate determinate recommendations. Without full idealization, public reason liberals argue, agents might disagree so much that they cannot converge on common laws or principles. I shall call the process of using idealization to determine agreement "normalization."[41] An example of normalization is the Rawlsian idealization of parties to the original position. If Rawlsian parties were not idealized radically, they might know more about their identities. If they did, it is very improbable that they could come to agree on any substantive point. Radical idealizers hold instead that idealization must be used to "translate" the preferences of diverse individuals into a simple collective ranking of options that makes the problem of political justification tractable.[42]

The diversity desideratum provides an argument against the standard conception by presenting it with a related dilemma. If the standard conception normalizes too much, then it will substantially reduce reasonable pluralism to achieve determinacy, generating significant diversity costs. But if the standard conception fails to produce normalization, then a powerful motivation for embracing it evaporates.

Before examining the dilemma, we must ask whether idealization has any diversity-based benefit. A benefit according to the second desideratum would result from an increase in the ability of citizens to converge on laws from their diverse perspectives. The only such benefit discussed in the literature is the putative increase in determinacy. By yielding determinate political principles, laws or recommendations generally, a conception of idealization generates norms that permit all agents to freely advance their diverse values. In doing so, such a conception accomplishes the goal of public justification—creating a society whose norms all recognize as justified despite their disagreements. Accordingly, determinacy is an immense benefit. But if radical idealization drastically normalizes, it can only be justified if it is the best method of securing determinacy, and perhaps not even then. I will argue later that determinacy can be generated without radical idealization. If so, the costs of normalization will outweigh the benefits, given that the benefits are low and the costs are high. Accordingly, the reasonable pluralism desideratum will rank radical conceptions of idealization below moderate conceptions of idealization.

To illustrate the dilemma, I will employ Rawls's prominent normalizing model of idealization, given its familiarity. As is widely recognized, Rawls's idealization normalizes until his parties completely agree by barring them from appealing to considerations that would differentiate them. The original position's point is to bracket comprehensive doctrines so that the parties can take a shared perspective to reach determinate principles of justice. But the costs of such idealization are clear: they attribute reasons to citizens that many would find alien, as so many of Rawls's critics have argued. Rawls advances several replies, but the one that I will focus on should prove illustrative. To grapple with reasonable pluralism, Rawls argues that parties must reach an overlapping consensus. Thus, the original position model generates a determinate conception of justice, which then needs to be justified to all reasonable comprehensive doctrines. The normalized model must prove acceptable to each reasonable point of view (recall Ch. 4, Sec. IV).

But this reply merely pushes the normalization question back a step. To put it in the form of a question: to what extent are members of the well-ordered society idealized when they evaluate whether the political conception is acceptable? On Rawls's view, whatever model of idealization we use must partially preserve the level of diversity present in real-world societies due to the burdens of judgment. Accordingly, Rawlsian idealization only normalizes in the first stage, which must then be tested against a non-normalized but idealized public.

In this way, Rawls faces the diversity dilemma I raise for idealization. Either radical idealization normalizes, in which case it seems to undermine reasonable pluralism, or it does not normalize, in which case it must appeal to other methods of generating determinacy, like widespread compliance with the duty of civility. And if radical idealization does not normalize enough to produce determinacy, then part of its rationale is undermined. It is easy to see why many radical idealization models will face this dilemma.

V. A Model of Moderate Idealization

We therefore have three reasons to reject the radical conception of idealization, namely that it borders on incoherence and runs afoul of our two desiderata. We now need a theory of moderate idealization that meet our two criteria. First, it must prohibit gross errors in reasoning and information (the error of populism) and prohibit undue integrity costs and normalization (the error of radical idealization). Second, in conjunction with other theoretical resources available to public reason liberals, it should generate a determinate set of legal recommendations. If moderate idealization meets these two criteria, it is superior to the standard view. I caution, however, that the point of my account is not to develop a detailed conception of moderate idealization. My aim is to solve the conflict between public reason and religion, so we only need a possibility proof that there is at least one plausible conception of moderate idealization.

My model of moderate idealization combines insights from Pollock and Harman. Pollockian agents differ from agents idealized in the standard way in several respects. They rarely optimize, they engage in nonterminating reasoning and they make defeasible inferences. They also make justified rather than warranted choices. "Harmanized" agents are circumspect about what they believe, avoid clutter, and only affirm values and beliefs required to satisfy their interests.[43] A *Pollock-Harman* agent combines these features into an idealized model. Pollock-Harman agents are only *moderately* idealized, given that they reason subject to significant environmental and processing constraints.[44] Given these constraints, they reason well, avoiding gross error.

A moderately idealized agent is rational if (i) she has only epistemically justified beliefs and (ii) she generally arrives at these beliefs via sounds rules of inference.[45] An agent need not affirm all beliefs that would be epistemically justified for her to have. Rather she must have *only* justified beliefs that may be overturned by further reasoning. In this way, moderately idealized agents forgo warrant. Instead, sound rules of inference include principles of practical reasoning like clutter avoidance and the interest condition. We can also add the access internalist conception of epistemic justification discussed in Chapter 4, Section I.

Moderately idealized agents do not fit neatly on the informational dimension. For one, different types of information will be relevant in different circumstances. As a result, moderate idealization necessitates a criterion of relevance that specifies which information is required to solve specific problems. I understand relevance in terms of information that will help agents to pursue their projects and follow their principles. Moderately idealized agents have projects and principles, much like their real-world counterparts, so they will have practical interests in pursuing them. These interests specify what information is needed. A standard of information idealization also requires a criterion of collection cost. Reasons cannot be attributed to citizens on the basis of information they cannot possibly collect. For example, we should not ascribe reasons to Newton based on Einsteinian physics, as he could not be expected to construct such a theory on his own. While knowledge of Einsteinian physics could help Newton satisfy his interests (perhaps his interest in knowing the true laws of physics), and so meet the relevance criterion, a real-world agent could not afford the collection costs. Thus, we should only ascribe information to agents that have low collection costs. Finally, we need a processing criterion. Sometimes information is hard to interpret and hard to reconcile with other bits of information, since even easily collected information may be costly to integrate. A technical manual for an entertainment device can serve as an example. The information is present in the manual, but integrating it requires a great deal of processing for those unfamiliar with the device. We should therefore ascribe information to Pollock-Harman agents according to criteria of (i) relevance, (ii) collection cost and (iii) processing cost.

As moderately idealized agents reason, they will make their beliefs *consistent* or coherent. We should therefore consider the conception of coherence that such agents will take to be regulative of their reasoning. First, it should be clear that global or perfect coherence is not the correct standard. Moderately idealized agents require time to render their beliefs consistent and only do so in response to challenges that arise as they attempt to satisfy their practical interests. Furthermore, some inconsistencies are hard to detect, even for intelligent individuals. Consider our discovery that slavery was immoral or that our folk physics was confused. These discoveries arguably resulted from harmonizing our beliefs, such as using our belief in human equality to critique racism or using a more comprehensive system of observation (early physics) to refute folk physics. But both achievements required a great deal of reasoning.

The best conception of coherence is therefore *local*, i.e., the relevant beliefs and values must be "close" to one another in an agent's network of beliefs. Beliefs and values are close or proximate to one another when they are connected via a relatively small number of simple inferences. To illustrate, suppose that John believes he left the front door unlocked, despite the fact that his wife just texted him to tell him that the door was locked. Suppose that John presently believes that the front door is unlocked, but would come to believe that the door is locked if he checked his iPhone and saw his wife's text. In this case, a moderately idealized John will believe that the door is locked, since the model possesses and integrates easily collected information like that encoded in John's wife's text message. Moderate idealization will generate local coherence in this way.

But the standard of local coherence requires a caveat in cases where an agent has locally inconsistent but deeply entrenched beliefs. In such cases, if the beliefs are made consistent, the agent's entire belief-value set will be fundamentally altered. For example, suppose that Reba is both deeply committed to having a good career and being a good mother. Suppose further that Reba overestimates how much time and energy she will have to attend to both goals and, as a result, will pay less attention to her family than she would like. Reba's two aims will often conflict with one another. But it would be inappropriate to render Reba's beliefs coherent in this case, as eliminating the inconsistency would eradicate one of the dynamic reason-generating features of her life. Due to this conflict, Reba may have reason to struggle with her priorities, engage in deep personal examination and perhaps even to go therapy for her workaholism or her fixation on family life. Since Reba struggles with this core life conflict, she acquires many reasons to engage in these practices. Consequently, we should avoid generating local coherence in this case. While Reba's contradictory beliefs may be local in the sense that only a small number of inferences are required to reveal the contradiction, Reba has likely maintained the contradiction over time by building up a large number of rationalizing beliefs, which help convince her that she can reconcile her aims. In this way, harmonizing Reba's beliefs will go beyond local coherence, as doing so will require removing or altering a vast edifice of these beliefs.[46]

Returning to reasonableness, recall that an agent is reasonable to the extent that (i) she complies with publicly justified principles and offers intelligible reasons for her proposals, (ii) she recognizes the burdens of judgment and (iii) she rejects repressing other reasonable points of view. The moderately idealized agent possesses all three of these dispositions. First, she will comply with publicly justified moral rules. In this way, she acknowledges that publicly justified rules have *priority* over her projects and principles in many cases. As a corollary, she will not employ coercion in publicly unjustified ways and so will not repress other reasonable points of view. In this way, the moderately idealized agent acts from a sense of fairness. However, like Rawlsian agents, she is not an unconditional cooperator. She will not necessarily obey publicly justified rules if others refuse to do the same. But moderately idealized agents wish to achieve their aims and will recognize that social cooperation improves their chances of doing so. So they will frequently cooperate. Finally, the agent recognizes the burdens of judgment because she understands that her intelligible reasons differ from the intelligible reasons of others.

In sum, moderately idealized agents (i) engage in continuous, defeasible reasoning, (ii) possess relevant, easily collected and processed information and (iii) have mostly locally coherent beliefs and values. Given public reason's foundational values and its conception of reasonableness, we can combine these conditions into the following two: the moderately idealized agent (a) rationally pursues her goals with integrity in an informed way, and (b) obeys rules she regards as publicly justified subject to the same epistemic constraints. In more familiar terms, she is rational and reasonable.

In this way, the reasons possessed by moderately idealized agents arguably model our own, as moderate idealization is explicitly built around extending the capacity of persons to act on the diverse considerations they identify as constitutive of their core projects and plans. A moderately idealized agent's strongest reasons are those that extend our capacities, and the reasons are formed in realistic ways, similar to how we actually formulate our beliefs about our reasons for action.

VI. Determinacy

The moderate idealization model deliberately forgoes the common aspiration of idealization theory: determinacy. Given that moderate idealization is tied to the agent's particular environment and perspective, her reasons will substantially differ from those affirmed by her fellow citizens. Consequently, idealization alone cannot tell us which laws or principles are publicly justified. Moderate idealization theorists must therefore appeal to other determinacy-generating mechanisms. I will now identify four methods of convergence that show how moderately idealized agents converge on common laws and policies, and therefore I will provide four ways that real citizens' reasons can converge on such laws and policies. These mechanisms are: (i) deliberation, (ii) bargaining, (iii) adjudication and (iv) evolution or convention making.

Public reason liberals commonly acknowledge that idealization alone cannot determine which laws and policies are justified. They believe that within the bounds of idealization, convergence can be reached through public deliberation. Deliberative mechanisms achieve convergence through explicit, communicative activity aimed at agreeing on a particular proposal. Deliberation is an attractive convergence mechanism because it explicitly aims at agreement, unlike the other methods, since the telos of deliberation in a liberal society is to reach agreement.

Deliberation is by far the most familiar method of convergence because the ideal of public justification is usually taken to imply a commitment to public deliberation (Ch. 1, Sec. VI). After all, what is public reason if not public *reasoning?* But as we have seen throughout the book, public justification and public deliberation are different (Ch. 1, Sec. VI; Ch. 2, Sec. II). Consequently, other methods of convergence can generate publicly justified outcomes. In lieu of deliberative agreement, we can appeal to bargaining, adjudication and convention making.

Bargaining contrasts with deliberation because it does not require that members of the public discuss which law or policy is best. Citizens do not engage one another as fellow deliberators but as trading partners. Each person enters public justification looking to achieve the outcome she regards as best, not necessarily according to her self-interest, but according to the outcome that best realizes her total set of values. But she recognizes that she may have to compromise, given that others regard different outcomes as best and given she needs their cooperation to achieve her own aims. Fred D'Agostino describes bargaining models as employing an "economic" conception of public justification instead of a "political" conception.[47] Political conceptions include deliberation, since justification rules form "from a consideration of the various issues at stake and that represent the common good."[48] This is opposed to the economic view, where the result of parties' deliberations is "a compromise between individuals' interests."[49] Perhaps the most famous example of a bargaining method of convergence is employed by David Gauthier's minimax relative concession decision rule for dividing the gains of social cooperation.[50] For Gauthier, self-interested parties converge on norms and distributions because their self-interest dictates that their most rational bargain occurs where they minimize the maximum concession they must make to convince other bargainers to cooperate. Any alternative bargain would require that at least one party give up more than any other party in the present bargain. Thus, while John can complain that he gave up too much, everyone else can respond that under any other arrangement one of them would have had to give up more than John as a proportion of her total initial endowment of assets. In this way, bargainers reach a distribution of goods that each regards as best from her own perspective and therfore publicly justified. Bargaining theory thus provides a method of convergence that may succeed where deliberation fails.

One concern about Gauthier's model is that it assumes background agreement on a number of matters, including the structure of the social world bargainers inhabit. In other words, agents have the same social ontology. However, bargaining theory is robust across different worldviews. Ryan Muldoon has constructed a bargaining theory that recognizes the "problem of diverse perspectives."[51] Due to reasonable pluralism, it is unlikely that a society can generate a common perspective within which social conflicts can be resolved. In response, Muldoon develops a bargaining model that avoids relying on a "neutral political perspective" and that requires "very little agreement between the parties involved."[52] Citizens engage one another from their own points of view. Bargainers, Muldoon argues, can negotiate even if they only understand the terms of the bargain from their own perspective. The negotiation process can still lead them to converge on a Nash bargaining solution, where the outcome of the bargain is the product of maximized utility gains.[53] While I cannot discuss Muldoon's model in more detail, I believe he demonstrates that bargaining theory is a robust method of convergence, given how little background agreement it requires. Bargainers can draw up agreements without a common perspective or a common evaluation of putative laws. This is a welcome result, since moderately idealized agents will disagree on a great many matters.[54]

Adjudication generates convergence when a third party, such as a referee or judge, resolves a conflict between two or more members of the public. Members of the public will appeal to adjudication when they need a determinate law or policy but anticipate that further deliberation or bargaining will not lead to an agreement. It is for this reason that in cases of unresolvable pluralism, a *decision procedure* can often be publicly justified to parties given their interest in reaching a solution (Ch. 3, Sec. V; Ch. 4, Sec. IV). For instance, in sports competitions, referees serve to oversee publicly justified decision procedures because self-interested sports teams will not be able to resolve disputes about proper calls. Similarly, because political deliberation is most often inconclusive, we require a decision procedure "to end the dispute, to bring it to practical closure even though we are still confronted with an open question," that is, a decision procedure can issue an authoritative "verdict."[55]

Adjudicative mechanisms are diverse. We need not restrict adjudicators to a single judge or group of judges. Voting rules can adjudicate, as can democratically elected representatives. Since these two adjudicative mechanisms can be combined, we can see that adjudicative mechanisms can be compounded.

However, while adjudication can supplement deliberation and bargaining, moderately idealized agents may still disagree about whether the adjudicator or umpire is publicly justified.[56] Accordingly, some decision procedures will not be justified for citizens. Surely we cannot agree with Hobbes that all people have reason to submit to an umpire no matter what, so long as the umpire (or Sovereign) does not require us to kill ourselves.[57] Moderately idealized members of the public will have reason to reject the authority of judges long before that point. As Gaus puts it, "a citizen has no obligation to obey a law if the umpire is enacting defeated proposals."[58] In these cases, members of the public may appeal to a fourth method of convergence.

A convention is, at a minimum, a norm or social practice that enjoys wide social recognition and compliance. Some conventions are moral, in that they license blame, resentment, punishment and the like. But laws and etiquette norms are conventions as well. Conventions can form in a number of ways, both through deliberate action, such as passing a piece of legislation, or through a spontaneous order process, such as when a new norm of etiquette evolves in an unplanned way. Since we are looking for a distinct, fourth method of convergence, let us focus on how conventions form from spontaneous order processes.

A spontaneous order process is one that is the result of human action but not of human design.[59] To put it another way, spontaneous orders explain the formation of a pattern or design when they show how some pattern, which we would have otherwise thought was necessarily the result of some agent or group of agents trying to generate the pattern, was created and sustained by a blind process, one that did not intend to produce the pattern.[60] Thus, when conventions form through spontaneous order processes, their formation gives the appearance of deliberate realization without deliberate realization taking place.

According to Robert Nozick, two types of spontaneous order processes can produce a particular pattern: "filtering" and "equilibrium" processes. For a given pattern P, a filtering process allows "only things fitting P, because processes or structures filter out all non-P's," whereas for equilibrium processes, "each component part responds or adjusts to 'local' conditions, with each adjustment changing the local environment of others close by, so that the sum of the ripples of local adjustments constitutes or realizes P."[61] If we specify Nozick's "pattern P" in terms of social

conventions, then we can see how spontaneous order processes can produce convergence via filtering or equilibrium mechanisms. To illustrate,
consider two cases where spontaneous order processes led to convention-
formation. The first case concerns the competition between VHS and
Betamax videotape formats between 1975 and 1985. Betamax died out
because of the increasing returns to scale of a particular videocassette
standard. The influence of cost structures and consumer choice were the
main causal contributors to convergence on the VHS format. VHS did not
defeat Betamax through explicit agreement or direct bargaining among
the parties involved, nor due to arbitration or adjudication. Instead,
VHS won due to the spontaneous evolution of a convention based on
the need for a single standard. The second case concerns the dramatic
moral shifts in attitudes about segregation and interracial marriage in
the 1960s and 1970s that led to convergence on the strong antiracism
norms that prevail in the United States today.[62] While discussion helped
to shift social attitudes about race, it cannot provide a complete explanation of how convergence happened so rapidly. Racist attitudes came to be
seen as morally blameworthy over the span of a few years, which seems to
be the result of an evolutionary cascade.

If a spontaneous order, via filtering or equilibrium, leads members
of the public to adopt a norm or law that is justified for them, then
the public justification of laws *and adjudicators* can be realized without
conclusive deliberation, bargaining or adjudication. In this way, spontaneously formed conventions have two attractive features: (i) they
can generate convergence without explicit agreement on issues, terms
or adjudicators and (ii) they exact a relatively low cognitive cost from
moderately idealized agents. Regarding (i), no one needs to explicitly
deliberate, bargain or adjudicate the dispute between VHS and Betamax, nor do they need to appeal to these methods of convergence to
reduce racist attitudes. Regarding (ii), conventions can form in cognitively cheap ways because they are the spontaneous by-products of
agents navigating the world as they otherwise would. For instance, conventions can form when some members of the public simply decide to
imitate the behavior of others for whatever reason they like.[63]

Public reason liberals may be hesitant to appeal to spontaneous
orders to generate public justification. As we have seen (Ch. 1, Sec. VI),
public reason liberals often run public justification and public deliberation together. But they are wrong to do so. Consequently, public
reason liberals should embrace several methods of convergence, even

unintentional, nonconscious ones. Spontaneous orders can generate public justification in cases where it is otherwise unavailable. Since public justification is a great good required by respect for persons, public reason liberals should be eager to find more resources to produce it. This goes double for moderate idealizers, as moderately idealized agents will both deeply disagree and wish to economize on costs of cognition.

One challenge for convention-based convergence is to locate a causal feedback system for social processes to operate on, specifically to reliably produce publicly justified law. Biological evolution utilizes survival and reproduction. When a trait spreads among a subpopulation and leads the subpopulation to grow with respect to another, a new biological trait can take over a population over time. Similarly, when prices are offered by businesses, consumer activity produces feedback that businesses can use to generate new prices that satisfy a broader range of consumer preferences; otherwise those businesses lose out to better-calibrated businesses.

The best candidate mechanism is *punishment*. Members who adopt moral and legal norms can sanction, blame or coerce those who refuse to comply with them. In this way, populations that comply with social norms can impose costs on those who deviate from the norms.[64] But how can it be rational for a moderately idealized agent to expend the energy necessary to punish others?[65] While the practice of punishment may have the overall effect of enforcing compliance with moral and legal rules (formed by spontaneous order processes or no), punishers will typically miss these macro-level effects. Fortunately, our model of moral reasoning (Sec. V) solves this problem by postulating that members of the public have reason to comply with moral and legal rules independently of their self-interest. Thus, moderately idealized agents may also be willing to blame and sanction others in order to enforce compliance with norms they regard as justified to all. Given deep-set and near universal punishing behavior within human populations, moderately idealized agents will likely be induced to punish as well. And if moderately idealized agents both comply with moral and legal rules and punish violators, spontaneous order convention-formation can occur. This means that they will prescribe similar cooperation-friendly reasons for ordinary citizens.

A second challenge for convention-based convergence is that it is unclear how *laws* can evolve. In other words, how can moderately idealized agents converge on a member of an eligible set of inconclusively justified *legal* norms? One answer is that laws evolve through acts of local adjudication. F. A. Hayek, in his *Law, Legislation and Liberty*, argues that traditional judge-made common law, characteristic of Western legal institutions, gradually generated standards whose application is not determined by any one legislative body.[66] Local judges make judicial decisions over time without knowing the direction of development. Similarly, publicly justified laws can evolve from judge-made laws so long as the laws are contained within an eligible set of proposals.

A third challenge for convention-formation accounts is that spontaneous order processes can converge on unjustified laws. Punishment can just as easily produce convergence on unjustified laws as justified laws. To address this concern, assume that we can determine which laws are justified (Sec. VIII). If so, moderately idealized agents will gravitate towards justified laws because they are motivated to comply with justified laws. If they discover that they have spontaneously converged on an unjustified law, then they will no longer comply with it and perhaps even alter or abolish it.

In sum, moderately idealized agents can converge on laws through deliberation, bargaining, adjudication and convention. The problem of determinacy can be solved.

VII. Five Concerns about Moderate Idealization

An important concern about moderate idealization is that it will collapse into radical idealization on examination. Eberle has argued that since any of an agent's beliefs might be based on ignorance or poor character, any belief can be subjected to idealization.[67] To deny this may imply an implausible form of belief infallibilism, which holds that some beliefs cannot possibly be compromised. Accordingly, a moderate idealizer must permit idealizing from any of an agent's beliefs concerning a law or proposal, given that all beliefs are fallible. Eberle claims that if we can idealize away from any of an agent's beliefs, we can idealize away from "*all* of [an agent's] beliefs about a given policy," which is tantamount to radical idealization.[68] He suggests that on moderate conceptions of idealization, we will have the same reason to idealize beliefs and reasons that the moderate idealizer may want to protect, as we will have reason to idealize beliefs and reasons that the moderate idealizer wishes to shed. Since any belief or reason is fallible, we have "the same reason" to idealize it.[69]

But a moderate idealizer can accept that any of an agent's beliefs "might be compromised" while resisting radical idealization. She need merely tease out the meaning of "might be compromised." Remember that moderately idealized agents only revise beliefs when it is in their practical interest to do so. They do not revise willy-nilly. And so the fact that a belief *might* be compromised is not by itself a reason to revise it. Consequently, while any belief "might be compromised," the modality differs across beliefs. Some beliefs might be easily revisable because agents have a strong interest in revising them and relatively little reason not to revise them. In contrast, agents may possess core beliefs that "might" be compromised only in a loose sense. In sum, the moderate conception of idealization is not committed to idealizing from any belief in the same way, at the same time or even in response to the same stimulus. Eberle's claim that we will have "the same reason" to idealize from different types of beliefs does not apply to Pollock-Harman agents.

Turning to our second criticism, Wolterstorff has criticized the standard conception of idealization on the grounds that what we would believe under idealized conditions has little to do with how we should be treated in politics. Laws coerce *me*, not my counterpart, after all. So what do the idealized person's views "have to do with how I, in my actually condition, am properly treated?"[70] With respect to the standard conception, the answer is very little. Severe upgrades in rationality poorly model citizens' reasons, as I argued extensively before. But moderate idealization protects citizens' integrity and diversity by identifying those reasons as justificatory, which protects and extends their ability to pursue their projects and principles. Thus, the state treats me appropriately if it treats me according to the reasons endorsed by my moderately idealized counterpart. Wolterstorff's concern places an upper bound on idealization, but it does not bar idealization altogether.

Our third criticism raises the problem of what I call the "marginally sub-rational member of the public."[71] One might worry that moderate idealization has the unhappy implication that people may be coerced into complying with laws that, had they been just a bit more reflective, they would reasonably reject. Generalizing this worry: for any level of idealization below the upper bounds, there will always be some marginal member of the public who would reject a law if she reasoned just a bit more. This may seem disappointing. I will grant that my view allows coercing the marginal member of the public, but I am not sure how we can do better. Moderate idealization is still superior to both populism and radical idealization. So if we rest with moderate idealization, it seems to me we have done the best we can. Furthermore, it's worth stressing that publicly justifying a law doesn't end with its initial ratification. If there are good objections to a law that we have missed, then theorists should listen to those objections and then propose reforming or repealing the relevant law.[72]

Some commenters have worried that moderate idealization, in virtue of its modest ambitions, cannot distinguish the reasons of cult members from the reasons of people with more ordinary, seemingly rational religious and secular reasons.[73] After all, someone raised in a cult might be able to sustain her beliefs given a modest upgrade in rationality and information. Since we presumably don't want to count cult members' reasons as justificatory reasons, my modest conception of idealization might run into trouble. I think that cult members' beliefs almost certainly do not survive rational scrutiny, given how much force and social pressure is required to sustain cultish beliefs. Furthermore, the requirement that such agents be reasonable by taking seriously the beliefs of others also seems at odds with cultish beliefs.

Finally, a critic might point out that so far I have only demarcated a range of eligible conceptions of moderate idealization. Any number of conceptions of moderate idealization might be viable. A critic could then argue that different conceptions of moderate idealization will attribute different reasons to citizens given that belief-value sets can be revised in many different ways in response to challenges. If so, then moderate idealization may be unable to non-arbitrarily ascribe reasons to citizens. This could count against my account of moderate idealization. It is hard to estimate the seriousness of this problem. Surely conceptions of idealization will make the same attributions in many cases. However, they will clearly diverge on a number of matters. Until a strong case can be made that the problem is debilitating, I am happy to accept multiple conceptions of moderate idealization as valid and then develop a specific conception of idealization to resolve problems as they arise.[74]

VIII. Discerning What is Justified

If we cannot discern whether a norm or law is publicly justified, then the Public Justification Principle cannot do us much good. One attraction of radical idealization is that it supposedly normalizes agents, until discerning what is justified is as simple as reading off the model's outputs. But moderately idealized agents are diverse and disagree, so discernment is more challenging. We should now consider some strategies for solving this discernment problem.

To begin, note that we can conceive of the project of public justification as proceeding in two ways. The first view employs public justification to construct principles of justice and constitutional essentials a priori. One might interpret the Rawls of *Theory* in this way. Rawls defends his two principles of justice by developing an abstract deliberative device that promises to harmonize our considered judgments about justice. On this view, public justification proceeds at the level of pure political theory and is determined through largely nonempirical considerations. The second view employs public justification as a method of resolving conflicts as they arise.[75] The early Rawls arguably held this view, as he claims that "perhaps the principle aim of ethics is the formulation of justifiable principles which may be used in cases wherein there are conflicting interests to determine which one of them should be given preference."[76] The second view poses a less insuperable epistemological problem for moderately idealized agents. On the first view, we must utilize moderately idealized agents to generate a priori justified principles of justice and constitutional essentials. But given the diversity of moderately idealized agents, building their diverse reasons into a model seems impossibly complex. On the second view, we need only evaluate laws in a piecemeal fashion when complaints are lodged against it in "cases of conflicting interests."[77]

I take the second approach, though it raises concerns of its own. First, it may be charged with excessive conservatism. Suppose that a society is suffused with oppressive norms that cannot all be subject to challenge at once. Under such conditions, my more gradualist approach may bar necessary revolutionary change. In this case, I argue that when people challenge the entire system, their complaints provide a basis upon which we can start to assess their claims. In such cases, revolutionary change may be required.[78] But in other cases, we should be wary of revolutionary change because the revolutionary implementation of political theories has often caused more problems than it solves. Revolutionary changes to the legal orders are potentially costly, as a society could lose its ability to coordinate on laws. In some cases, this would produce social chaos, as we have seen in a number of social revolutions.

A critic might also complain that the second view is relativistic. A conception of public justification that combines a convergence conception

of reasons with moderate idealization permits multiple publicly justified regimes. However, since the Public Justification Principle shows
that many laws are unjustified, it is not *objectionably* relativistic. Kurt
Baier describes his similar approach as follows: "My account is not relativistic in the sense that we cannot tell objectively whether [the morality
of a society or an individual] is sound or unsound. But it is relativistic
in the sense that what are sound moral guidelines in one moral order
may be unsound in another."[79] Public reason liberalism provides good
grounds to reject some laws, despite the fact that it will not always yield
a single true set of justified laws. So long as a political theory provides a
method of ruling out legal regimes that restrict the freedom and equality of persons, I fail to see the problem. Societies have many different
political norms, and rightly so. The second view of public justification
provides a method of criticizing these norms without imposing an
abstract uniformity on them.[80]

We may now turn to specific methods of assessment. These methods
apply to *real-world citizens* to help them discern what their moderately idealized counterparts would affirm. The most obvious method is
citizen deliberation, as we have seen throughout this book. While deliberation has limitations, it can help to assess complaints about laws. By
encouraging correction by others, sharing information and exchanging
arguments, real-world dialogue can sometimes approximate the reasoning of moderately idealized agents.[81] So despite the fact that I have
been at pains to stress the distinction between public justification and
public deliberation, deliberation may turn out to be a critical *epistemic*
method of discerning what is justified by getting our reasons out on the
table, so to speak. To be clear, though, this epistemic function of deliberation is far from constituting the process of public justification; instead,
it merely aids in revealing what is in fact publicly justified. What's more,
the forms of public discourse that we could use to discern what is justified need not conform to the strictures that more deliberation-oriented
public reason liberals advocate.

Determining what is justified might also proceed by studying the
evolution of norms in response to social changes, such as alterations
in family structure, economic institutions and technology. Sometimes
justified moral norms will adapt to social change. In other cases, new
norms will become justified as they replace older norms. One might
interpret changes in moral norms surrounding birth control in this
way. As Western societies became industrialized, children ceased being

economic assets and instead became major expenses for their parents. Furthermore, the potential for having more children increased substantially as infant mortality rates plummeted. In the past, norms against birth control may have contributed to parents' economic well-being, but as economic circumstances changed, more children may have started to reduce overall material well-being. Perhaps birth control use arose in response to a genuine need to control how many children couples produced.[82] Even most major religious groups did not resist such changes, indicating a broad consensus in favor of birth control that in turn indicates that a new norm prohibiting the use of birth control was publicly justified. The norm against birth control may have been justified in some times and places, but the public justification of the norm seems to have broken down as the balance of citizens' reasons changed. Of course, social change can be for the worse. But under broadly legitimate social conditions, history and social change will often track public justification.

Next, we can turn to specialized forms of media, as media culture often reflects the public evaluation of norms, policies and laws. Media figures gain prominence in many cases because they reflect opinions shared by their viewers, and so media culture will sometimes reflect what citizens take to be reasonable or unreasonable. Furthermore, discussion among members of the media can reach relatively high degrees of sophistication, elevating the quality of public discourse to the level of moderately idealized agents. Even vigorous debate among uncivil, sensationalistic and dishonest figures can help political institutions recognize which arguments are good and which arguments are not. My claims parallel John Stuart Mill's arguments for a diverse and vigorous public sphere, though I claim that open discourse can help uncover citizens' reasons rather than leading to knowledge of the truth.[83] Furthermore, sensationalistic, partisan and biased debate can be restrained by widely acknowledged moral rules that ground criticism of violators. This is what we see in the U.S. today, as American media is widely distrusted. This distrust impels members of the media to try to adhere to fair norms of argumentation.

The Internet nicely illustrates media tracking the reasoning of moderately idealized agents. First, the Internet reflects a wide divergence of opinion. And given the speed and public record of Internet debates, such discussions can approximate good reasoning. Consider how quickly bloggers fact-check one another and evaluate each other's

176 • Moderate Idealization

arguments. This process may lead to more rational policy discussions than television or newspaper outlets. An excellent case is the new media institution known as the "econoblogosphere," where hundreds of economists engage one another in constant, rigorous argumentation. While some previously prominent economists wield great influence (e.g., Paul Krugman), other economists who were relatively unknown prior to the econoblogosphere have risen to prominence through their reputation for evenhandedness and careful discussion (e.g., George Mason University economist Tyler Cowen). Thus to some degree economist bloggers earn their reputations through merit. Of course, bloggers do not always reason well and are not always civil. But one can still get a sense for which arguments have force by observing their discussions. The arguments they use, in my view, can be attributed to citizens more often than arguments that arise in many other media outlets.

Two objections bear mentioning. First, some claim that the American media *controls* rather than *reflects* the reasoning of citizens. Figures like Noam Chomsky have argued that the media "manufacture consent."[84] While it is true that media members often define debates in ways that exclude many voices, it is unclear what an alternative would look like. Public debates require simplification so that many individuals with diverse perspectives can take part in it. So to some extent, someone will always be excluded. It is true that some voices are unfairly excluded. But such exclusion only lessens the media's capacity to track the reasoning of moderately idealized agents, rather than demonstrating that the media is in control. Another concern is that the media increases diversity through polarization. For instance, the Internet has made it easier to filter out views with which one disagrees. This "echo chamber" phenomenon may contribute to the divergence of moral and social norms in the United States.[85] I admit that this is a potential problem, though I think it is hard to discern whether the Internet reflects rather than produces this divergence.

Pure political theory has a limited role in evaluating which norms, laws and policies are publicly justified because on our interpretation on the Public Justification Principle, citizens' reasons are *diverse* and *dispersed*. Consequently, it is hard to identify in the abstract which laws citizens have sufficient reason to endorse because it is hard to identify their justificatory reasons. That said, pure political theory could help to identify a *set* of potentially justified or eligible proposals and suggest mechanisms for selecting a member of the set. This task is eased if the standard of public justification is only meant to evaluate laws and policies as challenges arise.

Importantly, if we conceive of public justification as I have suggested, political theory must proceed in a different manner than it often has in the past, because "starting from where we are" requires a characterization of our present moral and legal practices. So, pure political theory must begin by describing our system of norms, laws and rights. Rawls was arguably moving in this direction toward the end of his career.[86] The goal of such an approach is first to provide a comprehensive description of our social practices and then and only then develop a method of evaluating or criticizing those practices.

IX. Conclusion

If we moderately idealize, convergence will not generate restraint because it permits a wide range of reasons to play a justificatory role. The complete theory I shall call *convergence liberalism*, that version of public reason liberalism that adopts a convergence conception of justificatory reasons and a moderate conception of idealization. We can now see that convergence liberalism promises *congruence* (Ch. 3, Sec. IV). A publicly justified polity satisfies a congruence standard when each moderately idealized agent has conclusive intelligible reason to accept and internalize its legal scheme. In this case, each citizen imposes the law for herself. Any restrictions on her free action will be regarded as compatible with her projects and principles.

But thus far the promise of congruence is only kept in theory. If we cannot translate theory into practice, theoretical reconciliation would be much less attractive. To remedy this concern, I will apply convergence liberalism to legal and policy questions. In Chapter 6 I apply convergence liberalism to dialogue and religious accommodation, and in Chapter 7 I apply convergence liberalism to the role of religion in public schools.

Notes

1. The standard account also includes a stipulation that idealized models be "reasonable," but I argue later on (Sec. I) that all viable conceptions of idealization contain this stipulation.

2. I should stress here that the standard conception of idealization is the standard conception *within public reason liberalism*. Idealization models in moral theory generally vary considerably from the standard view outlined here.
3. Rawls agrees. Rawls 2005, pp. 86–8.
4. I draw this summary of Rawls's conception of the reasonable from Gaus 1996, p. 132. See Rawls 2005, pp. 49–52, 53–8, 60, 76, 119, 162–3, 229.
5. Note that this does *not* mean that only people who endorse the Public Justification Principle are reasonable, just that reasonable people have a disposition, for whatever reason, not to repress other points of view. Such a disposition might have many bases. I thank Andrew Lister for this point.
6. Two of the major collective rationality theorists within political philosophy are Christopher McMahon and Philip Pettit. See McMahon 2001 and Pettit 1996. For an overview on the use of collective rationality within contemporary liberal political theory, see Gaus 2003, pp. 83–118.
7. D'Agostino 1996, p. 33.
8. Habermas 1999, p. 68.
9. Again, this is the conception of perfect rationality at work in the public reason literature, not moral theory generally. I thank Javier Hildalgo and Jess Flanigan for this point.
10. Gaus 2011, p. 236.
11. See ibid., pp. 233–56. Also see Fred D'Agostino's "wave model" as an alternative account of convergence on common norms. D'Agostino 1996, pp. 129–49.
12. Rawls 1971, p. 12, 124.
13. Gauthier 1986, pp. 145–6.
14. Ibid., p. 234.
15. Habermas 1995, p. 130.
16. Gauthier 1986, p. 234.
17. Habermas 1975, pp. 104–5.
18. Ibid., pp. 106–7.
19. Ibid., p. 108.
20. Ibid., p. 109.
21. I once included an ideal of coherence in the standard conception of idealization, as one could be an excellent reasoner with perfect information and not necessarily have coherent beliefs or desires. But it now seems to me that most of what matters for our purposes with respect to coherence is captured in the other two dimensions. For a discussion of belief coherence within public reason, see Gaus 1996, pp. 81–4.
22. Pollock 2006, p. 15.
23. Ibid., p. 4.
24. Ibid.
25. They can, however, complete the reasoning required to solve simple problems, like avoiding getting hit by a falling tree. I thank Robert Audi for this point.
26. Ibid.
27. Ibid., p. 5. Also see Gaus 2011, pp. 246–9.
28. Pollock, p. 11.
29. Ibid.
30. Railton 2003, p. 11.
31. Ibid., p. 37.

32. Ibid.
33. Ibid.
34. This is not to say there are no benefits, as I explain below.
35. Harman's account focuses on beliefs generally, but I only apply his arguments to developing a model of an agent's justificatory reasons.
36. Harman 1986, p. 55. This constraint concerns theoretical reasoning for Harman, which mostly means that it concerns belief, not goal formation (as it would in practical reasoning).
37. Ibid., p. 53.
38. Ibid., p. 55.
39. A commenter raises the possibility that a radically idealized agent may have very few moral commitments. But an indifferent idealized model will not sufficiently protect the real agent's projects and plans, and so seems to raise the same problems.
40. I thank Mark Murphy for pushing me to clarify this point.
41. D'Agostino 2003, p. 100. Rawls uses this term in his discussion of Rousseau in his *Lectures on the History of Political Philosophy*. Rawls 2007, p. 226.
42. D'Agostino 2003, pp. 95–104.
43. For brevity I will sometimes only speak of Pollock-Harman agents as affirming, revising and rejecting beliefs rather than beliefs *and* values.
44. I will now use the terms "moderately idealized agent" and "Pollock-Harman agent" interchangeably.
45. Or at least does not possess very many unjustified beliefs.
46. I grant that if these beliefs are epistemically unjustified, they can be altered. This may pose a problem.
47. D'Agostino 1996, p. 32.
48. Ibid.
49. Ibid.
50. Gauthier 1986, pp. 136–41.
51. Muldoon 2009, p. 122.
52. Ibid., p. 122.
53. Ibid., p. 140. Here "utility" is understood broadly to represent preferences over bundles of rights, not goods and services.
54. One might wonder whether bargaining is a reliable decision procedure; why think, for instance, that bargaining will reliably lead to publicly justified law? It is for the same reason that we think deliberation is reliable, namely the empirical observation that at least many citizens seem to care about taking the views of others into account.
55. Gaus 1996, p. 272.
56. Gaus 2003, p. 226.
57. For Hobbes' discussion, see Hobbes 1994, p. 142.
58. Gaus 2003, p. 228.
59. Hayek 1973, p. 21.
60. Nozick 1974, p. 18.
61. Ibid., p. 21.
62. It is of course true that legal and political elements were a part of social evolution, but they were surely insufficient for convergence on our present moral practices. Government coercion alone rarely results in the degree of social and moral change that accompanied the change in social attitudes about race in the United States.

63. See Boyd and Richerson 2005, pp. 19–52 for a discussion, among other things, of the role of imitation in the spread of norms across populations. Also see Bicchieri 2006, p. 204.
64. See Boyd and Richerson 2005, pp. 166–88 and Bicchieri 2006, pp. 1–51 for extensive discussions of how punishment leads to norm equilibria.
65. For a direct answer to this question, see Boyd and Richerson 2005, pp. 189–203.
66. Hayek 1973, pp. 35–54.
67. Eberle 2005, p. 180.
68. Ibid., p. 180. Emphasis mine.
69. Ibid., p. 182. Emphasis mine.
70. Wolterstorff 2007, pp. 153–4.
71. Where "marginal" is understood in the decision-theoretic sense, not as a "marginalized" or oppressed member.
72. I thank Mark Murphy for raising this case.
73. I thank Paul Woodruff in particular for raising this matter.
74. Mark Murphy has raised the possibility that a competitor model of idealization might *index* the degree of idealization to citizens' own commitments about how they are to be idealized. In this way, citizens committed to high degrees of scientific reasoning could allow more idealization in contrast to other citizens, who may not be committed to idealization that radical. Insofar as it is distinct from my proposal, Murphy's suggestion requires that citizens have commitments about what form of idealization they're committed to. But this seems implausible, as idealization is a technical concept within a relatively obscure political theory. If Murphy's proposal does not involve a commitment this detailed, my model should accommodate it simply in virtue of tracking how citizens understand themselves and their projects.
75. See James 2005 for an argument that Rawls saw himself as engaged in the second project.
76. Rawls 1951, p. 186–7.
77. Ibid. Gerald Gaus calls this view the "testing conception." See Gaus 2011, pp. 424–7.
78. I thank Chad Van Schoelandt for this point.
79. Baier 1995, p. 274.
80. In this way, I somewhat follow Rawls's claim that there is a family of reasonable liberal political conceptions of justice. Rawls 2005, p. xxxvi.
81. That said, such methods may systematically fail. See Pincione and Tesón 2006.
82. Lest this suggestion smack of social Darwinism, I am only arguing that publicly justified *norms* may have been selected for by societal changes, emphatically *not* that certain social *groups* are or should be selected for given certain social conditions.
83. Mill 1978, p. 50.
84. Perhaps the most prominent argument that media outlets "manufacture consent" can be found in Chomsky and Herman 2002.
85. Sunstein 2011 provides a classic study of this phenomenon.
86. Rawls notes in *Political Liberalism*, "There are many liberalisms and related views, and therefore many forms of public reason specified by a family of reasonable political conceptions." Rawls 2005, p. 450. Rex Martin explicitly adopts this approach in his *A System of Rights*, as does Gaus in his recent book, *The Order of Public Reason*. See Martin 1993, pp. 323–39; Gaus 2011, pp. 424–47.

CHAPTER **6**

Reconciliation in Law
Deliberation and Accommodation

This chapter applies convergence liberalism to deliberation and religious accommodation. I develop a convergence-based principle of exclusion and apply it to dialogue, individual political action and religious accommodation. I believe that convergence liberalism provides a compelling, original approach to these issues.

With respect to dialogue, public reason imposes no unique restraint on citizens' deliberations. However, legislators and judges must resist imposing coercive laws and policies on citizens that those coerced have sufficient intelligible reason to reject. This stricture I call the Principle of Convergent Restraint (PCR). With respect to accommodation, public reason requires that all laws be sensitive to whether citizens have intelligible defeaters for them. I call this restriction the Principle of Intelligible Exclusion (PIE). The vast diversity of intelligible defeaters requires an extensive set of religious accommodations to forestall laws from defeat. In cases where exemptions prove infeasible, public reason requires that we reform or repeal the laws themselves.

This chapter has nine sections. In the first three sections I develop the Principles of Intelligible Exclusion and Convergent Restraint and apply them to the conduct of legislators and judges. The next five sections focus on religious accommodation by developing Intelligible Exclusion–based interpretations of the two principles of religious exclusion in the U.S. Constitution, the Free Exercise and Establishment clauses. I then apply the resulting principles to three prominent legal cases concerned with religious accommodation, *Wisconsin v. Yoder, Employment Division v. Smith* and *Mozert v. Hawkins*. I next argue that the Principle of Intelligible Exclusion does not require excessive accommodation and that the law should treat nonreligious moral requests for accommodation the same as religious requests for accommodation. The ninth section concludes.

I. The New Master Argument and the Principle of Intelligible Exclusion

Despite rejecting the Master Argument, we can construct a new argument for restraint based on the intelligibility requirement. Let's call this the New Master Argument:

(1) Public Justification Principle → Intelligibility Requirement
(2) Intelligibility Requirement → Principle of (Intelligible) Exclusion
(3) Principle of (Intelligible) Exclusion → Principle of (Convergent) Restraint

While the New Master Argument requires restraint, it is quite limited. Since all intelligible reasons can enter into public justification, restraint *at most* requires citizens to offer intelligible reasons for their positions. Given that a great many of citizens' reasons (including religious reasons) probably survive the scrutiny of moderate idealization, then restraint will apply to relatively few reasons. So even if we adopt a direct approach to public justification, requiring that citizens contribute in some deliberate way to publicly justified outcomes, the burden of convergence-based restraint is light. Convergence-based restraint is further weakened by the fact that it only applies to proposals, not reasons, and only to persons who can make a significant causal contribution to whether proposals become law. Given an indirect approach, objections to restraint should evaporate altogether.[1]

The first two premises of the New Master Argument are true. We saw in Chapters 3 and 4 that the intelligibility requirement is implied by the very idea of public justification, so premise (1) holds as a conceptual truth. And we never disputed the second premise of the original Master Argument, which connects a conception of justificatory reasons to a principle of exclusion. Premise (2) thereby holds as well. But the content of the convergence-based principle of exclusion is as of yet unclear. We must first draw out the implications of premise (2) by specifying the sort of exclusion entailed by intelligibility.

To do so, let's revisit the intelligibility requirement:

Intelligibility: A's reason X is intelligible for members of the public if and only if members of the public regard X as epistemically justified for A according to A's evaluative standards.

Intelligibility Requirement: A's reason X can justify coercing members of the public only if it is intelligible for them.

To illustrate the application of the intelligibility requirement, consider reason ~H, John's reason to ban homosexual marriage.[2] ~H is intelligible to members of the public if and only if they regard John's reason as epistemically justified for him according to his evaluative standards. Assume that John adheres to a conservative form of Protestant Christianity, such that his reading of Romans 1 leads him to conclude that homosexual sex is immoral. He also believes that a law validating homosexual marriage in the eyes of the state provides a general impression that society approves of homosexual sex. Given that John's evaluative standards include the New Testament, members of the public must regard John's reason to ban homosexual marriage as intelligible and so must allow it to figure in a public justification for a law. So while reason ~H is not shareable or accessible to members of the public, it is intelligible to them, and so may be used in public justification.

But a reason can only justify coercing members of the public if the law the reason supports is justified to each member of the public given their diverse evaluative standards. Consequently, ~H, while intelligible, cannot justify banning homosexual marriage for those whose evaluative standards reject it. While ~H may require legislatures to make an exemption for John to comply with and fiscally support the public provision of marital benefits to homosexual couples, ~H cannot justify coercing others to comply with restricting state benefits to forms of marriage that privilege heterosexual relationships.

We can now formulate the principle of exclusion that follows from the intelligibility requirement. I call this the Principle of Intelligible Exclusion (PIE):

The Principle of Intelligible Exclusion (PIE): law-making bodies must (i) only impose laws on members of the public that members of the public have sufficient intelligible reason to endorse and (ii) repeal or reform laws that members of the public have sufficient intelligible reason to reject.

Intelligible Exclusion is designed to ensure that citizens are coerced only in ways compatible with the Public Justification Principle. It prevents coercive bodies from employing coercion save when all people have sufficient intelligible reason to endorse the coercion in question. Thus law-making bodies and their associated agents must strive to only impose laws that can be publicly justified and remove or reform laws that are not publicly justified. Intelligible Exclusion therefore ascribes ~H significant, but limited, power. ~H by itself can only defeat laws. To justify laws, it has to figure into a patchwork of intelligible reasons that members of the public have to endorse the law.

The Principle of Intelligible Exclusion has implications for both deliberation and accommodation. First, it limits deliberative restraint. The only forms of restraint that can be justified are the minimal degree of restraint required to satisfy Intelligible Exclusion. Restraint must ensure that citizens are only coerced in line with laws that they have sufficient intelligible reason to endorse. Since most citizens have almost no impact on legal outcomes, restraint will not apply to them. But those who significantly impact the law should restrain themselves from advocating proposals that cannot be publicly justified. Similarly, Intelligible Exclusion impacts accommodation because it requires that legal bodies reform or repeal legislation that violates the Principle of Intelligible Exclusion, such as by assigning accommodations to minority dissenters. To move forward, let's distinguish different forms of restraint.

II. Reason Restraint, Proposal Restraint and Convergent Restraint

I distinguish between restraint on reasons and restraint on proposals. A principle of *reason* restraint restricts the reasons that one can offer and act upon in public life. But a principle of *proposal* restraint only restricts which coercive laws or policies citizens and officials can support.[3] If I must endorse reason restraint, I can at most require citizens to offer and act upon intelligible reasons, making my principle of restraint the weakest in the literature. But reason restraint probably does not apply to ordinary citizens because they contribute little to the satisfaction excluding unintelligible reasons. The case for proposal restraint is somewhat different.

Given the laxity of Convergent Restraint, we might wonder whether public reason liberals should affirm any principle of restraint. Why not just let citizens do what they like? In my view, the only reason that can decisively override the presumptions in favor of respecting liberty and diversity is that citizen and/or official behavior helps to determine which laws are coercively imposed on others. Any adequate expression of the ideal of public reason must significantly contribute to the end state of publicly justified coercion. The claim of the restraint proponent, then, must be that publicly justified institutions can more effectively exclude unjustified coercion if some subset of citizens refrains from advancing proposals that they take to be unjustified. That is the *only* way to vindicate premise (3) of the New Master Argument, which holds that the Principle of Intelligible Exclusion entails a principle of restraint. We may need a weak principle of restraint to ensure that public justification can be reached and publicly unjustified law reformed or repealed.

Given this, here's a preliminary formulation of the Principle of Convergent Restraint:

Principle of Convergent Restraint (PCR): A should not publicly advocate law L if [some] members of the public have sufficient reason R_n to reject L.[4]

Convergent Restraint restricts A from advancing a law defeated by the diverse reasons of members of the public, with reasons indexed to members of the public via the R_n variable. Thus, if some small sector of the population has sufficient reason to reject L, then A should not advocate it.[5] This standard may seem too stringent, as the great diversity of views among members of the public may frequently provide defeater reasons, even for much-needed laws. However, whether that is so depends upon the relevant conception of sufficiency, and for our purposes I leave this conception open.[6]

The initial formulation of Convergent Restraint is defective for two reasons. First, it fails to identify a causal connection between advocacy and outcomes. Any citizen not holding political office has a vanishingly small impact on whether L is imposed, via her votes or even her concerted political organization. If so, then why should citizens restrain themselves according to Convergent Restraint? After all, the Principle of Convergent Restraint restricts their liberty without any clear benefit. To illustrate, consider Gerald Gaus's case of a voter in Hawaii who votes for president long after the U.S. national elections are decided.[7] Given that the Hawaiian voter cannot possibly have an impact on the outcome, it is hard to see why we should restrict his voting behavior any more than we should restrict his ordinary private action. And if we cannot restrict his *votes* due to their lack of direct impact, we surely cannot restrict his *speech*.

An obvious reply is that while no one citizen affects coercive outcomes, citizens do as a whole. Convergent Restraint could be grounded on its salutary macro-level effects, since widespread compliance with it might help prevent publicly unjustified coercion. But this suggestion is speculative in the extreme. We lack sound empirical reason to suppose that widespread citizen compliance with Convergent Restraint will aid in the exclusion of publicly unjustified coercion, given the complex social processes by which citizens' advocacy is translated into legislative outcomes. If we are to charge anyone with such responsibility, then, it should be legislative representatives of the public. It is they who have an identifiable impact on outcomes, not ordinary citizens.

Perhaps this reply is too dismissive. Consider, for example, the rise of effective general restraints on the use of sexist and racist reasons in public discourse over the last fifty years. While one person deviating from these restraints will not harm the pursuit of sexual and racial equality, general restraints have had salutary aggregate effects, and those effects seem sufficient to justify antiracist and antisexist discursive norms. Perhaps, then, these discourse norms have significant impacts on policy outcomes. Presumably the spread of antiracist and antisexist speech norms has made it more difficult for politicians to appeal to citizens' baser instincts and so have had a positive impact on the shape of the law.[8] Given that racist and sexist laws cannot be publicly justified, moral restraints on sexist and racist speech can be justified based on their impact on public justification.

Three replies are in order. First, antisexist and antiracist speech norms were arguably adopted because people thought that holding sexist and racist views were in themselves wrong, so that expressions of those views were wrong as well. But this is not the case with restraint on citizens' nonpublic and non-justificatory reasons generally. Political liberals have always protected the individual's right to be driven by reasons that are sound, moral *and* inappropriate for public discourse. Second, in the case of racist and sexist norms, it's still not clear we have an adequate case for restraint based on *policy outcomes*. While restraint on racist and sexist reasons may account for some part of the variance between laws concerning race and sex over the last fifty years, we don't know how much. Therefore, even arguments for ethically restricting racist speech to reduce racist policy need more empirical support than public reason liberals typically provide. Finally, even if we had the requisite evidence, it's not clear that we can extrapolate from the policy impact of antiracist and antisexist norms to the policy impact of allowing citizens to act on the broad range of reasons that Convergent Restraint allows.

A second problem with the Principle of Convergent Restraint is that it supposes that citizens should regulate their actions in accord with whether other citizens *actually* have sufficient reason to endorse the coercion in question. But justificatory reasons are diverse and dispersed and so hard to discern. Convergent Restraint thus appears to be too informationally demanding. We can weaken it, then, by basing restraint on *beliefs* about which coercive laws citizens have sufficient reason to endorse. Furthermore, since we want to add a causal connection to Convergent Restraint, we should also base restraint on beliefs about whether a citizen's advocacy will be causally efficacious. Thus, restraint will depend on two types of beliefs: beliefs about sufficient reasons, and beliefs about causal efficacy. Importantly, these beliefs should have good epistemic credentials.

I now modify the Principle of Convergent Restraint to cover citizens' beliefs about their own causal efficacy and their beliefs about whether citizens have sufficient reason to endorse some coercive law or policy:

PCR′: A should not publicly advocate law L if she justifiably believes (a) that members of the public lack sufficient reason R_n to endorse L and (b) that A's public advocacy effectively contributes to L's imposition.[9]

PCR′ is more plausible because it is indexed to citizens' justified beliefs. But it has a critical implication: since Convergent Restraint only applies to those who justifiably believe they have an impact on coercive laws, it applies to few individuals in large-scale elections. Ordinary voters cannot justifiably believe that their political activism affects outcomes, if for no other reason than that their vote is an incredibly small proportion of vote totals. If PCR' is true, it has little impact on citizens' political lives in these contexts. In this way, we adopt an indirect approach to public justification (Ch. 2, Sec. II).

PCR' has problems of its own, however. First, it rules out strategic advocacy because citizens cannot advocate laws based on what other citizens will do. To see why this is problematic, consider Gaus's case of Alf, a citizen who believes that a policy of extensive free trade and government aid to displaced workers is publicly justified, but not a policy of free trade alone.[10] Alf also recognizes that the public sphere is full of complicated messages and that if he advocates his preferred policies, nuances and all, he will be ineffective. So he decides to talk only of the benefits of free trade and let others advocate aid to displaced workers, believing that his advocacy will push political opinion towards the policy he believes is justified. Note that Alf aims at producing publicly justified laws. That is, he honestly supports public justification even if he is seemingly *dishonest* in his actual speech. Has Alf done anything wrong? In my view, he has not. Alf has noble goals and shows considerable political savvy. Public reason liberalism should not block citizens from engaging in such thoughtful, honest political activities.

PCR' should be emended accordingly:

> *PCR"*: A should not publicly advocate law L in order to contribute to M's becoming or remaining law (where L may be equivalent to M) if A justifiably believes (a) that members of the public lack sufficient reason R_n to endorse M and (b) that A's public advocacy effectively contributes to M's becoming law.

Gaus's case is now accommodated. Alf is free to advocate for a pure free trade policy because his ultimate aim is to generate publicly justified law. As long as he believes that his end result is publicly justified, his advocacy seems not only permissible but shrewd and prudent. Note an important implication of *PCR"*: it permits complex forms of strategic advocacy with multiple steps. That is, it makes the permissibility of advocacy turn on its effect on the outcome of frequently opaque, multistage political processes. The importance of appropriate inputs into the political process now seems less important vis-à-vis effective institutional design.

Now that we are focused on the functioning of political institutions, we might attend to advocacy for particular candidates and officials, who will directly impact the imposition of laws. In most cases, citizens base their votes on the range of proposals the officials are likely to support. To apply Convergent Restraint to voting for officials, it should be updated as follows:

Convergent Restraint for Officials (PCRO): A should not publicly advocate politician P in order to contribute to the election of politician Q (where P may be equivalent to Q) if she justifiably believes (i) that politician Q will contribute no less than the alternatives to the imposition of proposals that members of the public have sufficient reason R_n to reject and (ii) that A's advocacy for politician P effectively contributes to politician Q's election.[11]

Convergent Restraint for Officials introduces a new complication. Voting for or publicly supporting proposals is simple—aye or nay. But politicians contribute to the imposition of a vast range of proposals and *some* politician will be elected (voting "no" is rarely an option). As a result, citizens must choose between politicians based on their competitors and based on the range of proposals these politicians will likely implement. We might further emend the Principle of Convergent Restraint for Officials to include a threshold requirement, as some politicians may be so bad that abstaining from voting is required.

A potential problem for PCR″ and Convergent Restraint for Officials, as we have seen, is that they probably do not apply to citizens in most political contexts, since citizens cannot justifiably believe that they have a significant impact on outcomes inside or outside the ballot box. But I find this a happy result, since restraining citizens' advocacy is often a poor way to bring about publicly justified laws. Knowledge of other citizens' reasons is hard to come by. On convergence, reasons are *diverse* and *dispersed*. If so, we should encourage citizens to clearly and forcefully broadcast what they take their reasons to be.[12] It is vital for political systems to encourage citizens to be forthright and open about their reasons. Even poor reasoning may be evidence of general dissatisfaction with a law. The problem with principles of restraint is that they "distort the dispersal of information: the most reasonable voters may self-censor their views, leading to wide-spread misconceptions about the real issues and the breadth and depth of consensus."[13] Mainstream principles of restraint may misrepresent good information, partly because many reasonable citizens may keep their reasons to themselves, producing misinformation about matters of import and reducing the social resources to draw on diversity in solving political challenges.

I believe that we can explain why mainstream public reason liberals are attracted to restraint by eliciting their implicit model of politics. To see this, consider Jon Elster's distinction between politics as a forum and politics as a market.[14] In politics as a forum, citizens debate, discuss and change their views in response to the reasoning of others. At the extreme, the task of electoral and legislative institutions is simply to adequately register the results of forum discussion. In contrast, the market view takes views that reflect a variety of concerns and interests as inputs and then uses institutions to transform them into a justified political outcome.[15] Mainstream public reason liberals implicitly view politics as a forum, and this is why they are so focused on tweaking deliberative inputs to produce publicly justified outputs. But tampering with citizens' behavior is morally unattractive on liberal grounds. We do better to understand politics as a market, as an attempt to transform information about citizens' reasons into publicly justified outputs.[16]

III. Legislative and Judicial Restraint

If we see politics as a market rather than a forum, we may wish to rely on institutional design alone to satisfy Intelligible Exclusion. However, the deliberate choices of political officials directly impact whether citizens are coerced. So the Principle of Intelligible Exclusion may require restraining their choices. To demonstrate, let's focus on legislators and judges.

I take a legislator to be any member of a coercive government body who directly votes to propose, amend, pass or repeal coercive laws, policies and proposals. Her aim is not primarily interpretative, as is the case with judicial bodies. Instead, legislators aim to legislate, which most often is an aim to coerce. And in most cases, the votes of legislators are causally efficacious—their votes make a predictable, substantive contribution to outcomes.[17] It is true that legislators do not always make a substantive contribution to coercive outcomes, as they may be in a persistent minority, but legislators vote on many issues while in office, and in a great many we can expect that they contribute to the passage of legislation. One in several hundred is a small contribution, but it is many orders of magnitude greater than the contribution made by ordinary citizens.

Institutional design can go a long way towards satisfying the Principle of Intelligible Exclusion. But institutions only provide prescriptions that ordinary legislators are free to ignore. If enough legislators reject the institutional constraints imposed upon them, then they will legislate in ways that violate these constraints. The U.S. Congress provides many such cases, most egregiously in foreign policy, where Congress has allowed the president to initiate military conflicts without congressional approval, despite the fact that the Constitution requires a congressional vote to declare war. The general point: unless legislators adopt some norms regulating their conduct, institutional design cannot satisfy Intelligible Exclusion. Legislators should only enact legislation that they believe is publicly justified.[18] Accordingly, PCR" applies to them.

We can simplify the principle as follows. First, legislators usually justifiably believe that their advocacy effectively contributes to which laws are passed, so we can drop condition (b). Second, we can confine our focus to actual votes. While public debate is important, even legislative discourse can be lost in public discussion (consider legislative speeches on C-SPAN given to mostly empty rooms). Finally, we can replace the generic variable "A" with legislators. Let us call the new principle the Principle of Convergent Restraint for Legislators (PCRL):

Convergent Restraint for Legislators (PCRL): A legislator should not vote for law L in order to contribute to M's becoming or remaining law (where L may be equivalent to M) if he justifiably believes that members of the public lack sufficient reason R_n to endorse M.

Notice that Legislative Convergent Restraint retains sensitivity to strategic voting, so strategic concerns do not count against it. As long as compliance with legislative restraint contributes significantly to conforming laws to the ideal of public reason, it is sound. This has an important consequence, for legislative restraint based on convergence is only a principle of proposal restraint, not reason restraint. Legislators are permitted to vote based on *whatever reason they like*, including sectarian religious reasons. So long as legislators justifiably believe that the law they support is publicly justified, their votes are permissible.[19]

Four worries deserve comment. The first is that Convergent Restraint is too permissive because it allows citizens to be insincere and dishonest.

Since citizens can act on whatever reasons they like and offer whatever reasons they like, it does appear that the Principle of Convergent Restraint permits dishonesty and insincerity. And we might reasonably think that counts against Convergent Restraint as an expression of respect for persons as free and equal. But we can admit that dishonesty is disrespectful without concluding that requiring, say, reason restraint is an implication of the ideal of public reason. Not all moral norms governing civic life need have the same basis. Of course, it might well be that norms restricting, say, rudeness and principles of restraint *are* rooted in the same weighty moral values, making it unlikely that restraint can be justified without simultaneously justifying restrictions on insincerity and dishonesty. But our question is whether Convergent Restraint is objectionable because it permits insincerity and dishonesty and the answer appears to be no. If anything, the fact that restraint and other moral prohibitions share a common moral basis means that we cannot justify Convergent Restraint and dishonesty and insincerity at the same time, which is all to the good.

The second worry is that legislators and citizens who internalize Convergent Restraint will not add to the public justification of laws. Knowledge of citizens' reasons will inevitably be dispersed and decentralized, sharply limiting legislators' ability to tell whether citizens have reason to reject particular proposals. The point of Convergent Restraint, however, is not that legislators must painstakingly gather such information (though that would be nice), but rather that they become sensitive to such information as they run across it. Thus, if legislators become aware of defeaters for their preferred proposals, they will have a tendency to stop advocating them. This sensitivity will augment the process of exclusion.

Yet we can still imagine cases where legislators' internalization of Convergent Restraint makes them worse contributors to publicly justified laws than otherwise. For instance, we might think that legislators who represent large minority populations will do best if their advocacy on behalf of their group is unrestricted. Perhaps their unbridled passion will force the polity to be fairer to their group. But this case seems exceptional. If Convergent Restraint is internalized, then legislators will not push for publicly unjustified coercion in general, which will make imposing unjustified coercion much more difficult. Some public advocates may be able to produce better outcomes if their behavior is unconstrained, but it is hard to see how these cases could be prevalent enough to override the benefits to public justification brought about by widespread compliance with Legislative Convergent Restraint.

Finally, some will worry that requiring conduct from legislators that is not required of their constituents will render legislative restraint infeasible. My view allows citizens to act on whatever reasons they like, and yet holds that officials should restrain themselves. But how plausible is this recommendation given the fact that representatives will have an incentive to vote for whatever their constituency supports? Consider the case of abortion activism in Texas. On my view, citizens can advocate for abortion restrictions even if such restrictions are defeated, but legislators may not.[20] Can we really expect representatives not to do something a large majority of their constituency demands?[21] The short answer is yes, we can. Representatives are routinely expected to comply with much more complex normative standards than their constituents, such as legislative procedures. This means they aren't always permitted to act as their constituents demand, so even if Texas representatives oppose abortion privately, and agree with their constituents, they might still have a duty to protect their constituents and other members of the public from publicly unjustified legislation. On analogy, we can and should expect representatives to resist restricting free speech rights based on their understanding of the First Amendment, even if their constituents insist that they do otherwise. If we are to have any constitutional restraints on democratic procedures, we must expect legislators to cast hard votes, since sometimes representatives must protect the constitutional order against the present will of the majority.

Worries answered, legislative restraint based on convergence is quite attractive given public reason's foundational values. Convergent Restraint for Legislators imposes fewer integrity costs than *any* competitor principle in the literature. First, it is a principle of proposal restraint, not reason restraint. As a result, legislators are permitted to vote based on religious considerations alone. So long as they justifiably believe that the law they support is publicly justified, their votes are permissible. Second, legislators are a vanishingly small proportion of citizens, so restraint applies to a greatly restricted class of individuals. Finally, I am aware of no religion that requires their adherents to run for or hold political office. So in cases where one's office requires an integrity violation, politicians are free to resign. For this reason, I am not simply recreating the problem of restraint for legislators. As I remarked in Chapter 2 (Sec. IV), no one cares about splitting the identity of a judge if we ask her not to rule based on her private religious convictions. This is due to the fact that it is easy to avoid being a judge, in contrast to being a citizen.

Speaking of judges, Intelligible Exclusion and Convergent Restraint have something to say about their conduct as well. I take a judge to be a political official responsible for interpreting passed legislation and policies in accord with broader legal standards, such as constitutional constraints. Judges must also consider whether their decisions are compatible with previous rulings. Consequently, they must engage in subtler forms of reasoning than legislators. Now one wants to know whether the Principle of Intelligible Exclusion imposes a unique requirement on judicial deliberation and, if so, what that imposition consists in. To proceed, consider how judges contribute to the imposition of coercion. In most cases, they either reaffirm the legitimacy of coercion already imposed or stop coercion by ruling some new law unconstitutional or otherwise improper.[22] For this reason, legislative restraint based on convergence is not appropriate for them.

Rawls has argued that the Supreme Court is the "exemplar of public reason."[23] On his view, public reason (that is, shared reason) is the court's characteristic and, indeed, only appropriate form of reasoning. While citizens and legislators need not always justify their activities in terms of public reasons, the justice must do precisely this, having "no other reason and no other values than the political," though they may appeal to shared practices, traditions and historical texts.[24] Thus, judges cannot appeal to their own personal morality or ideals or invoke the same views of others. Rawls discusses a number of reasons for this restriction, among them that the Supreme Court sets the tone of political debate by identifying some issues as salient rather than others, and that the Court must speak in public terms because it is often a center of controversy. These arguments explain our outrage at a justice who issues a ruling based on her private religious, moral or political view. Our expectation of judges differs even from legislators. This is why, as Kent Greenawalt notes, we rarely find explicit religious arguments in opinions, even when the courts appeal to history and tradition or even conceptions of social benefits, for we expect "judges to rely on arguments they believe should have force for all judges. In our culture, this excludes arguments based on particular religious premises."[25]

I believe this expectation can be justified. The reason why religious justifications should not figure into the rulings of judges is that their rulings are the grounds for future law. This is to say that the *reasoning they use* can be utilized to justify coercion in the future. I should be clear that judicial reasoning is not a required basis for future judicial rulings in American courts, or at least whether this is so is a matter of dispute. The key issue is that by offering certain kinds of arguments, judges make certain forms of coercion more or less likely in the future. The arguments that legislators employ are quickly lost to historical memory, but judicial arguments are crystallized on public record in a way that is at least often taken to be normative for future decision making, such that the distinction between reasons and proposals partially breaks down. Judicial decisions are partly constituted by the reasoning they employ; reason restraint, therefore, applies to judges, at least in part.

Judicial reasoning is therefore subject to something like a consensus requirement, as we expect judges to rule on shareable or accessible considerations. As Rawls says, justices are to rule based on political values. Why? Because, again, judicial reasoning is an influential basis for future laws. And since the reason-proposal distinction breaks down, convergence on proposals means convergence on reasons as well. The result of convergence is an agreement on which considerations are salient and relevant, a restriction similar to accessibility and shareability requirements.[26]

How then should judges promote the satisfaction of the Principle of Intelligible Exclusion? They should offer what they take to be shareable or accessible reasons for their decisions. Conversely, they should not offer decisions that they believe couldn't be supported by shareable or accessible reasons. We can now formulate a principle of judicial restraint. Let us call this the Principle of Convergent Restraint for Judges:[27]

Convergent Restraint for Judges (PCRJ): Judges should not issue decisions concerning the constitutionality of coercive laws that appeal to reasons they justifiably believe are not shareable (or accessible) for members of the public.[28]

Judicial convergent restraint expresses our conviction that the idea of public reason requires restraint on judicial reasoning. It is not overridden by integrity or fairness considerations. Judges can reasonably be expected to compartmentalize their commitments in light of the direct, reason-based role they play in imposing coercion. Contra Rawls, the Supreme Court is not the exemplar of public reason, but rather a special case. Nonetheless, he was right about the application of shared and accessible reason to the judicial system.

Given that legislative and judicial restraints provide plausible social mechanisms for satisfying Intelligible Exclusion, we can further specify the New Master Argument:

(1) Public Justification Principle → Intelligibility
(2) Intelligibility → Principle of Intelligible Exclusion
(3) Principle of Intelligible Exclusion → Principle of Convergent Restraint (for legislators and judges)

The New Master Argument requires restraint, but only a limited sort. Restraint does not *touch* ordinary citizens, and legislators need only comply with proposal restraint. Restraint only significantly affects judges, but no one finds such restraint problematic.

I conclude that *the best interpretation of the Public Justification Principle requires no restraint whatsoever,* save for mild restrictions on legislators and judges. We have established the primary claim of the book. But we cannot stop here, for convergence has more work to do. To demonstrate that reconciliation between public reason liberals and their religious critics is possible in practice, we should also show that convergence resolves important contemporary legal controversies. For this reason, I turn to religious accommodations.

IV. Accommodation and Exclusion

Religious accommodations are exemptions from laws based on specifically religious objections. Prominent examples include exempting pacifists from the draft, exempting Christian Scientists and Jehovah's Witnesses from laws requiring certain medical procedures and allowing religious groups exemptions from antidiscrimination law in clerical hiring.[29] I now develop an approach to religious accommodation that answers three questions: (1) What is the basis for religious accommodation within public reason liberalism? (2) What considerations determine how to institutionalize religious accommodations? (3) Are religious accommodations special, that is, do nonreligious considerations form a valid basis for accommodation? My primary purpose is to illustrate the differences between convergence and consensus approaches to accommodation and to show that religious objectors should find the convergence view attractive.

The approach I develop should apply to a number of past and present legal controversies. However, I caution against using it to determine what the law should be independently of real-world social and legal processes, like judicial precedent. As we saw in Chapter 5 (Sec. VIII), discerning which laws are justified is partly a historical and empirical matter. That is why I focus on the principles of exclusion embedded in American constitutional law to assess several classic court decisions on the appropriate extent of religious accommodation.

The primary factor in delineating religious accommodations is the Principle of Intelligible Exclusion. We can apply Intelligible Exclusion to religious accommodation by acknowledging the centrality of religious reasons to personal integrity. Consequently, coercive state bodies can only satisfy the Principle of Intelligible Exclusion with respect to religion if they provide strong protections for religious freedom and prevent religious sects from co-opting state power. These prohibitions form the legal basis for religious accommodation in liberal democratic societies because they reflect a concern not to coerce people of faith in ways they have sufficient intelligible religious reason to reject.

Fortunately, all liberal democratic constitutions contain explicit protections for religious freedom and, to varying degrees, restrictions on the establishment of religion. The American constitutional approach to religious accommodation is based on two fundamental principles, the Free Exercise and Establishment clauses of the First Amendment. These principles empower and require judges to overturn legislation that unjustifiably restricts the free exercise of religion or that establishes religion, and bars the legislature from passing laws that violate free exercise or constitute establishment. In this way, the Free Exercise and Establishment clauses specify how state coercion satisfies the Principle of Intelligible Exclusion.

The second factor in delineating religious accommodations is Convergent Restraint as applied to legislators and judges. Legislators and judges should avoid imposing coercion on citizens that cannot be publicly justified. In endeavoring to do so, they must recognize that citizens' defeaters are diverse and *dispersed*. Consequently, legal bodies cannot always discern whether citizens have defeaters for laws. To approximate citizens' reasons, they should use social signals to make educated guesses about which laws are defeated. Public religious objections to laws should therefore signal not only that the objector has a defeater for the law but also that others may as well. Objections in deliberation are often the only evidence that a law is not publicly justified. In cases where further evidence is absent, the Principle of Convergent Restraint requires that political officials err on the side of liberty.

The third factor in determining the scope of religious accommodations is that officials have a duty to not impose unequal burdens on citizens. A publicly justified polity must ensure that citizens are treated equally before the law. So if its citizens reasonably object that more burdens are placed on them than others, their polity must take such "fairness" objections seriously (Ch. 2, Sec. V). Fairness objections come in two types: (1) complaints that the law unfairly burdens religion and (2) complaints that the law unfairly privileges some religious group. Both are serious. Type-1 fairness objections are widely acknowledged as valid, type-2 objections to a lesser extent. Type-2 is often not an issue, since in most cases religious exemptions apply to a small number of individuals, such as Sikhs who receive exemptions from British motorcycle helmet laws. But as exemptions increase as a proportion of the population, more citizens are likely to resent the fact that they must bear burdens that other citizens do not. So type-2 fairness objections can wield great force.

I should allay the concern that religious accommodations are prima facie inegalitarian simply because they favor religious groups. Some have argued that religious beliefs are "expensive tastes" that the law has no business protecting.[30] Just because some citizens happen to care a great deal about religion is insufficient to ground an exemption, these critics complain. After all, I could care a great deal about being free to eat gourmet cakes, but this would not entitle me to special legal protection. To rebut this criticism, recall the conception of equal treatment embodied public reason. On the Public Justification Principle, citizens are treated equally in the most fundamental sense if no citizen is coerced when she has an intelligible defeater for the coercion in question. Given citizens' diverse commitments and reasons, some citizens will have more defeaters than others. It follows that when treated equally, some citizens will have more impact on the law. But public reason liberalism is still egalitarian because it is equally sensitive to the reasons of each citizen.[31] What's more, citizens cannot secure religious exemptions for themselves if they think the law should apply to others but not to themselves. The key point is that religious objectors typically prefer no law at all on some issue to having the law apply to everyone; they prefer the law to apply to *no one* rather than to themselves.[32]

Legislators and judges can take four approaches in response to accommodation requests validated by these factors. I use Kent Greenawalt's terms for the first three approaches: *neutral-restrictive, targeted accommodation* and *neutral accommodating.*[33] The neutral-restrictive approach maintains that the state has an overriding interest in securing uniform compliance with the law, such that all persons should bear the burdens of the law equally, religious or no. The targeted accommodation approach only allows those with specific religious objections to opt out of a law. The state's interest in equality takes a backseat to its duty to respect liberty of conscience. The neutral-accommodating approach provides a general opt-out provision for anyone to whom the law applies. Citizens cannot opt out for any reason, but the exemption is not directed specifically at a group or individual, such as the Amish.

The fourth approach to accommodation is to repeal objectionable laws due to the defeaters of religious citizens, or what I shall call the *repeal* approach. I believe that liberal states should take the repeal approach much more often than they do. But in some ways the repeal approach is not an approach to accommodation *per se* but rather a response to an inability to produce particular accommodations. For this reason, I set the fourth approach aside for now.

V.   Free Exercise and Establishment

Given that this book is not a work of constitutional law, I will not discuss the history of religion clause jurisprudence. Instead, I shall simply review the two general principles that govern accommodation, the Free Exercise and Establishment clauses. The content of these two principles is widely disputed, along with disputes about how and when they conflict. However, we can still safely conclude that any liberal constitution must contain a version of both principles in order to ensure that citizens are not unjustifiably coerced based on religion, for or against. Once we have established this, we can analyze some legal cases to illustrate how convergence handles religious accommodation in ways salutary to both liberal and religious concerns.[34]

The first sentence of the First Amendment reads: "Congress shall make no law respecting an establishment of religion, or prohibiting the free exercise thereof." The Free Exercise Clause bars Congress from using legal coercion to restrict the various facets of religious belief and practice.[35] Freedom of exercise has been interpreted expansively, extending far beyond freedom of worship to protecting styles of dress in the workplace and in prison, exempting citizens from some forms of public education and the use of controlled substances. In general, the courts have always protected religious citizens from many coercively imposed hardships that they suffer "just because of their religious beliefs and practices" on free exercise grounds.[36] Thus the Free Exercise Clause serves as a principle of exclusion: it bars the state from coercing citizens based on the importance of protecting a person's ability to act in accord with her deepest reasons of integrity, at least if such reasons are religious.[37] Legal bodies acknowledge that core religious reasons serve as defeaters for coercion. As Greenawalt puts it, a central goal of the Free Exercise Clause is to acknowledge the value that "many people care deeply about their religious beliefs and practices, and they feel that their religious obligations supersede duties to the state if the two collide."[38]

To make matters more concrete, let's review a paradigmatic free exercise violation. In *Church of the Lukumi Babalu Aye, Inc. v. City of Hialeah* (1993), the Supreme Court reviewed an ordinance that banned animal sacrifices engaged in by adherents to Santeria, a religion that synthesizes elements from Roman Catholicism and West African and Caribbean indigenous religions. Adherents of Santeria practice animal sacrifice (including but not limited to chickens, ducks, goats and turtles). The other citizens of Hialeah reacted negatively when they learned that such practices were taking place in their town and passed an ordinance banning animal sacrifice, though they allowed animal killing for any number of other reasons, such as reasons based on kosher restrictions. Writing for the Court, who overturned the law, Justice Kennedy claimed that the law in question is not appropriately neutral because its aim is to "restrict practices because of their religious motivation." Thus the Free Exercise Clause renders the law unconstitutional because there is no "compelling interest" on behalf of the state in banning animal sacrifice.[39] *Hialeah* is an unusual ruling because it is rare for a law to so explicitly target a religion. But it is a core case that helps to illustrate the exclusionary function of the Free Exercise Clause. The Free Exercise Clause excludes as a ground for coercion that some people find the religious practices of another group offensive because they slaughter animals for religious reasons.

While there will be disputes about hard cases with respect to free exercise, it is not hard to see how Intelligible Exclusion requires a similar constitutional protection, since it makes the law sensitive to religious defeaters and so appropriately defeats many coercive laws based on religion.

Now let's turn to the Establishment Clause, both to explain how it functions as a principle of exclusion and why a similar principle is likely required by the Principle of Intelligible Exclusion. The Establishment Clause is the first of the two religion clauses, reading: "Congress shall make no law respecting an establishment of religion." It is not always clear what "respecting" comes to and it is for this reason that the Establishment Clause is in many ways the more controversial of the two religion clauses. Originalist judges tend to interpret the Establishment Clause to only prohibit the federal government from establishing a state church. Justice Scalia, for example, has written "there is nothing unconstitutional in a State's favoring religion generally, honoring God through public prayer and acknowledging or, in a nonproselytizing manner, venerating the Ten Commandments."[40] In sharp contrast, more liberal judges believe the Establishment Clause requires courts to overturn a vast range of laws that contribute to the promotion of a particular religion or religious group. The controversial *Lemon Test* for establishment roughly reflects their approach.[41] Despite these deep disagreements, there is a consensus that the Establishment Clause is intended to block the imposition of laws that require "someone to contribute to the upkeep of a religion he does not support," because such upkeep may violate his conscience.[42] Furthermore, judges widely agree that laws promoting establishment can violate free exercise if they require "forced instruction" because, while one's freedom of worship may not be restricted, one's conscience can "be violated if one is instructed regularly in the doctrines of the established church" or even a church not officially established.[43]

The Establishment Clause is thought to embody a number of different moral values. One commonly accepted value is that the Establishment Clause helps to protect free exercise and religious conscience. Other examples include the promotion of autonomy, the recognition of government's incompetence regarding religious judgments, avoiding a source of corruption of religion, avoiding government corruption, avoiding unhealthy intermingling, avoiding religious conflict that could threaten social stability and promoting a sense of equal dignity among citizens.[44] All interpreters of the Establishment Clause acknowledge that some of these values provide good grounds for interpreting and applying the Establishment Clause to exclude certain justifications for coercive laws.

An illuminating example of Establishment Clause jurisprudence is the prohibition of federal funding for groups who engage in in proselytization. Sometimes judges distinguish between "faith-saturated" and "faith-centered" providers of social services.[45] Faith-saturated providers have "explicit, extensive, and mandatory" religious content in their programs.[46] But faith-centered providers "have programs that include religious messages and activities, but may allow participants to opt out of them and do not assume that a positive outcome depends on involvement in the religious aspects."[47] There is controversy over whether the Constitution permits funding faith-centered programs, but there is widespread agreement that the Constitution prohibits funding faith-saturated programs. Funding faith-saturated programs is tantamount to funding attempts to convert others, such as funding mandatory worship service attendance to receive social services.

In the case of faith-saturated organizations, a publicly justified establishment clause functions as a principle of exclusion by preventing reasons that support funding such groups from figuring into a public justification. But how can funding stand in need of public justification? After all, it does not seem coercive. For one thing, funding does not restrict the free exercise of religion. For another, while taxpayers must fund such activities against conscience, their financial contributions are miniscule. I believe that despite appearances to the contrary, a publicly justified establishment clause excludes an important form of coercion with respect to funding faith-saturated organizations. But this can only be seen if we distinguish, as Robert Audi does, between *primary* and *secondary* coercion. Primary coercion is familiar, as it requires a particular action. Secondary coercion is more complex, for it "depends on primary coercion, such as when tax payments are spent partly in ways one disapproves of, so one is in a sense funding something against one's will."[48]

To gloss the issue: primary coercion forces you to do something, whereas secondary coercion uses the proceeds of that force to support something you oppose. Audi thinks that primary coercion "is more in need of justification than is secondary coercion" as it is harder to show that coercion is justified than showing that particular uses of the benefits of coercion are justified given that the coercion itself is justified.

However, if, say, "a tax revenue is to be used for a purpose inconsistent with the rationale for imposing the tax, then the secondary coercion in question is (apart from the special excuse) impermissible."[49] I agree that secondary coercion stands in need of justification, especially as part of justifying primary coercion, as the justification of primary coercion may consist in the benefits of coercion being used in some specific manner. Consequently, state bodies are not permitted to use the benefits of coercion in other ways.

Intelligible Exclusion blocks funding that violates a publicly justified establishment clause in precisely this way. A publicly justified establishment clause therefore serves as a principle of exclusion for *secondary coercion*. It bars the use of taxable funds to support causes that citizens have intelligible defeaters for, such as an atheist who objects to the use of her tax money to fund Christian organizations that proselytize. She is coerced in the secondary sense and given that she is an atheist, she probably has intelligible defeaters for the coercion in question.[50]

If secondary coercion must be publicly justified, Intelligible Exclusion requires a nonestablishment requirement to bar the use of coercion to fund organizations with agendas that promote values incompatible with citizens' core integrity-based reasons. Consequently, the Establishment Clause resembles an appropriate principle of exclusion.

We can further develop these two principles of exclusion—Free Exercise and Establishment—by combining them with the various considerations raised in Section IV. First, since legislative bodies are responsible for applying these two principles, we can specify the way in which they satisfy the Principle of Convergent Restraint. Legislators comply with the Principle of Intelligible Exclusion by blocking coercion incompatible with principles of free exercise and non-establishment. They should therefore err in favor of less coercion rather than more. I will focus on legislators here, as second-guessing judicial procedures is much more problematic. Judicial bodies are bound to follow a number of procedural restrictions for enforcing constitutional law that may bar them from directly crafting an exemption. So I am on better ground recommending that we leave the crafting of exemptions to the legislature. But when a law is defeated, legislators are under a duty to craft an exemption when repealing or reforming legislation is infeasible or unwise for other reasons. I believe American courts and legislative bodies do a fairly good job respecting free exercise and nonestablishment of religion. So the main moral recommendation public reason liberals should make it that nonreligious citizens should have the same broad protections as religious citizens.

VI. Exemptions—Three Cases

In light of the foregoing, I shall analyze three famous legal cases that concern religious accommodation, *Wisconsin v. Yoder, Employment Division of Oregon v. Smith* and *Mozert v. Hawkins*. While the details of these decisions are complex, I believe that they are sufficiently clear to show that religious accommodations were merited in each case. I will *not* claim that the courts rightly or wrongly decided each case, given the variety of adjudicative rules they labor under. Instead, I am concerned with whether the burdened parties in each case (the *Yoder* and *Mozert* parents and the plaintiffs in *Smith*) merited religious accommodation based on the reasoning cited in the court cases. The reason I focus on court cases is because they provide written evidence of what moderately idealized reasoners would endorse, and so help us to determine whether the burdened parties have defeaters. On convergence, the burdened parties have defeaters for all three proposed legal requirements. The *Yoder* parents merit an exemption for their children from public high school, the *Mozert* parents from using the controversial Holt reader, and the *Smith* plaintiffs from being denied unemployment benefits.

Note that I focus on cases regarding free exercise as a principle of exclusion, not establishment, for establishment issues raise complexities that would take me too far afield.

By evaluating the reasoning of the courts, I am only assessing whether they reveal defeaters for the relevant coercion in accord with the Principle of Intelligible Exclusion and the Public Justification Principle. In other words, I am illustrating how my approach to accommodation should determine the final legal outcome of certain cases, not whether the court reasoned properly according to the multifaceted considerations that they must routinely take into account.[51] As such, when the court appropriately finds contrary to Intelligible Exclusion, legislatures or citizens generally should enact the necessary legal reforms.

Before I analyze these cases, I should be clear about the relevant *comparison class*. As stated in Chapter 1 (Sec. IV), laws are only defeated if some members of the public have sufficient reason to regard them as morally inferior to *no law at all* regulating the matter. In the case of many religious complainants, they rank all laws lacking an accommodation below no law at all on the matter. They might rank the accommodating law below no law, but the generic law must fall below no law in their ranking. So their rankings can take at least two forms, from highest to lowest rank:

No law, Accommodating law, Generic law
Accommodating law, No law, Generic law

In the *Yoder* and *Mozert* cases, the parents clearly preferred no law at all that would regulate their religious liberty to laws regulating them in ways they found objectionable. In the *Yoder* case, the Amish parents preferred no law requiring their children to attend secondary schooling, whereas in the *Mozert* case, Vicki Frost and others preferred no legal restriction that conflicted with their religious beliefs via the education of their children to any law requiring one. So we compare the public justification of a law that burdens them to no law at all on the matter in question.

A critic might attempt to undermine this framing of the issues by arguing that other parties have a veto for the law that permits accommodation, presumably on the basis that they are adversely affected by the accommodation in question. In other words, other members of the public may have either of the following rankings:

Generic law, No law, Accommodating law

In this case, if the objectors have genuine intelligible defeaters for the accommodating law, then the only legal option is not to have a law at all. So even in this case, religious objectors will not be burdened. But in most cases of accommodation, the law's supporters are sufficiently committed to the law that they'd prefer it to apply nearly universally than not at all. So in most cases those who object to exemptions actually have the following ranking:

Generic law, Accommodating law, No law

And this is because it is rare that someone is so bothered by a religious accommodation that they'd *give up* the other benefits of the law to avoid it. One reason they probably have this ranking is because in general, the requested accommodations have little impact on them or anyone else, as we shall see.

Given that we can assume that the accommodating law is eligible for the general public, even if most prefer the generic law, our question is whether the objectors have defeaters for the generic law.[52] Thus we can in one way separate the coercion applied to the *Yoder* and *Mozert* parents and children from the coercion involved in applying the rest of the law to everyone else. This gives us a method of coherently asking whether coercion should be applied to these specific religious groups. Since the exemptions in both cases have little causal impact on others, we ask whether the parents in both cases have sufficient reason to prefer the accommodating law to the relevant or similar burden involved in complying with the generic law. We can distinguish the generic law from the accommodating law for two reasons. First, the public justification of a free exercise principle allows us in principle to selectively exempt individuals from following laws that impose a significant burden on their free exercise of religion. So while we might not be able to selectively apply laws *without* a free exercise principle, we can with a free exercise principle in place.[53] Second, we can selectively apply the law because the effects of the law on religious objectors can be isolated from the other effects.[54]

In what follows, then, I will compare the generic law to the accommodating law for *Yoder* and *Mozert*. We should go with the accommodating law when the religious members of the public in question prefer it to no law and prefer no law to the generic law. We must establish that they have the following ranking: Accommodating law, No law, Generic law.[55] For the most part, we do not have to worry about other alternatives because granting an exemption or retaining the relevant burden are the only legal options on the table. If someone proposes an intermediate alternative, we might need to evaluate it, but these cases present more limited choices.

Smith is more complicated, as the plaintiffs sued for unemployment benefits, which comes at taxpayers' expense. But as we shall see, I assume for the sake of analysis that the laws that made the controversy possible are publicly justified. If so, then we can isolate the request of the *Smith* defendants in the same way as we isolate the requests of the *Yoder* and *Mozert* parents.

Finally, I should allay a concern that in evaluating these cases I'm assuming that public reason can generate more determinate recommendations than I allow in Chapter 5. In that chapter, I made clear that determining what reasons members of the public have is a complicated matter. There is a great deal of indeterminacy in cases of moderate idealization, and it is hard to discern what is justified even in cases where moderate idealization yields clear results in principle. So how can I hope to determine whether the burdened parties in these cases have defeaters? Consider two of my resources. First, by focusing on free exercise cases of conscientious objection, I focus on especially strong reasons for action at the core of persons' belief-value sets. Free exercise cases are not based on mild objections, but on concerns at the root of individual integrity, so we can expect the strong reasons derived from such objections to survive moderate idealization. Second, we have judicial record to explain the reasoning of the burdened parties, which gives us unusually good evidence of what reasons the burdened parties have. That is how we overcome the indeterminacy mentioned in Chapter 5.

Now to the cases. *Wisconsin v. Yoder* concerns three Amish students whose families removed them from New Glarus High School in New Glarus, Wisconsin, at the end of the eighth grade (represented by Jonas Yoder, one of the fathers). The parents acted on the basis of their religious conviction that secondary schooling would have a negative impact on their children's ability to understand and live by the values of the Amish community. The Amish never objected to primary schooling for the purpose of teaching basic reading, writing and arithmetic. But they believed that secondary schooling would excessively expose their children to "worldly influences" and so interfere with their religious development and integration into the Amish community; therefore, forcing them into public schools "contravenes the basic religious tenets and practice of the Amish faith, both as to parent and the child."[56] In other words, to force these children to attend two years of high school would effectively take them away from their community. The state of Wisconsin refused the parents' request after the families appealed to a Green County Court ruling, which convicted the families of breaking the law. The Wisconsin Supreme Court came down in favor of the Amish, but then the state appealed the case to the Supreme Court. The Supreme Court ruled unanimously in Yoder's favor, citing a number of reasons for their decision. First, they held that the state of Wisconsin violated the Amish's free exercise of religion. In this case, the *Yoder* parents' beliefs were sufficiently sincere and deep that the First Amendment covered them. The Court also determined that an eighth-grade education plus the Amish's further educational services were adequate to prepare citizens for participation in American political institutions. The decision of the parents also in no way burdened society as a whole.

The *Yoder* parents merited an exemption because their intelligible defeaters satisfied the Principle of Intelligible Exclusion in this case. Even if the Supreme Court acted wrongly for procedural reasons, the *Yoder* parents were given an exemption they morally merited. To see why, we must ask whether the *Yoder* parents had intelligible defeaters and whether the court had good reason to think as much. I believe that the *Yoder* parents had intelligible reasons because such reasons are epistemically justified for them, given their religious evaluative standards. The Amish are well educated in their religious tradition, deeply familiar with the Bible and their hermeneutical tradition for interpreting it. Perhaps at high levels of idealization, the Amish parents would renounce their religious commitments, but at moderate levels of idealization they seem to have engaged in a respectable amount of reasoning, such that it would be inappropriate to charge them with irrationality, especially in light of the fact that multiple Amish communities have come to similar conclusions (the *Yoder* parents were in no way exceptional).[57] Given reasonable pluralism, it is hard to see how we can deny that they have a reasonable view. Furthermore, it is within the epistemic capacities of members of the public to recognize these reasons as such. So, given the definition of intelligibility (Ch. 4, Sec. I), the *Yoder* parents have intelligible reasons. I also believe that their reasons defeated competing considerations, such as their recognition of the state's interest in secondary education. The Amish argued from their deep religious convictions, convictions around which they build their entire lives. Few reasons in their epistemic system could override these integrity-based considerations. Furthermore, we have good reason to think that their reasons were intelligible defeaters. First, it is clear that their beliefs were sincere. The Amish religious tradition requires that its adherents pay extensive social and economic costs by segregating themselves from the rest of society (though the Amish might deny that these are costs). Few commitments are held so strongly that their adherents so profoundly separate themselves from their fellow citizens. Second, the reasoning was clear to the courts, as evidenced by the facts that the courts scrutinized their reasoning and repeatedly found it comprehensible and sensible.

Given that many other parents lacked similar exemptions, and that the courts believed the state had a compelling interest to compel non-Amish parents to educate their children at the secondary level, fairness considerations might lead us to wonder whether the court should have adopted a neutral-restrictive approach. But we have seen that according to the Public Justification Principle, fairness considerations require respecting citizens' intelligible defeaters. Fairness considerations might lead us to exempt more than just the *Yoder* parents via a neutral-accommodating approach. But with respect to the *Yoder* parents, the courts assigned them a publicly justified exemption from public secondary schooling.

Yoder also raises the question of the integrity and moral development of the children in the case. Children are difficult cases for liberal theories that require respecting the developed convictions and autonomy largely available only to adults. While many children lack the capacity for integrity, they will eventually develop that capacity, and there are good reasons to protect the development of that capacity. Suppose that being raised Amish prevented children from developing their own projects and plans; if so, we might have reason to resist Amish parents' wishes. While this may be a genuine worry in cases where, say, parents deny their children basic medical care, I cannot see that it applies to *Yoder* (or *Mozert*), where the well-being of children is not at stake. Being raised Amish does not debilitate a child's ability to make autonomous choices (nor does being denied access to a particular textbook, as with *Mozert*). For this reason, I believe we can set worries about the integrity of children aside for our purposes, which is to illustrate the convergence approach to religious exemptions.

Our next case is in many respects *Yoder's* opposite, as the Court overrode the religious objections of the defendants, taking a neutral-restrictive approach. *Smith* concerned two men, Alfred Smith and Galen Black, who adhered to the teachings and practices of the Native American Church. They were counselors at a private drug rehab center and had been fired as the result of ingesting peyote, a hallucinogenic substance used in their religious ceremonies. At the time, the possession of peyote was a criminal offense in Oregon. So when Smith and Black filed for unemployment compensation, Oregon denied their request on the grounds that they were fired for poor conduct (breaking the law). The Oregon Court of Appeals reversed the state's decision on the grounds that the state had violated free exercise. The Oregon Supreme Court largely agreed. Oregon then appealed to the Supreme Court on the grounds that using peyote violated legitimately imposed law. After the Supreme Court returned the case to Oregon, who sent the case back to them, it overruled the Oregon Supreme Court on the ground that the state's interest in imposing the law was paramount with respect to the provision of unemployment benefits. The law, the Court said, was not intended to restrict free exercise, and the fact that it had negative unintended effects did not constitute a free exercise violation.

It turns out that the Court was deeply divided. Justice Scalia wrote for the majority, arguing, "We have never held that an individual's religious beliefs excuse him from compliance with an otherwise valid law prohibiting conduct that the State is free to regulate."[58] If a criminal law has a "public justification" and does not target a specific group, the law is legitimate. In this case, Scalia rejected the standard practice of the Court in recognizing that free exercise could only be restricted if a compelling state interest was present. The compelling interest test was too permissive, said Scalia, as it is often difficult to see how a state interest can override an individual's conscience: "What principle of law or logic can be brought to bear to contradict a believer's assertion that a particular act is 'central' to his personal faith?"[59] The Court should not be in the business of making such judgments. That said, Scalia did not argue that such exemptions were inappropriate, merely that exemptions must be left to the legislative process.

Smith led to public outcry, especially from groups like the ACLU and a number of members of Congress, and arguably prompted the passage of the 1993 Religious Freedom Restoration Act (RFRA) by overwhelming margins, which was later signed by President Bill Clinton. The purpose of RFRA was to require the courts to adhere to the compelling interest test. But in 1997, the Supreme Court significantly truncated the RFRA on two grounds: (a) that due to state's rights, Congress lacks the authority to expand constitutional rights to control states, and (b) that the Congress lacks the authority to tell the Supreme Court how to interpret the Constitution.[60]

Let us set aside the legitimacy of the RFRA and its truncation and focus on whether Smith and Black merited an exemption. Assume for the sake of argument that three laws were publicly justified at the time of the ruling: (i) a law restricting the general use of peyote, (ii) a law requiring unemployment compensation for certain types of layoffs and (iii) a law banning religious discrimination.[61] Given these assumptions, I argue that Black and Smith merited exemptions because they possessed the relevant intelligible defeaters for the denial of unemployment benefits because peyote serves a sacramental role in their church.[62] Members of the public can arguably see that Smith's and Black's reasons to use peyote were epistemically justified for them given a moderate degree of idealization. So Smith's and Black's religious objections satisfy the intelligibility requirement. Given that their interest in engaging in sacred rituals provided them with core reasons for action, they likely had a defeater for the laws (or portions of the laws) that allowed them to be fired without compensation for participating in their sincerely affirmed religious practices, assuming that laws (i)–(iii) are already publicly justified. A publicly justified free exercise principle properly identifies Smith and Black as having intelligible defeaters. So even if the court ruled rightly according to procedure, the legislature should have provided them with an exemption.

While the Court probably could not have anticipated public outcry over their decision or Congress's nearly unanimous vote to force them to use the compelling interest test, these events help determine whether defeaters were present. The great diversity of beliefs among congressional officials did not prevent them from working together to oppose *Smith*, suggesting that defeaters were present for the coercion permitted by the Court.[63] So even if *Smith* was rightly decided, legislative bodies should be sensitive to the evidence of widespread defeaters revealed by public outcry and legislative reaction. And as with *Yoder*, a neutral-restrictive approach is inappropriate. Even if a neutral-accommodating approach is unfair, Smith and Black still merited an exemption.

While *Yoder* is widely regarded as legitimate and *Smith* is widely regarded as illegitimate, no such consensus exists with respect to our next case. In *Mozert*, "fundamentalist" Christian parents sought an exemption for their children from using a textbook they believed advanced ideals that would undermine their ability to raise their children in their faith. The *Mozert* parents believed that the textbook threatened their children's religious beliefs.[64]

The controversy leading to *Mozert* was the result of parent Vicki Frost's discovery of a discussion of mental telepathy in a textbook used in her daughter's sixth-grade class. Further exploration of this textbook in the "Holt" series led her and other parents to conclude that the series promoted ideas favorable to evolution and hostile to religion.[65] The *Mozert* parents also argued that the Holt textbook gave insufficient attention to Protestant Christianity. Finally, they argued that the Holt readers endorsed secular humanism. Consequently, the parents asked their school to excuse their children from having to use the books. The school board responded negatively, not only continuing to use the Holt books but also requiring the *Mozert* children to attend classes.

The Sixth Circuit Court of Appeals rejected the *Mozert* parents' request for an exemption. The decision preceded *Smith*, so the court still appealed to the compelling interest test. All three judges concluded that the state had a compelling interest in educating the *Mozert* children, and all three rejected the claim that the parents had demonstrated a burden relevant to free exercise. Judge Lively argued that exposing children to these materials did not burden free exercise on the grounds that the parents' objections probably could not have been satisfied by alternatives.[66] Judge Kennedy joined Lively in his decision but argued that the state had a compelling interest in requiring the *Mozert* children to participate in courses with the Holt readers, because it was the least obstructive manner to teach them critical thinking and reading, along with the capacity to discourse about social and moral issues. Allowing the *Mozert* children to exempt themselves would both "disrupt the classroom" and "cause religious divisiveness."[67]

Before we can assess these claims, we must recognize that the *Mozert* parents' complaints were very limited. As John Tomasi notes:

> The case record states clearly that the Tennessee parents did *not* consistently object to the mere exposure of their children to the ideas in the reader. Nor even did the parents consistently object to their children acquiring critical skills such as those needed for political purposes from the reader. Rather, the *Mozert* complainants objected consistently only to the *repetitiveness* and the *depth* of the exposure. They saw the overall effect of the reader, whether intended or not, as denigrating to the faith-based form of reasoning on which their nonpublic worldview depended.[68]

The *Mozert* parents had no problem with their children learning about other views. Again, as Tomasi notes, the problem was objectionably *intense* exposure. It is also crucial that the *Mozert* parents only wished to protect their own children's faith, as "they never sought to use the state apparatus to impose their religion on other people's children."[69]

Mozert should divide consensus and convergence liberals. Stephen Macedo, perhaps the paradigmatic consensus liberal, agrees with the *Mozert* court. According to Macedo, the purpose of the Holt series was not to take a stand on the truth or falsity of various religious claims, since the Holt series only taught students to engage in civil toleration, not that all faiths were on a moral par.[70] Thus, the *Mozert* parents had no legitimate legal objection to the required use of the Holt series. So long as the schools do not advance particular religious teachings, even those that support shared civic institutions, they are not required in principle to create a unique curriculum that all religious groups can equally accept.[71] For consensus liberals, as we shall see in Chapter 7, the liberal state has a vital interest in creating a common, shared civic culture based on public (that is, shared or accessible) reasons. To promote stable liberal institutions that protect liberal freedoms, the United States needs a common school system to teach children liberal political values. If the law must respect claims like those offered by the *Mozert* parents, "the most basic forms of liberal civic education would be swept aside on the basis of the uncritical embrace of multicultural respect."[72] While the *Mozert* parents appeal to the liberal values of freedom and equality, consensus liberals have to emphasize the overriding importance of shared political goals.[73]

Convergence approaches reject coercive attempts to promote a shared civic culture in the face of intelligible defeaters. Accordingly, a convergence approach supports the *Mozert* parents on the grounds that they have intelligible reason to reject to the subjection of their children to ideas they sincerely believe are dangerous. Why think that the *Mozert* parents had intelligible defeaters? Two reasons. First, the complainants had careful, detailed objections to the Holt readers, which suggests that they would likely affirm these objections at a moderate level of idealization. During her testimony, Vicki Frost claimed to have studied the required reader for over two hundred hours and was thereby able to name seventeen distinct types of objectionable content.[74] Her testimony was extensive and full of cross-referenced examples. Clearly Mrs. Frost made a respectable effort to reason well with regard to her children's well-being, far beyond what is arguably required for a citizen to have epistemic justification for her beliefs. Accordingly, Mrs. Frost's reasoning meets the intelligibility requirement at a moderate level of idealization. Second, her reasons had defeater-level force due to her core project of raising her children well by her own lights. The state imposed a significant burden on her (along with the other parents).[75] Frost, among others, suffered an offense by being ordered by a coercive power to allow her children to be subjected to ideas she regarded as false and dangerous. It is hard to see how the state could have a compelling interest that could override these defeaters, especially given that the *Mozert* parents objected to a minute part of their children's curriculum. Perhaps if their complaints had been broader the schools would have sufficient reason to ignore them on the grounds that the state has a compelling interest in providing all children with an adequate education. But the *Mozert* parents made a simple request: to have their children excused from using textbooks that the parents found hostile to their right to educate their children as they saw fit. We can conclude that the Sixth Circuit Court overrode the intelligible defeaters of the *Mozert* parents under the free exercise application of Principle of Intelligible Exclusion. That is, even if the courts acted properly according to judicial procedure, the *Mozert* parents merit an exemption.

Ironically, *public reason liberalism itself* requires that we demand religious exemptions for Smith, Black and the *Mozert* parents. This will likely please the religious critics. While religious critics reject the Public Justification Principle, convergence protects the integrity of religious citizens and treats them as equals with respect to secular citizens. With regard to the other side, I suspect we convergence liberals shall have to drag our mainline brethren along kicking and screaming. Of consensus liberals, Macedo not only agrees with *Mozert* but rejects *Yoder*: "the *Mozert* families have no right to be accommodated" and "we should hope that *Yoder* remains a 'dead end' in American Constitutional Law."[76] This view should not surprise, as shared reasons and the corresponding need to promote a shared civic culture will have much more weight on the consensus view. Religious reasons do not have the same weight, for "honoring the authority of public reasons means that we should avoid relying on 'private' grounds when fashioning the principles that underlie the basic political institutions of society."[77] And more directly: "it is illegitimate to fashion basic principles of justice on the basis of religious reasons—or reasons whose force requires that one accept a particular religious or philosophical framework—for those are matters about which reasonable people disagree."[78] The convergence interpretation of the Public Justification Principle presents a strikingly different approach to legal practice. And since it is a *superior* interpretation, Macedo and other public reason liberals are committed to it by their own lights, along with its legal implications.

VII.   Too Many Exemptions?

Given that convergence liberalism favors extensive religious accommodation, it is natural to wonder whether it places any limits on exemptions. If not, it seems vulnerable to two objections: first, convergence threatens anarchy and, second, convergence will create smaller, but still severe, pragmatic problems in creating and enforcing law. We have already addressed the more general concern that convergence will create too many empty sets with respect to important policy issues (Ch. 4, Sec. V), but we can now assess similar objections as applied to political practice.

Justice Scalia advanced a version of the anarchy objection in *Smith*. If the state must always show a compelling interest to justifiably burden religious citizens, it would be "courting anarchy" because it would commit itself to "deeming *presumptively invalid*, . . . every regulation of conduct that does not protect an interest of the highest order." The resulting prospect would generate exemptions from "civic obligations of almost every conceivable kind."[79] But surely Scalia exaggerates. Judges often accommodate religious complaints, and while courts have not always articulated principled reasons for these accommodations, we need not worry about a sharp slippery slope even under our present institutions.[80] To add to this point, recall that members of the public are often rationally committed to complying with decision procedures to settle their disputes (Ch. 3, Sec. IV), so we need not regard many accommodation requests as a threat given that they can be settled in publicly justified ways.

However, while consensus liberals can reject the threat of anarchy, they will likely claim that a regime of extensive accommodation would undermine the rule of law. Politics cannot be merely a matter of "particularistic requests for exceptions" based on complaints of unfairness, for otherwise "governance in even a moderately heterogeneous society would be impossible, and there would be no such thing as the rule of law."[81] There are two practical problems here. First, on the convergence view, the informational and adjudicative demands of assessing citizens' diverse and dispersed claims may significantly burden judges and legislators. When accommodations are confined to small groups like the Amish, these judicial and legislative burdens are low. But convergence seems to substantially increase these burdens. Second, the cumulative effect of religious accommodations may undermine the rule of law because coercive laws may need many exceptions, such that the law as a whole loses its ability to provide clear and general behavioral guidelines.

I offer two replies. First, these problems assume that religious accommodations are largely made during or following the legislative process. But the Principle of Intelligible Exclusion permits almost any institutional solution that prevents citizens from being unjustifiably coerced. The drawbacks of legislative and judicial tinkering should lead us to support institutions that reliably avoid imposing problematic laws on the populace in the first place. The costs of ex post accommodation require that our institutions be less friendly to the use of coercion in general. Consider how *Yoder, Smith* and *Mozert* might have been handled by publicly justified political institutions ex ante. If public reason does not require a largely government-operated school system, parents could more easily separate into schools compatible with their values. Under a system of school choice, *Mozert* would not have happened. Furthermore, while choice-based educational systems might still mandate high school education, the *Yoder* parents would probably have had access to secondary schooling more compatible with their values, in no small part because Amish communities provide their own schooling. And if the government were less interested in prosecuting a paternalistic drug war of questionable efficacy, then the use of peyote would never have been regulated in the first place, such that *Smith* would not have arisen.[82] A more limited government could avoid the pragmatic problems associated with extensive accommodation.

Citizens of contemporary liberal democracies probably overestimate the importance and justifiability of coercion, given the fact that defeaters are diverse and dispersed. The public will not always be aware of the defeaters for laws lurking in the rational commitments of a diverse citizenry. Furthermore, too few political officials are concerned with whether coercion can be justified to each person. Legislators should follow the Principle of Convergent Restraint, becoming more sensitive to the justifiability of coercion, thus more effectively controlling the pragmatic problems raised by religious accommodation.

A second option would be for legislatures to more clearly articulate principles on which religious accommodations are based. With clear principles, it would be easier for legislators to fashion legislation that would avoid raising concerns about religious accommodation. Furthermore, judges could more easily evaluate religious complaints. For example, the arguments in *Yoder* and *Smith* seem to be in tension, as in one case a conscientious objection overrode the state's interest and in the other the opposite occurred. A more consistent approach could alleviate the problems associated with our piecemeal practice. For instance, if the Court hewed to a compelling interest test and gave clear conditions for what counts as a compelling interest, Scalia's arguments in *Smith* might be more easily dismissed.

VIII.   Is Religion Special?

Before ending, I should also address an important, controversial issue in the contemporary religion and politics literature, i.e., whether the current practice of affording special protection for religion can be justified.[83] While liberal political theory tends to be prejudiced in favor of secular citizens, liberal political practice tends to be prejudiced in favor of *religious* citizens. The Constitution protects the free exercise of *religion* and not secular moral philosophies. A commonly cited example is the exemption that the Amish received in *Yoder*. The courts would almost certainly not protect secular persons who offered similar objections.[84]

Some argue that by giving special preference to religion, U.S. constitutional law establishes an inequitable privilege for religious over secular forms of life. But this preferential treatment of religion is inconsistent with the Equal Protection Clause of the Fourteenth Amendment. We can illustrate with a prominent counterexample—conscientious objections to the military draft. For a significant stretch of U.S. history, conscientious exemptions were only given to pacifist Christian denominations. In the 1940s, conscientious objector status was extended to all theistic religions.[85] Two decades later, conscientious objector status was extended to nontheistic religions and finally to nonreligious, moral doctrines.[86] American lawmakers often resisted this broad extension of conscientious objector status on the grounds that such an extension would permit too many exemptions and encourage deception on the part of objectors. But equal treatment won out.

Several legal theorists have argued that preferential treatment of religion is morally unjustified. Michael Perry has defended a right of "moral freedom" that is symmetrical with the presently recognized right of religious freedom.[87] If he is correct, the reasons that count in favor of the legal protection of religious conscience apply no less forcefully to moral conscience: the features that make religion worthy of protection (such as its central role in structuring values and practices) apply to moral doctrines as well. Greenawalt has countered that a number of practical, legal and moral reasons appropriately motivate courts to give religion a special status. For instance, many judges may have trouble distinguishing sincere conscientious objections from less important moral objections unless they use religion as a standard of demarcation.[88] Legal tradition itself might provide reason to protect religion's special treatment as well. And in comparison to nonreligious moral claims, the standard true believer seems to have more at stake, since "God may punish wrongdoers when this life is over."[89] But in the end, even Greenawalt holds that if nonreligious claims of conscience are sufficiently similar to religious claims and if there are not overriding independent concerns, the Equal Protection clause combined with the Establishment clause should be read as requiring that religious and moral claims be treated symmetrically.[90]

Since intelligible defeaters can be either religious or secular, convergence draws no distinction between the two. It follows that the case for the asymmetric treatment of religion and morality in the law is philosophically weak. Having said that, I argued above that we must evaluate norms by testing present laws based on our best understanding of citizens' reasons. Therefore, we cannot justifiably demand that lawmakers immediately revise all laws that assign religion a special status. Instead, we should look to present legal tradition and legal institutions to gradually extend the law to cover nonreligious, moral complaints.

It will be useful to contrast my view with Brian Leiter's recent argument that religion should not receive special legal treatment.[91] Leiter contends that religion does not deserve special treatment because there is no feature essential to religious belief that requires the sort of respect that would justify special treatment. In particular, religion is not worthy of "affirmative" respect, where religious belief is respected based on some virtue or merit of people who typically hold such beliefs.[92] Instead, religious belief merely requires "recognition" respect, understood as the simple toleration of religious belief. This is because most contemporary religious beliefs are "culpably false," given the force of Enlightenment critiques of religion.[93] Religious belief is culpably false belief in part because it is an essential property of religious belief that it does "not answer ultimately . . . to *evidence* and *reasons*, as these are understood in other domains concerned with knowledge of the world."[94] Since, plainly, there is no reason to affirmatively respect culpably false belief that is essentially insulated from evidence and reason, there is little reason for the law to give religion special treatment. In part because Leiter seeks to *downgrade* respect for religious belief, he takes what Greenawalt terms the neutral-restrictive approach, where there is no presumption on behalf of protecting claims of conscience.[95] Religious belief is not to be singled out and "there should not be exemptions to general laws with neutral purposes, unless those exemptions do not shift burdens or risks onto others."[96]

My view stands in *stark* contrast to Leiter's. I seek to *upgrade* respect for nonreligious comprehensive and moral belief to the level presently extended to religious belief. Following Rawls, I extend reasonable pluralism to cover most forms of religious belief and deny that political theory should proceed based on the assumption that religious belief is culpably false. Leiter assumes without argument that even contemporary analytic philosophical views like Reformed epistemology or Thomistic natural law ethics are based on culpably post hoc attempts to defend religious belief in the face of counterevidence.[97] In contrast, I have argued that the epistemology appropriate to political theory allows that, at the right level of idealization, members of the public will *non-culpably* affirm such views, despite the purported force of Enlightenment critiques of religion.[98] If we hold that even philosophically sophisticated members of the public have culpably false views, then we deny reasonable pluralism, a foundational assumption of political liberalism.

It is no surprise, then, that Leiter views Rawls's political turn as "unfortunate" because political liberalism does not permit dismissing as culpably false (half of) the views that instigate the religion and politics debate.[99] Because Leiter does not recognize reasonable pluralism in this robust sense, it is natural to find his view off-putting, even condescending. That is a deep demerit of his view and a reason I think his position may generate more heat than light in an already acrimonious debate. Given Leiter's rejection of reasonable pluralism, then, we should reject his neutral-restrictive approach in favor of a compound neutral-accommodating and repeal approach.

IX. Conclusion

I have argued that convergence is friendly to religious dialogue and political activity based on the legal and discursive application of the Principle of Intelligible Exclusion. Specifically, the Principle of Convergent Restraint is a principle of civic virtue that applies to legislators and judges. These principles are *extremely* permissive: citizens may employ whatever reasons they like whenever they like. Convergent Restraint even permits legislators to use religious reasons if they believe the proposals they advance are publicly justified. Only judges face significant restraint, and this restraint is not objectionable. I then argued that Intelligible Exclusion requires extensive religious accommodations by taking either a targeted-accommodation or neutral-accommodating approach to religious exemptions. I also showed that Intelligible Exclusion draws no distinction between moral and religious reasons. Consequently, convergence requires the gradual elimination of the legal distinction between moral and religious conscience.

So far, reconciliation between public reason liberals and their religious critics has been borne out in both theory and practice. But we can strengthen the case for practical reconciliation. Convergence liberalism can resolve disputes about religion in the American educational system. If so, then in both theory and practice, public reason liberalism is friendly to an expansive role for religious conviction and activity in the public life of liberal democracies.

Notes

1. The integrity, fairness and divisiveness objections should evaporate, at least. As discussed in Ch. 4, some religious citizens will dislike the fact that convergence is hostile to laws that can only be justified on a religious basis. So convergence is not friendly to all the goals of some religious citizens. Obviously I do not think this impugns the view, however. Liberalism draws the line at religiously-based coercion.
2. Specifically, excluding gay couples from the benefits of state marriage.
3. Like reason restraint, proposal restraint is a principle of civic virtue, not a constitutional requirement. Furthermore, I shall not discuss restraint on noncoercive proposals, as it would unnecessarily complicate our discussion. Thanks to Kyle Swan for pressing me to make this point explicit.
4. This and other formulations of Convergent Restraint bar the use of coercion when only *some* nontrivial set of members of the public have sufficient intelligible reasons to reject said coercion, rather than all, but I will suppress using "some" for the sake of parsimony.
5. I leave open how small this group may be, though presumably the group is not as small as an individual, as this may make my view too demanding.
6. For a developed definition of sufficient reasons that does not debilitate the political process, see Gaus 2011, pp. 244–51.
7. Gaus 2010a, p. 24.
8. I thank an anonymous referee for this objection.
9. I leave cases of effective private advocacy to the side here.
10. Gaus 2010a, p. 27.
11. I allow that fulfilling condition (i) allows the relevant parties to weight their preferred political issues more heavily in their political calculus about whether a politician will contribute to publicly unjustified outcomes.
12. Gaus and Vallier 2009, pp. 68–9.

13. Ibid., p. 69.
14. Elster 1997.
15. Gaus and Vallier 2009, pp. 66–7.
16. I should stress that understanding politics as a market does not exclude the use of deliberation. On my view, citizens deliberate based on comprehensive, diverse reasons, and this deliberation can help generate publicly justified outcomes.
17. Let us focus on their legislative votes, as opposed to votes for officials like judges, party officers and leadership positions like Speaker of the House. I assume that these intermittent votes are covered by Convergent Restraint.
18. An ambiguity arises: should legislators care more about whether laws are publicly justified for *all* members of the public, or merely for their constituents? I am not sure.
19. It is true that each legislator often knows that her votes are unlikely to matter. Nonetheless, her impact is still nontrivial: even if the probability of her making a difference is low, it is not *very* low, as are the votes of citizens. So Convergent Restraint for Legislators need not make explicit a caveat that ineffective legislators are exempt. I thank an anonymous referee for this point.
20. I assume here that abortion restrictions cannot be publicly justified only for the sake of argument. Determining whether abortion restrictions can be publicly justified is rather complicated. See Ch. 4, Sec. IV, n. 71, for my explanation.
21. I thank Andrew Lister for raising this objection.
22. Of course, the net effect of their rulings may change the complex balance of coercion imposed by a law, but let us set this complexity aside.
23. Rawls 2005, p. 231.
24. Ibid., pp. 235–6.
25. Greenawalt 2008, p. 506.
26. The shareability requirement may be weakened by the fact that reasonable justices could have partially distinct evaluative standards, say, depending on whether they are constitutional originalists.
27. While judges are subject to something like a consensus requirement, I still use the term "convergence" in Convergent Restraint for Judges because it is grounded in the application of convergence to judicial decision making.
28. Kyle Swan points out that we can distinguish between the reasons that judges issue decisions and the reasons that judges express in their decisions. Judicial restraint applies to the latter, not the former.
29. I'm including here secular cases where, say, nonreligious citizens are exempt from the draft in the United States.
30. For a conditional defense of this position, see Bedi 2007, esp. 246–7. For discussion and criticism of this position, see Taylor and Maclure 2011, pp. 69–80.
31. Some will worry that on my interpretation of the Public Justification Principle the law is non-neutral because it imposes burdens on citizens unequally. But public reason liberals have long had to struggle with the issue of legislative neutrality. I have nothing to add here. For a recent, extensive and illuminating discussion, see Gaus 2011, pp. 400–8.
32. Thanks to Chad Van Schoelandt for discussion on this point.
33. Greenawalt 2006, p. 166.
34. On the history and interpretation of these two principles, I am enormously indebted to Kent Greenawalt's two volume work, *Religion and the Constitution*.
35. Though the Supreme Court does place limits on free exercise in many cases.

36. Greenawalt 2006, p. 2.
37. Though in many cases this bar is interpreted only as a *prima facie* limitation.
38. Ibid., p. 3.
39. Ibid., p. 533.
40. *Van Orden v. Perry*, 545, U.S. 677, 692 (2005).
41. See Greenawalt 2008, pp. 45–7, for a succinct explanation of the *Lemon* test.
42. Ibid., p. 5.
43. Ibid., p. 5.
44. Ibid., p. 7.
45. Ibid., p. 381.
46. Working Group on Human Needs and Faith-Based and Community Initiatives, "Finding Common Ground: 29 Recommendations of the Working Group on Human Needs and Faith-Based and Community Initiatives," January 2002, www. dlc.org/documents/Working-Group_FBO_Report.pdf.
47. Greenawalt 2008, p. 381.
48. Audi 2000, p. 88. Audi goes on: "Secondary coercion may also be only conditional, as where it applies in circumstances that citizens may avoid, say by deciding not to drive and so avoid being forced to go through the process of licensing."
49. Ibid.
50. I will argue (Ch. 7, Sec. VI) that we cannot expect the state to avoid all the indirect effects of revenue use. For this reason, the restriction on secondary coercion may need to be relaxed a bit from my statement above. Thanks to Kyle Swan for this point.
51. So I will not here focus on the reliability of judicial review. For a helpful discussion of public reason liberalism and judicial review, see Gaus 1996, pp. 279–85.
52. One might read these cases as instances of deciding how to individuate coercion. But that's not quite right. We're not individuating parts of laws but determining whether the law applies to all members of the public or not.
53. Jerry Gaus raises the worry that relying on free exercise to permit selective application of laws might bind me to the historical practice of treating religion as special, a practice I want to reject. My response is that the Principle of Intelligible Exclusion gives us reason to broaden the scope of the Free Exercise Clause insofar as the Free Exercise Clause is publicly justified. I am not entirely happy with my answer here.
54. Note that fairness outcomes do not count as negative effects here because, as I have suggested, fairness objectors typically prefer the accommodating law to no law at all. For example, those who oppose granting certain types of religious exemptions to the Health and Human Services contraception mandate associated with the Affordable Care Act almost certainly prefer the ACA with exemptions to no ACA at all.
55. We might also defend accommodation based on a [No law, Accommodating law, Generic law] ranking, though it is controversial whether public reason has much to say about how to treat comparisons between laws below the no-law default. My inclination is to say that in such a ranking objectors are owed an exemption until the law in question can be repealed.
56. *Wisconsin v. Yoder*, 406 U.S. 205, 218 (1971).
57. I appeal here to Gaus's conception of a "respectable" amount of reasoning as a method for tracking citizens' justificatory reasons. See Gaus 2011, pp. 254–7.

58. *Employment Division, Dept. of Human Resources of Oregon v. Smith*, 494 U.S. 872, 879 (1990).
59. Ibid., p. 886.
60. RFRA is still applied to the federal government. See *Gonzales v. O Centro Espirita Beneficente Uniao do Vegetal*, 546 U.S. 418 (2006). I thank Mary McThomas for this point.
61. Without these laws as a legitimate background, the unique nature of the case cannot be assessed. For what it's worth, in my view, (i) was not publicly justified, (iii) was publicly justified and (ii) was probably publicly justified.
62. Assuming they were honest, which is consistent with their willingness to endure a Supreme Court battle.
63. Arguably the political coalition that supported the RFRA no longer exists. But so long as a sizeable number of legislators would support the law, we can still use their support as evidence that there is rational support for religious exemptions among large sectors of the population. I thank Micah Schwartzman for helping me understand the unique conditions of the RFRA's passage.
64. Greenawalt 2006, p. 89.
65. Not that evolution and religion were necessarily opposed in their minds. In other words, their complaints did not derive from creationism.
66. Greenawalt 2006, p. 106.
67. Ibid., p. 107.
68. Tomasi 2001a, p. 92.
69. Ibid., p. 93.
70. Macedo 2000a, p. 177.
71. Ibid., p. 168. Emphasis in original.
72. Ibid., p. 163.
73. Ibid., p. 175.
74. Tomasi 2001a, p. 91.
75. Greenawalt concurs that "the *Mozert* parents did suffer a burden on their exercise of religion, and constitutional relief from some burdens of that kind is appropriate." Greenawalt 2006, p. 107.
76. Macedo 2000a, pp. 205, 208. Macedo does disagree with *Smith*, however. See p. 198.
77. Ibid., p. 189.
78. Ibid., pp. 177–8.
79. *Smith*, 110 Sup. Ct. 1595, 1605 (1990). Cited in Macedo 2000a, pp. 192–3.
80. Interestingly, even Macedo thinks that Scalia exaggerates. With expansive exemptions, "we are not on a quick slide into the abyss." Macedo 2000a, p. 195.
81. Ibid., pp. 204–5.
82. Of course, Smith and Black's employer may still have fired them, but Oregon would have had no grounds on which to deny them unemployment benefits.
83. The literature on this question is rather large. Reviewing it would detract from my main line of argument. I raise the issue of whether religion is special to illustrate how my theory approaches the issue. For a helpful overview of the literature, see Schwartzman 2012.
84. Leiter 2013, p. 3.
85. See *United States v. Kauten*, 133 F. 2d 703 (1943) and *Berman v. United States*, 302 U.S. 211 (1937).

86. In *United States v. Seeger*, 380 U.S. 163 (1965) and *Welsh v. United States*, 398 U.S. 333 (1970), respectively.
87. Perry 2010, p. 996.
88. Greenawalt 2006, p. 906.
89. Ibid., p. 914.
90. Ibid., p. 917.
91. Leiter 2013. I review Leiter's work largely to illustrate the distinctiveness of my approach by comparing it with a sharply contrasting view, not because his view is widely held.
92. Ibid., pp. 77–85.
93. Ibid., p. 77.
92. Ibid., p. 34.
95. Ibid., p. 130.
96. Ibid., p. 4.
97. Ibid., pp. 81, 90.
98. Note that I do not extend this respect to religious belief *simply because it is religious*, but rather because on my convergence-moderate idealization account of justificatory reasons, religious reasons will almost certainly count as justificatory in a great many cases.
99. Leiter 2013, p. x.

CHAPTER 7

Reconciliation in Policy
Public Education

There is no reconciliation between public reason liberals and their religious critics without reconciliation in the American public school system. As Stephen Macedo rightly notes, "the tension between diversity and the felt need to promote shared values has played out most dramatically" in American public schools, due largely to the fact that it is the primary method by which the state creates a shared political culture out of the great diversity of religious, racial, ethnic and class groupings in the United States.[1] In this way, the American public school system has been used for what many regard as legitimate "public" purposes, not merely to teach children basic skills but also to produce democratic *citizens* on the basis of shared principles. It helps a political liberal culture engage in what Amy Gutmann calls "conscious social reproduction."[2] The consensus liberal approach provides strong ground for using the public education system to promote a shared, civic culture based on shared reasons and values. But given that public reason liberals have defeaters for the consensus view, I contend that they have defeaters for the correlative approach to education.

Convergence liberalism requires a transformation of liberal democratic educational systems. Because religious reasons enter into public justification, so-called "public purposes" can be more easily defeated by diverse concerns, including controversial worries about the teaching of evolution. I shall argue that respecting diverse, dispersed defeaters requires transforming the American public education system into a school choice system. While the state is permitted to mandate a civic minimum, it cannot justifiably restrict school choice because many parents have defeaters for restrictions on their authority to select educational institutions that respect and promote their conscientious commitments.

The goal of this chapter is therefore twofold: first, to show that the present educational system cannot be publicly justified and second, to demonstrate that an alternative system of school choice can be publicly justified. I begin by examining work by Stephen Macedo and Amy Gutmann on civic education to illustrate the consensus liberal approach to education policy (Sec. I) and then critique the view based on convergence liberalism (Sec. II). I next analyze a key source of conflict in public schools—the teaching of intelligent design—as an example of a curriculum-based controversy that cannot be easily solved in a publicly justified fashion within the traditional public school model (Sec. III). Controversies about intelligent design, along with many others, illustrate that many parents have sufficient reason to prefer no public education system to the coercion involved in sustaining the present public school system (Sec. IV). I present school choice as a publicly justified institutional alternative to public schooling (Sec. V) and address some objections to school choice, including claims that it constitutes an establishment of religion, fails to quiet the relevant controversies and produces illiberal citizens (Sec. VI). I conclude by arguing that school choice can reconcile public reason liberals and their critics in political practice.

I.   The Consensus Approach to Civic Education

Recall from previous chapters that the mainstream interpretation of the Public Justification Principle includes a consensus conception of reasons—it imposes accessibility and/or shareability requirements on the reasons that can enter into the process of public justification.[3] The consensus view emphasizes the importance of shared rationales for the use of state coercion and attaches great importance to citizens' willingness to restrain their political discourse and activity in accord with shared principles. The liberal polity should embody, respect and promote shared political values. Accordingly, good citizens should support the liberal polity in its endeavors as in their political activities. *Consensus education* flows naturally from these commitments because it is based on *consensus civics* or the conception of civic aims based on consensus. Consensus civics is rooted in a view Macedo calls "civic liberalism," a political program "that gives freedom its ample due while taking reasonable steps to promote good citizenship and thereby to preserve the social and political supports that freedom needs for future generations . . ."[4] The aim of civic liberalism is to put into practice a deep insight about the limits liberalism places on diversity, namely that "diversity needs to be kept in its place: diversity is not always a value and it should not, any more than other ideals, be accepted uncritically."[5] Instead, liberalism should embrace "the positive constitutional project of shaping diversity toward the demand of a *shared public life*."[6]

Pursuing this project requires the liberal policy to create liberal citizens by educating diverse citizens to focus on shared civic purposes. Political order is essentially aimed at creating common ends and goals, including preserving liberal liberties. Thus, the liberal polity must actively sculpt citizens to have certain liberal values. It must "mold people."[7] The liberal polity does so by deliberately and actively requiring that citizens share constructive political aspirations and support institutions that realize these aspirations. Liberal citizens should thus both embrace and act on the basis of shared liberal values and a distinct liberal "character."[8]

What is it to have a liberal character? We can identify three core features: (a) liberal citizens must have a disposition to engage in a "self-critical process of giving and demanding reasons, a process in which all substantive commitments are provisional and none are beyond political challenge."[9] That is, liberal citizens must be sophisticated and fair deliberators. (b) Liberal citizens should engage in political life by "seek[ing] mutually acceptable reasons for the way they direct [state] power."[10] Thus, liberal citizens deliberate in shared terms. Finally, (c) liberal citizens prioritize their responsibilities as citizens over a number of competing concerns. If they are to respect public reasons' authority, they must not attempt to base their institutions on principles tainted by private commitments. We must not let the presence of reasonable pluralism "shake our confidence in the overriding weight of shared public principles."[11] In sum, to have a liberal character is to be a consensus deliberator who assigns priority to consensus values.

The foregoing entails that consensus civics *simply overrides* religious considerations. It is inevitable that liberal civic goals will make it more difficult for advocates of some moral and religious views to gain adherents. But consensus liberals regard a society's ability to privatize religious values and practices as a profound achievement.[12] Given how grand privatization is, we should be suspicious of citizens who seek wholeness in their lives by concentrating their loyalties on their private doctrines.[13] A publicly reasonable citizenry recognizes that we must not shape principles of justice with religious reasons, since reasonable people disagree about their normative force. In response to concerns about integrity, consensus liberals admit that many will find restraint burdensome. For even if some religious citizens adjust to prioritizing public reasons, restraint still has moral significance.[14] In the end, liberals may simply have to face the sobering fact that, when it comes to the religious critic, they have nothing to say save that devout religious believers are poor citizens.[15]

We could not ask for a clearer application of the consensus view to civic life.[16] Consensus civics requires that citizens be sophisticated and fair deliberators, who both deliberate in shared terms and recognize that the importance of doing so overrides their private convictions in the political sphere. Accordingly, consensus civics requires that a liberal polity unapologetically mold children into consensus liberal citizens. Such molding must be the explicit aim of public schools, to which we now turn.

Throughout its history, the public education system has been the most important institutional device "for creating a shared political culture amid religious, racial, ethnic, and class diversity."[17] Or as John Tomasi has put it, "Civic education is one of the most dramatic places where the broader legitimacy-directed components of liberalism touch down and make a distinct institutional impression."[18] It does so by contributing "to the creation of a common civic identity" by bringing "children from many backgrounds together" to make them sufficiently liberal and tolerant. By teaching civic virtue and forcing children to encounter and grapple with their differences, public school teachers and administrators imbue them with a liberal character.

While no consensus liberal denies that the American public education system has many flaws, they insist that common or public schools must be a central part of any system of consensus education because the public school system is based on the need to enclose and restrain a society's diverse views within a tolerant and respectful legal and social framework.[19] Public schools have the advantage of independence from the sectarian views of families and small communities, and so can better equip children to respect and understand one another despite their differing views. As a result, public schools might be able to successfully teach the liberal virtues of tolerance, respect, self-criticism and public reasonableness.[20] The public schools are well equipped to bring children together and teach them that common values predominate, despite the fact that their parents disagree about what is of ultimate importance in life.[21]

Gutmann goes so far as to claim that "public schools can . . . foster what one might call a *democratic civil religion*: a set of secular beliefs, habits, and ways of thinking that support democratic deliberation and are compatible with a wide variety of religious commitments."[22] Liberal democracy requires that citizens affirm a set of political doctrines as strongly as they might hold to a religion, since that is what is required to produce truly liberal citizens. And secularism is a core part of that civil religion. In a religiously pluralistic society like ours, we must focus on secular standards of reasoning because they provide a superior foundation for common education than private religious views provide. Secular standards provide both more stable and fairer methods of conflict resolution.[23] Thus, the state can legitimately promote secularist civil religion because governments should provide subsidies and impose schooling requirements in order to equip students to employ their civil rights and comply with their civic duties.[24]

Consensus liberals must not allow parents like Vicki Frost to have their way. Exposure to multiple ideas "is a necessary and well-selected means for teaching a basic civic virtue, objections to it cannot support a fundamental moral or constitutional right to be exempted from an otherwise reasonable educational regime."[25] The interest of the democratic state is paramount. If it does not have the authority to override the wishes of sectarian parents, then the schools could regress into sectarianism and prejudice.[26] Gutmann insists that unless the state provides and regulates education, children will not learn to mutually respect one another or to dialogue with those who are different because their parents will prioritize their salvation.[27] The consensus education approach is thoroughly *statist*. While not all schools must be owned and operated by the state, the state has a compelling interest in shaping the minds of children in ways that will perpetuate and strengthen its power and legitimacy. Since on the consensus view the democratic state is legitimate, and its shared civic culture is a key instrument in maintaining the legitimate state, the government must be given extraordinary power over children in order to make them liberal.

II. The Convergence Approach to Civic Education

Convergence offers an attractive approach to civic education that sharply contrasts with the Macedo-Gutmann view. As we have seen, consensus liberal citizens must be (i) sophisticated and fair deliberators who (ii) deliberate in shared terms and (iii) assign the aim of creating a shared public culture overriding weight with respect to their religious convictions that bear on political life. Convergence citizens are not required to meet any of these conditions.

Against (i), convergence imposes no restraint on citizens, so while convergence citizens may have reason to be fair and kind to their fellows, the Public Justification Principle does not require that they develop complex deliberative capacities to engage one another in public discussion. Deliberation is merely one way for a society to achieve public justification (Ch. 5, Sec. VI). Convergence civics is also friendlier to politics as a market, rather than as a forum (Ch. 6, Sec. II). For example, given that bargaining is a permitted form of public justification (Ch. 5, Sec. VI), convergence citizens should be free to bargain to bring about publicly justified outcomes. It follows that good citizens are free to build coalitions with one another and engage in interest-based political activism. Third, and most surprising, the ideal of public reason does not require citizens to care about politics *at all*. Instead, one can be a good citizen without engaging in political life. Perhaps one can even be a good citizen without voting. Jason Brennan has recently argued that political philosophers have an excessively *political* conception of civic virtue, where a citizen best expresses respect and care for his fellow citizens by engaging in political activity. Brennan develops an "extrapolitical" conception of civic virtue to contrast with theirs.[28] Convergence civics similarly permits people to exercise their liberal democratic citizenship in nonpolitical ways. In this way, convergence civics is less statist than consensus civics.

Regarding (ii), consensus citizens must deliberate in shared terms. But convergence citizens have no such duty, if and when they decide to deliberate. Instead, they can deploy any intelligible reason they like. Citizens should generally present what they take to be their best reasons for acting as they do, or for affirming a particular position, but they need never shy away from offering their private, sectarian and religious reasons, or acting on them. Convergence citizens therefore have enormous freedom to deliberate as they see fit.

Finally, with respect to (iii), convergence citizens are in no way obligated by the ideal of public reason to prioritize shared values. Convergence citizens can be as sectarian and partial as they like, so long as they are prepared to comply with publicly justified policies.[29] Furthermore, convergence citizens will more easily recognize that what we take to be shared is itself a matter of dispute. To say that we must appeal to shared values often hides the fact that we disagree about what we share and how important our shared values are with respect to one another.

Convergence civics stands in *stark* contrast to consensus civics. Consensus citizens are deliberation-focused statists who prioritize shared values, whereas convergence citizens are free to shape and formulate their own conceptions of civic virtue, deliberative or no, statist or no, and based on what they share or on what makes them unique. Liberalism means *it's up to them.* As you might imagine, the educative implications of convergence are significant. To see this, let's further contrast consensus and convergence liberal education. On the consensus side, consider the words of Justice Brennan in the case of *Abingdon Township v. Schempp*, who argues that the American public school system is supposed to serve a "uniquely *public* function," where citizenship is promoted in an "atmosphere free of parochial, divisive, or separatist institutions of any sort" in order for children to learn about their shared heritage, a heritage that is "neither theistic nor atheistic, but simply civic and patriotic."[30] Consensus liberals agree. The public education system should train children to be good liberal democratic citizens who can set aside their parochial, sectarian values to deliberate in shared terms. This arrangement is perfectly liberal, "civic and patriotic." But the convergence liberal is sympathetic to claims that public education is not neutral or universal.[31] As we have seen throughout this book, the consensus liberal's tendency to equate the shared with the publicly justified is mistaken. From the convergence liberal's perspective, consensus liberals are simply one more sectarian group attempting to impose their views on others. Consensus is the sectarianism of the shared.

Loren Lomasky characterizes the spirit of convergence education by reminding us of the deep connection between citizens' children and their projects:

> [H]aving children is often an integral component of persons' projects . . . And having children in whom one invests one's devotion is to undertake a commitment that spans generations and creates personal value for the parent that transcends his or her own span of life . . . Few people can expect to produce a literary or artistic monument, redirect the life of a nation, garner honor and glory that lives after them. But it is open to almost everyone to stake a claim to long-term significance through having and raising a child.[32]

If we recognize the obvious fact that citizens' reasons of integrity often involve raising children, then it is easy to see how citizens could have defeaters for state intervention in child development. Consensus liberals emphasize the state's interest in sculpting children in its image, but on the convergence view shared civic ends are more easily undermined by intelligible defeaters. State-run education comes under suspicion insofar as it conflicts with the wishes of parents. And to the extent that the state claims a monopoly over education, it will be able to impose a politically determined uniform institutional arrangement on all consumers.[33] When the consensus liberal demands that the state impose shared values on children so long as the imposition of these values is the result of democratic choice, the convergence liberal dissents, as collective choice cannot override the intelligible defeaters of citizens qua parents.[34] Convergence defeats many of the coercive proposals characteristic of consensus education, and is thereby friendlier to school choice and market-based methods of education.

III. Inevitable Conflict—The Case of Intelligent Design

I believe that convergence liberalism implies that a school choice system is legitimate and that traditional public schooling is illegitimate. That is, the set of eligible education systems does not include public education, at least at the secondary level, because citizens have diverse defeaters for most curricular choices made by government-run schools. We can illustrate this point by reviewing controversies that lead citizens to withdraw their children from the public school system. The inability of public school systems to resolve these controversies in a way satisfactory to all reasonable parties helps to explain why citizens take themselves to have sufficient reason to prefer no public education than to some modified forms of government schooling. If I can show that there are controversies, like the teaching of intelligent design, that give parents defeaters for a range of curricular choices, then I should be able to vindicate the more general claim that various forms of public schooling are defeated by members of the public.

In the remainder of this chapter, I shall focus primarily on conflicts in secondary education, with cases like the teaching of intelligent design, which do not usually arise in the context of primary education. What's more, even the *Yoder* parents, to my knowledge, did not object to sending their children to public primary school. Since values issues don't typically arise in primary education, and they're the source of the defeaters I point to, convergence may not show that the eligible set of public education arrangements is empty for primary schooling. That said, many homeschooling families never place their children in public school in the first place because they hope to include religious instruction in their children's education from early on. What's more, there have been attempts to introduce sex education and prayer into primary schooling. So value conflicts certainly arise at the primary level. For this reason, I believe my arguments show that many parents prefer no public education to public education in general, but I am most confident in my conclusions as they apply at the secondary level.[35]

As in Chapter 6, I should stress the critical role of the *comparison class* in determining which arrangements are defeated and which are merely suboptimal. Showing that a coercive arrangement is not compatible with parents' highest ranked educational choices is insufficient to show that it is defeated. Instead, we must show that many parents have sufficient reason (at the right level of idealization) to reject public schooling altogether. In what follows, I will not argue that parents have defeaters for some particular form of public education or a particular curricular choice. Instead, I use these controversies to illustrate the claim that for any standardized public education curriculum, C, there will be some member of the public with a defeater for C.

As I mentioned in Chapter 6, Chapter 5 presents a somewhat murky model of idealization. It is not always clear on moderate idealization whether members of the public have defeaters for coercion, given indeterminacy in the model. I appealed to cases of free exercise in Chapter 6 because I thought it was clear that the burdened parties in the cases I discussed had defeaters for the coercion in question, as evidenced by the judicial record. That evidence helped us to overcome the indeterminacy in moderate idealization. In this chapter, I make a similar move. I shall argue that parents have defeaters for public education based on the fact that millions of parents take the rather radical step of withdrawing their children from public education systems on the grounds that public schools fail to adequately promote moral and religious values.

The change of schedule and cost of homeschooling illustrates the seriousness of these objections, much as the objections of the *Yoder* parents illustrated the power of their objections, given the austere nature of the Amish lifestyle.[36] To illustrate, in 2007, 1.5 million children were homeschooled in the United States, an increase from 850,000 since 1999 and 1.1 million in 2003. Of parents of homeschooled children, 36% cited the need for moral and religious instruction as their reasons for homeschooling.[37] While many parents may lack sufficient reason at the right level of idealization to withdraw their children from public school, given the importance of raising their children in line with their comprehensive doctrines, many surely do.

One way to illustrate this is to show that certain issues having to do with religious and moral values create unavoidable controversies within the public school model. I focus on intelligent design as my key illustration because it has been the subject of enormous rational scrutiny. Further, I believe the issue is considerably more complicated than many public reason liberals are prepared to admit. While public reason liberals rightly recognize that intelligent design is bad biological science, they forget their commitment to recognizing that there are many reasonable religious comprehensive doctrines that generate religious defeaters. So if some religious comprehensive doctrine generates reasons to endorse intelligent design, then adherents of that doctrine may have defeater reasons for coercion *based on bad science*.

So let me be clear: in what follows I will *not come close* to claiming that intelligent design is good science, *much less* that it is correct. In fact, from a purely scientific point of view, *it is almost certainly false*. I merely aim to show that some theistic parents have good reason to object to evolution-alone science education on the grounds that it frequently runs together naturalistic interpretations of science with the teaching of science, obscuring what they take to be the critically important story about human origins. Thus, the *only* reason I raise intelligent design is to help explain why many parents have defeaters for public education for their children. I now move to review the moral and legal controversy surrounding intelligent design.

As the reader is no doubt aware, the teaching of evolution has been the subject of considerable controversy since the 1968 Supreme Court case *Epperson v. Arkansas,* where the Court struck down an Arkansas law that prevented the teaching of "the theory that mankind descended from a lower order of animals."[38] While the 1925 *Scopes* trial cannot be overlooked, states could still restrict the teaching of evolution until *Epperson.* After *Epperson,* a number of groups sought to have creationism taught along with evolution, but the courts struck down these attempts. The contemporary challenge concerns whether teaching *intelligent design* alongside evolution can be legally justified, so I shall focus on clarifying the objections that intelligent design–believing parents have to the teaching of evolution alone. To begin, let's review the intelligent design theorist's claim.

Michael Behe, a molecular biologist and perhaps the most prominent proponent of intelligent design (ID), defends ID based on the claim that some biological systems are *irreducibly complex.* A biological system is irreducibly complex when is "composed of several well-matched, interacting parts that contribute to the basic function, wherein the removal of any one of the parts causes the system to effectively cease functioning."[39] Purported examples include the bacterial flagellum, blood clotting and the immune system. Behe argues that gradual modifications of prototype systems cannot produce irreducibly complex systems because the prototypes will miss the relevant parts and will therefore fail to be functional.[40] Behe's argument can be formulated in a number of ways. Alvin Plantinga has reconstructed the argument by holding that it is exceedingly improbable that there is a "series of steps through 'design space'" that begin with a precursor mechanism and proceed by a series of heritable, adaptive genetic variation, unguided by any intelligence, to the irreducibly complex system in question.[41]

To be fair to the ID theorist, let me be careful to properly characterize her claim. ID maintains that at least one intelligent intervention in the evolutionary process was required to produce an irreducibly complex system. *Any* sufficiently intelligent being or beings could have intervened at *any* point in the billion years–long evolutionary process, and they need not have done so more than a handful of times. The claim of the ID theorist is that unguided evolution via natural selection cannot explain *every single step* from the beginning of life to its present diversity. So ID largely consists in the negative thesis that "neo-Darwinian theory, as it now exists, does not have an adequate explanation for the rich complexity of many organs and individual cells."[42] ID theorists also advance a positive thesis, namely that intelligent design "is the causal explanation for many important aspects of life's development over time."[43] But the positive thesis requires only the slightest interference in the evolutionary process. ID does not even violate methodological naturalism, the nigh universally accepted scientific methodology where scientists proceed as though the world were composed entirely of matter and energy, and that all features of the world have an explanation in those terms, because it does not assume that the designer is a nonnatural being.

Questions about the constitutionality of teaching ID are presently taken to depend on whether ID counts as science.[44] If ID is not science, its critics claim, then it is likely an implicitly religious view, and so teaching ID will count as establishing a religion. With regard to whether ID is science, the vast majority of scientists believe that ID is not a scientific theory because it fails to satisfy a reasonable threshold of specificity in its explanation.[45] ID is also unscientific because it tells us almost nothing about the designer, save that the designer has great power and it cannot tell us much about why the designer acted as he or she did or how the designer will act in the future.[46] Courts have rejected the constitutionality of teaching ID on similar grounds. In the 2005 case, *Kitzmiller v. Dover Area School District*, the U.S. District Court for the Middle District of Pennsylvania struck down the Dover Area School District's policy of teaching ID as an alternative to evolution. Judge Jones found that ID does not count as science for three reasons:

(1) ID violates the centuries-old ground rules of science by invoking and permitting supernatural causation;
(2) The argument of irreducible complexity, central to ID, employs the same flawed and illogical contrived dualism that doomed creation science in the 1980s;
(3) ID's negative attacks on evolution have been refuted by the scientific community.[47]

Jones also emphasizes that ID has almost no adherents in the scientific community and, that it has never been tested or researched.

Judge Jones and many opponents of ID infer from the fact that ID is not science that the case for teaching it is implicitly based on religion. Consequently, teaching ID is said to be unconstitutional because it violates the Establishment clause. Judge Jones found that "the evidence at trial demonstrates that ID is nothing less than the progeny of creationism."[48] Thus, the teaching of ID goes beyond merely making students aware of it, as teaching ID legitimizes it along with the religious view (creationism) on which it is implicitly based.

While in fact there is no *direct* connection between whether ID is science and whether teaching ID constitutes an establishment of religion (the latter plainly does not follow from the former), I shall assume for the sake of argument that teaching ID as science would be problematic from a constitutional perspective.[49] Instead, I shall interpret the request that schools teach ID as a request to teach students about the *limits* of scientific explanation. ID postulates what Greenawalt terms a "contingent limit" on science, a limit on what science can explain "within the domains that scientific inquiry covers."[50] Accordingly, I will evaluate a proposal to teach ID within a classroom period focused on the limits of science as such, including other more metaphysical limitations.

I believe that parents and groups who defend ID would be happy for ID to be taught in any form at all. At base, I do not think they are motivated by a desire that good science be taught, but rather by a desire that some curricular counterweight be given to the attempt by schools to teach that humans evolved without any intelligent guidance, a doctrine that many parents regard not merely as false but morally pernicious. So under this proposal, ID would be taught as part of a theology or philosophy portion of secondary schooling that could be legitimately mandated by local school boards, or by state or federal departments of education.[51]

Before evaluating my proposals, we should identify how coercion is employed in this case. I shall set aside the coercion involved in forcing teachers to comply with local or state educational guidelines and the coercion used against students to keep them in school and to encourage them to learn the relevant material. Instead, let us focus on the coercion used against *parents*. To ensure that a particular public school educates her child, governments typically claim the authority to coerce a parent in four ways. First, she is forced to have her child attend school. Second, she is forced to have her child attend a state-accredited school within a restricted area. Third, she is forced to fund the school in question.

Fourth, she is forced to have her child taught in accordance with standards that she does not directly determine.[52] The first three forms of coercion are primary coercion, whereas the fourth is secondary coercion (Ch. 6, Sec. V).

According to the Public Justification Principle, all four forms of coercion must be publicly justified. Let us assume the first form of coercion, compulsory education, is publicly justified in the discussed range of cases, as this is nigh universally agreed upon. I shall focus instead on the three other forms of coercion, i.e., whether the state is publicly justified in forcing parents to fund the public school system, to have their children attend particular state-accredited schools and to significantly restrict parents' power to determine their children's curriculum.

Imagine now two parents, Alvin and Daniel. Alvin is a Reformed Christian. His core life project is to serve God and Jesus Christ to the best of his ability. Included in this project is raising his children to be good Christians. Consequently, Alvin wants his children to learn about God's creation and theories about how creation works, including modern biology. However, he approaches the teaching of biology with some trepidation. Alvin is a theistic evolutionist and is open to divine intervention at points in the evolutionary process. He wants his children to believe the same. But he recognizes that many biologists are atheists and that, as a result, they often fail to carefully distinguish between the science of evolution and the philosophical naturalism associated with it. As a result, biology textbooks often claim that science shows that evolution is essentially unguided. But Alvin believes that God used evolutionary mechanisms to create life, and so sees these textbook claims as metaphysical rather than scientific. He believes that his children will suffer from being taught that a metaphysical position incompatible with Christianity is a matter of scientific fact. Doing so is an affront to his values and is all the more unacceptable given that such teaching occurs against his express wishes and on his dime. Alvin supports the teaching of ID on the grounds that it creates a space for children to think about the limits of science and the relationship between faith and science. His goal is not for the public school system to convert students to Christianity. Instead, he simply wishes his school to clearly distinguish between matters of science and matters of faith and value. He thinks teaching ID is a good way to do this.

Contrast Alvin with Daniel. Daniel is a New Atheist. He not only believes that all religions are false and that there is no God but that careful reflection on religious claims will decisively reveal them to be false and perhaps even unjustifiable. Daniel prizes the values of reason, openness, creativity and individual freedom. He believes religion opposes his fundamental values. Daniel is also a father and his children attend the same school as Alvin's. Daniel thinks it is vital for children to learn science unpolluted by nonscientific questions. He has no problem with his children reflecting on the limits of science, but he thinks such a focus will tend to obscure the beauty of science and serve as a backdoor method of introducing religion into public school curricula, something he finds pernicious and immoral. Daniel thinks that children must be taught Darwin's theory of evolution clearly and forcefully because it is one of the greatest ideas in history, regardless of the protestations of "fundamentalist" religious parents. Sadly, some parents are simply too parochial to be responsible for the entirety of their children's education. Consequently, the state has a duty to present a diversity of views to students on the public dime and to help them understand how to reason well. Science is the best model of good reasoning we have, Daniel believes, and so attempts to obscure or undermine its teaching must be vigorously opposed.

Alvin and Daniel send their children to Sweet Philosophy High. They are both coerced to do so in the latter three ways described above. Both are forced to fund Sweet Philosophy High, both are directed to have their children attend the school in question and neither has much influence on their children's curriculum. Alvin and Daniel are free to send their children to private school, but both find that they cannot afford private school tuition and so are reliant on their local public school system. Now, suppose that the Sweet Philosophy School Board is deciding whether to mandate the teaching of ID, not as science, but as part of a course on the limits of science.

Daniel has good reason to protest the mandate. He will be coerced not merely to fund the teaching of ID but to have his child learn it and regurgitate it on a test. The school offers Daniel the ability to have his child opt out, but Daniel thinks this is not enough. His child will have to pay the social consequences of separating herself from the class, and her Christian classmates may ridicule her. Coercive pressures remain in place. Daniel is also worried that the teaching of ID is simply a way of teaching religion in disguise, something he considers dishonest. He has engaged in a respectable amount of reasoning on the matter. Surely he has a good objection to the coercion the school board and the state use against him by teaching curriculum to his children that he strongly objects to. He is understandably upset about the coercion employed to teach his child ID.

In contrast, Alvin has good reason to advocate the teaching of ID. He believes that without ID as a counterweight, the teaching of evolution will give his children the impression that anyone who takes science seriously must believe that humans evolved unguided. Understandably, he does not trust teachers to make the fine metaphysical distinctions necessary for children to learn that evolution is not a philosophical theory but a scientific one. The teaching of ID in a theology or philosophy course would alleviate his concern that secular education authorities are effectively propagandizing his children. Surely he has a good objection to the coercion the school board and the state use against him to fund a school that not only fights his ability to pass his values onto his children but also expropriates his salary to do so. He is understandably upset about the coercion employed to teach his child unqualified Darwinism.

On the convergence view, Alvin and Daniel do not necessarily have defeaters for the mandate or the absence of a mandate. It is hard to see, for instance, that Daniel prefers not teaching evolution *at all* to teaching evolution as science and having the mandate in place. What's more, it is hard to see that Alvin prefers not teaching evolution *at all* to teaching evolution without the mandate. Both are sufficiently committed to having evolution taught that they arguably lack *defeaters* for the mandate. The problem is that both Daniel and Alvin know that these are not the only controversies over which school boards deprive them of control over their children's education. They recognize that the same concerns they have about teaching or not teaching intelligent design are similar to concerns about teaching or not teaching other matters, such as abstinence education. They have both engaged in a respectable amount of reasoning and see the power of the school board as generally endangering their fundamental project of raising their children in accord with their values. Consequently, Alvin and Daniel may reasonably judge that they have reason to withdraw their children from public school entirely in order to ensure that local school boards and the cultural norms of their school districts do not exercise undue influence on their children. No matter how the school board exercises its power, it threatens coercion that both Alvin and Daniel justifiably believe sets back their children's education. In sum, the power of government under the present public school system may eventuate in unjustifiable coercion used against Alvin, Daniel or both.

IV. Public Education—An Empty Set

Both Alvin and Daniel have strong convictions about the way that evolution is taught in schools. But both recognize that their conflicts extend beyond evolution to other issues. I argue that the presence of these and other value conflicts leaves the state with an empty set of permissible coercion when it comes to the structuring of public education. If so, there is a strong case for an alternative institutional arrangement.

Consider sex education as a second case. Daniel believes that it is important for his child to be taught about sexual matters at a relatively early age. He is realistic. Young teens have sex and it is no use ignoring it. If parents pretend that their children are not engaged in sexual activity, then they will fail to adequately prepare them for the consequences of their choices. Teaching abstinence is hopeless and, what's worse, it encourages children to deny themselves the opportunity to explore their sexuality. In contrast, Alvin believes that sexual intercourse is a sacred act between a man and woman that must be oriented towards procreation. The unitive and procreative acts of sex should not be separated. And since young teens are too young to be married, teaching them about safe sex effectively gives them permission to engage in irresponsible and immoral sexual behavior. Alvin also sees the rationale for teaching safe sex as self-fulfilling. By teaching safe sex through the public schools, children feel more comfortable engaging in it, which helps create the problem that sex education is meant to ameliorate. As with ID, both Daniel and Alvin have engaged in a respectable amount of reasoning and both have strong reason to reject the sort of sex education the other would like to be available for all children.[53] Of course, the school could refuse to teach sex education altogether, but both Alvin and Daniel believe that some education would be useful, especially for children whose parents are either unwilling or not competent to help them. They may also agree that there is a gain from the division of labor and specialization in education, so that children will often learn more, and at lower cost, from education at school than education at home. They simply deeply disagree about what shape sex education should take.

The problem for Alvin and Daniel, however, is that they both think the fact that their children could be compelled to take the other's sex education courses is one more reason to give up on the public education system entirely. Alvin would prefer to provide sex education to his children himself or through his church rather than have teachers tell his kids that sex before marriage is OK. Daniel would prefer to provide sex education to his children himself as well rather than have them propagandized about sex based on an archaic and medieval philosophy of abstinence. On sex education, the Sweet Philosophy School Board faces one more controversy, giving public reason theorists yet another reason to worry that on convergence the set of public education systems may be empty.

From these two cases, then, we can infer that the public schools will often confront an empty set given the various value conflicts raised by public education. This is largely due to the fact that our four forms of coercion ensure that educational choices must be made as collective despite (i) pervasive disagreement within the collective and (ii) no easy way to opt out of the collective in order to make an individual choice. Michael McConnell explains the problem: "If students of different cultures and creeds are to be educated according to a common curriculum, then it is necessary to determine what the content of that curriculum is. The diversity of opinions about the content of education makes that difficult."[54] The result is that schools coerce some parents into arrangements they reject and so those who dissent have only two choices: allow those with contrary values to educate their children or pay for alternative arrangements from their own pockets on top of their taxes. The result is a coercive arrangement that is in tension with liberal commitments.[55] This point is obvious when applied to domains of social life outside of education, such as religious practice. If Al and Dan were members of a democratic collective that can mandate that all attend a particular *church* rather than a school, that they would use the same *sacred text* rather than the same textbook and teach the same *theology* rather than sex education, the eligible set of churches, sacred texts and theologies would be empty.[56]

To put it in economic terms, the problem with an education monopoly is its tendency towards supplying uniform and politically determinate services on all consumers, such that they are stuck with a product many of them find unattractive. This directly restricts their liberty to select their own product.[57] Subjecting education to extensive democratic choice virtually guarantees that some citizens will be coerced in ways that cannot be justified to them given the deep diversity of educational values.

Modern school systems typically respond to collective choice conflicts by watering down school curricula and removing controversial elements. But this is an unacceptable "mush alternative" because it effectively "capitulates to the often anti-social values of mass youth culture."[58] Educational institutions have reason to teach some scheme of values to prevent children from being bandied about by the forces of vice and immorality.[59] Thus, declining to teach values is itself an unattractive policy. McConnell formulates the foregoing as a dilemma which forces schools to choose between imposing a scheme of values, rendering it illiberal, or avoiding "comprehensive doctrines and [abandoning] the hope of supplying a morally coherent structure for its teaching of democratic values."[60]

A critic might reply by denying that citizens have defeaters for all policy alternatives available to public school systems. Instead, complaints offered by parents like Alvin and Daniel only shows that they rank their curricular choices as superior to those offered by the other. All of these proposals are in this way inconclusively justified rather than defeated.[61] The problem with this response, as I have alluded, is that to have a defeater for a law is simply to have sufficient reason to regard the law as inferior to no law at all on the issue.[62]

The critic could reply by offering a concrete alternative that both Alvin and Daniel might rank above restricting educational choice to public schooling, namely allowing parents to opt their children out of controversial issues by requiring that parents pay for private instruction in the area or do it themselves, but allowing them to opt out of education only in those limited cases. On this proposal, both sides would get public education and have the values education they endorse. Plus, by paying for private instruction, parents demonstrate their strong commitment to special values education for their children.[63] So long as both Alvin and Daniel place value on having a public education system generally, then they might both rank this opt-out-and-pay model ahead of no public education system at all.

Given how unusual this proposal is, I shall not spend too much time on it. But I have two concerns. First, Alvin and Daniel are coercively required to pay twice for education on areas they care most about, since they must still pay for public schooling. The scheme appears to place more burdens on Alvin and Daniel than parents with less intense views on the importance of values education for their children. Second, the proposal is only uniquely justified if Alvin and Daniel have sufficient reason to reject public education on controversial issues, but lack sufficient reason to rank school choice ahead of it. Yet it is not plausible that either Alvin or Daniel have this ranking. After all, if choice is good for controversial issues, then why not education generally? This is particularly clear for Alvin. If Alvin prefers choice to compulsory education on evolution and sex ed, then he will likely prefer choice for other subjects as well. He would be able to offer his children a religion-infused education without paying extra for it. But these concerns aside, whether the proposal is justified will depend on how highly Alvin and Daniel value public education. If they value it highly enough, then yes, the modified proposal may outrank a school choice system. But many reasonable parents in a diverse society arguably do not have this ranking.

Some consensus theorists do not worry enough about these complexities, partly because they think that democratic choice alone can legitimize even highly controversial decisions. Amy Gutmann argues that "the values we are teaching are the product of a collective decision to which you were a party. Insofar as that decision deprives no one of the opportunity to participate in future decisions, its outcome is legitimate, even if it is not correct."[64] But the convergence liberal rejects the claim that collective decisions based on shared reasons can override the intelligible defeaters of parents.

Accordingly, present educational arrangements in the United States cannot be publicly justified to diverse, reasonable parents. We should explore alternative arrangements, like school choice.

V.   School Choice

I believe that school choice systems can solve the problems of public justification that the present public school system cannot. School choice is generally understood as a market-based system in which parents can use either tax breaks or vouchers to pay for tuition at a school of their choice. It differs from the present public school system because the government is not a major *producer* of education. Parents are free to purchase educational services in an open and competitive education market.[65] However, the government would still have a significant educational role. On this proposal, the state could require that schools be accredited in order to guarantee minimal educational quality and civic competence. The state would also guarantee that all children have an opportunity to receive educative services.[66] Thus, the distinguishing feature of school choice is that it reduces the state's role in producing education, while permitting it to accredit schools and provide everyone with the means to participate in the market.

We can place John Stuart Mill in the choice camp. In *On Liberty*, he defends a similar arrangement. Mill argues that "the State should require and compel the education, up to a certain standard, of every human being who is born its citizen."[67] However, the government should still "leave to parents to obtain the education where and how they pleased, and content itself with helping to pay the school fees of the poorer classes of children, and defraying the entire school expenses of those who have no one else to pay for them."[68] Public exams should extend "to all children and beginning at an early age."[69] If children cannot pass the exams, then parents could be fined. Beyond the minimum, students should take "voluntary examinations on all subjects, at which all who come up to a certain standard of proficiency might claim a certificate." To prevent state interference in public opinion, the knowledge required to pass even the higher level exams should be limited to "facts and science exclusively." Exams on disputed topics should not be based on the "truth or falsehood of opinions, but on the matter of fact that such and such an opinion is held, on such grounds, by such authors, or schools, or churches."[70]

School choice insulates the education system from extensive democratic control and allows parents to make their own decisions about their children's education. In doing so, it introduces a new set of arrangements into the eligible set of educational systems. Without school choice, Alvin and Daniel have three alternatives for educating their children: (i) public schooling according to Alvin's values, (ii) public schooling according to Daniel's values and (iii) public schooling without values education, perhaps with private values education. By introducing school choice, we give them a fourth option, namely (iv) one school promotes Alvin's values and another school promotes Daniel's values. I argued above that alternatives (i) and (ii) are defeated. Option (iii) may be defeated as well, as both parents have an interest in their funds being used to inculcate their preferred scheme of values. If (iii) is defeated, then only (iv) can be publicly justified. And even if (iii) is not defeated, (iv) is still superior to (iii) from the perspectives of both Alvin and Daniel, given the high value they place on values based education. Since by stipulation they want schools to promote their values, the school choice system is superior because it facilitates the teaching of moral values more easily than (iii).

Setting (iii) aside, (iv) should be eligible for just about everyone, not only because parents will not want their children propagandized to adopt others' views but also because it keeps any one view from gaining dominance.[71] While Daniel and Alvin must give up their power to determine the education of the other's child, they can safeguard their own. Consequently, school choice respects diversity and reasonable pluralism by allowing each person or group to make her own choices.[72] Liberal societies take this approach with respect to many domains of social life, such as higher education, communication, art and religious worship. Convergence holds that education should be treated similarly.

VI.   Objections

School choice will meet resistance for at least three reasons: (i) school choice constitutes an establishment of religion, (ii) school choice does not resolve the controversies its defenders suppose and (iii) school choice will produce illiberal citizens. The first objection to school choice is that it constitutes an establishment of religion and so violates the Principle of Intelligible Exclusion. The argument is that by providing parents with public money to finance religious school, the state establishes religion (albeit indirectly) by helping religious institutions to produce pervasively sectarian religious education.

Since *Everson v. Board of Education* (1947), the Supreme Court has continuously concerned itself with state aid to religion. Prior to *Everson*, the Court rarely addressed government aid to religious schooling. But as the American welfare state expanded, government and religion became more entangled, calling for judicial review. The most important case respecting school vouchers is *Zelman v. Simmons-Harris* (2002), where the Supreme Court sustained the constitutionality of the city of Cleveland's voucher program for low-income families.[73] At the time, the state of Ohio gave parents vouchers as checks that would cover up to 90% of tuition costs extending to $2250. Eligible schools could not discriminate against attendees based on religion, but they could have a religious curriculum. The majority argued that the aid is too indirect to constitute establishment. As Kent Greenawalt explains, "the standards for aid were neutral, and it was irrelevant that religious schools receive most of the aid."[74] But Justice Souter, writing for the minority, argued that the effects of vouchers were not neutral because many poor students had only religious alternatives. He also argued "public funding was bound to bring more state control, already evidenced by the rule that no school receiving vouchers could discriminate on religious grounds."[75]

Consequently, there are two versions of the establishment objection. I interpret both objections as potential defeaters for the coercion involved in providing vouchers. Such coercion is purportedly defeated on the grounds that (a) the funding goes to support religious institutions whose values taxpayers do not share, and (b) the funding undermines the autonomy of religious institutions in ways that many citizens (mostly adherents) have reason to reject. Let us call the first version the *liberal* objection and the second version the *libertarian* objection.

The liberal objection seems to rest on an implausible version of neutrality of effect. Since the law was not generally or publicly intended to fund any particular religion and does not officially favor religion as such, the only grounds on which to object is that, in practice, voucher money goes to support either a particular religion or religion over non-religion. The more worrisome objection comes from secular citizens who recognize that they are a minority in a largely religious society and so worry that vouchers favor religious education over secular education. But the connection between secular parents' taxes and religious institutions is remote. The state cannot reasonably be expected to avoid all the indirect effects of funding it engages in. Food stamps can be used at religious grocery stores, health insurance can be used at religious hospitals and tax exemptions can be used to tithe to churches. Funding vouchers is not fundamentally different. Were the state to directly pay religious schools, an establishment complaint would be more plausible.[76] But so long as money is given directly to parents who can freely choose to support religious or nonreligious institutions, the liberal objection fails.[77]

The libertarian objection holds that religious institutions that receive voucher money will gradually lose their autonomy to an ever-expanding state. Given the importance that liberals (especially libertarian liberals) place on the importance of the autonomy of non-state intermediary institutions, this objection is potentially serious, especially because we have already assumed that the state has the authority to mandate basic quality standards. Thus, if public money goes to religious schools, the state may claim authority to ensure that religious education is nonsectarian. The problem with the libertarian objection, however, is that there are plausible methods of insulating intermediary institutions from state control other than refusing to allow parents to use vouchers to fund them. Social norms protect families, churches and other non-state organizations against state interference even when the law does not. If we make the effort, we can protect schools just as well. Perhaps the present state overregulates religious schools (it arguably does). Yet this fact, even if combined with familiar libertarian concerns about encroaching state power, is insufficient to justify denying parents an expansion of their educational freedom. Given how much libertarians value free choice, they make the perfect the enemy of the good. Furthermore, even if libertarians are correct that certain voucher *types* lead to government control over religious institutions, there may be policies that approximate the educational freedom secured by vouchers that avoid these problems, such as tax breaks or a more generic voucher that could be used on goods and services other than schooling.

Moving to the second objection, Gutmann describes permitting government to set minimal curricular standards as "civic minimalism" and the minimal curricular standard as the "civic minimum." She objects that "competing conceptions of the civic minimum itself are reasonably contestable" and therefore that "civic minimalists cannot therefore credibly promise that their conception of schooling is the key to ending heated public debates over schooling."[78] I will block this move.

The first step of Gutmann's argument is that school choice advocates bear the burden of proof. Civic minimalism must be publicly justified against the default of more extensive "democratic" education: "Civic minimalism must publicly justify denying citizens the legitimate authority to mandate more than a specific civic minimum."[79] For civic minimalism "denies democratic citizens the discretion to mandate more than a minimal civic education in schools."[80] Without the power to "collectively influence the purposes of primary schooling," education is undemocratic and so publicly unjustifiable.[81] For Gutmann, then, restrictions on collective choice, but not collective choices restricting individuals, require public justification.

But this gets public justification precisely backwards. It is not individual choice that requires justification but the coercion involved in democratic control. Coercive, collective choice can only be publicly justified when it solves serious social and political problems that individual and small group choices cannot. Favoring the individual, family or civic organization over the democratic state follows from our rejection of consensus civics. On convergence, the diverse intelligible defeaters of persons and groups subordinate the shared democratic will of the people. Consequently, a more demanding civic minimum must be justified against a less demanding civic minimum.

I have argued in favor of school choice partly on the grounds that it reduces controversy. But Gutmann denies this because interpretations of the civic minimum are reasonably contestable. Given her conception of the burden of proof, the civic minimum cannot be publicly justified. Instead of reviewing her argument further, I will accept her claim that there are many reasonably contestable interpretations of the civic minimum, but deny that this is problematic. To see why, consider that the case for a particular interpretation of the civic minimum can either be defeated or inconclusive.[82] Contestation alone can be evidence of either option. A proposed civic minimum is defeated only if all interpretations of it are defeated. But if the set of interpretations contains two or more undefeated members, then decision procedures can select one of them.

Consider a parallel objection to a free speech principle. The fact that interpretations of a free speech principle are reasonably contestable does not show that the free speech principle cannot be publicly justified. If the free speech principle is publicly justified, then we all have an interest in having some interpretation of the principle on the books even if it is not the interpretation we think best. We can use a decision procedure like the court system to vindicate a particular interpretation. We can do the same thing with a plural set of interpretations of the civic minimum. Thus, for her argument to succeed, Gutmann must demonstrate that the eligible set of interpretations of the civic minimum is empty rather than plural. But she does no such thing. Thus, given my arguments in the prior section, we have reason to think the set will be nonempty.

Gutmann also offers the third objection, namely that a school choice system will produce illiberal citizens. On her view, one can infer from history that unless the state provides and regulates schooling, children will learn neither "mutual respect among persons nor rational deliberation" because their parents will prioritize teaching them to avoid "eternal damnation," since some religious parents believe other forms of life are sinful and will therefore lead their children to disrespect those who are different.[83] To put it another way, if parents are allowed to make diverse educational choices, many will expose their children to only one set of values. This concern is amplified in the case of religion, as parents may believe their children's salvation depends on whether they adhere to those values. School choice systems will therefore balkanize the public and lead citizens to retreat from liberal democratic institutions. In contrast, the "symbolic significance" of the American public school system gives it the unique capacity to inculcate the importance of shared civic life.[84] To abandon public schools would be to abandon public recognition of the importance of producing good citizens. In response to McConnell, Gutmann argues that while market reforms have great effects in various domains of commercial life, they fail to recognize that "primary schools serve public purposes as well as private ones and fulfill public obligations to children."[85]

There are two versions of this objection, one that holds that a school choice system will produce illiberal citizens in virtue of permitting parents to self-sort, and the other that holds that a school choice system will signal that the creation of liberal citizens is not important. But we have no evidence for either claim. Even Macedo admits that "the actual effectiveness of public schools at teaching toleration is hard to gauge" and cites a study which claims that Catholic schools are more effective than public schools at producing religiously tolerant students that endorse civic liberties.[86] Given that even Macedo admits that the evidence for Gutmann's claim is elusive, we probably lack sufficient empirical evidence to justify overriding citizens' authority to make educational choices for themselves and their children.

But perhaps more importantly, even strong evidence that public schooling promotes a shared sense of civic community cannot override the intelligible defeaters of many parents. Despite such evidence, some parents are plainly justified in prioritizing their child's salvation over their democratic citizenship.

VII. Conclusion

Convergence education is *considerably* friendlier to religious citizens than consensus. It does not require that children be taught to prioritize shared values as determined by the nation-state. Instead, it protects religious parents' rights to make their own educational choices. For instance, convergence not only sides with the *Mozert* parents, but also legitimizes complaints couched in purely religious terms.

True public reason liberalism once again sides with religious citizens by protecting their liberty and treating them fairly.

Chapters 6 and 7 demonstrate that the theoretical reconciliation between public reason liberals and their religious critics extends to political practice. In Chapter 6, we saw that convergence carves out an extensive range of religious accommodation in response to diverse, dispersed defeaters. Chapter 7 demonstrates that convergence likely requires a school choice system, again protecting the liberty of religious citizens. The book's thesis is vindicated: in both theory and practice, public reason liberalism is far friendlier to religious citizens than its proponents and opponents suppose.

Notes

1. Macedo 2000a, p. 39.
2. Gutmann 1987, p. 14.
3. We can set aside the symmetry and radical idealization components of the mainstream view in this chapter.
4. Macedo 2000a, p. 13. I should note that Macedo also resists a "civic totalism" that attempts to snuff out the private sphere in favor of democratic political life (a view Macedo ascribes to John Dewey). Ibid, p. 139.
5. Ibid., p. 3.
6. Ibid., p. 14. Emphasis mine.
7. Ibid., p. 15.
8. Ibid.
9. Macedo 2000a, p. 12.
10. Ibid. Again, "we owe our fellow citizens reasons they can share with us." Ibid., p. 186.
11. Ibid., p. 197.
12. Ibid., p. 15.
13. Ibid., p. 143.
14. Ibid., p. 181.
15. Ibid., p. 186.
16. Kyle Swan raises the possibility that the consensus theorist would recognize, as I claim below, that we disagree about what we share. Armed with that recognition, the consensus theorist might be hostile to shared civic education, given that few shared reasons support such institutions. That is, perhaps the consensus approach isn't as uniform as Macedo or Gutmann would suppose. I grant that the consensus approach may not straightforwardly entail consensus civics or consensus education. But given that consensus liberals draw such connections themselves, I will critique them on those grounds.
17. Macedo 2000a, p. 186.
18. Tomasi 2001b, p. 216.
19. Macedo 2000a, p. 232.
20. Ibid., p. 125.

21. Ibid., p. 232.
22. Gutmann 1987, p. 104. Emphasis mine.
23. Ibid., p. 103.
24. Gutmann 2001b, p. 23.
25. Macedo 2000a, p. 201.
26. Ibid., p. 232.
27. Gutmann 1987, p. 30.
28. Brennan 2011, pp. 43–67.
29. Again, save for legislators and judges, as I argued in Ch. 6.
30. *Abingdon Township v. Schempp*, 374 U.S. 203, 241–2 (1963) (Brennan, J., concurring).
31. McConnell 2001, p. 105.
32. Lomasky 1987, p. 167.
33. Ibid., p. 174.
34. Gutmann 1987, p. 61.
35. I thank Jerry Gaus for pushing me to distinguish between primary and secondary education here, which follows established legal practice.
36. I am grateful to Chad Van Schoelandt for this point.
37. National Center for Education Statistics 2013.
38. Greenawalt 2008, p. 137.
39. Behe 1996, p. 39.
40. Ibid.
41. Plantinga 2011, p. 227. Note that even Alvin Plantinga, the dean of Christian philosophers, rejects Behe's argument. The clarification Plantinga offers should not be construed as an endorsement on his part, *or mine* for that matter.
42. Greenawalt 2008, p. 144. They also believe that future versions of neo-Darwinian theory will fail as well.
43. Ibid.
44. For a philosophical argument that ID does not count as science, see Audi 2009b.
45. The U.S. National Academy of Sciences claims that "creationism, intelligent design, and other claims of supernatural intervention in the origin of life or of species are not science because they are not testable by the methods of science."
46. Greenawalt 2008, p. 147.
47. Ibid., p. 64.
48. Ibid., p. 31.
49. However, I will neither endorse nor reject the Establishment clause reasoning that Judge Jones employed.
50. Greenawalt 2008, p. 148. Science also has "intrinsic" limits, limits it seems to have by nature, such as its inability to explain why anything exists at all and whether we should be moral.
51. I shall assume that all three institutions are publicly justified for the sake of argument.
52. Her vote for school board members does not count as direct determination of curricula, though PTA meetings might.
53. For a detailed account of a respectable amount of reasoning, see Gaus 2011, pp. 254–8.
54. McConnell 2001, p. 97.

55. Ibid., p. 104.
56. See D'Agostino 2003 for a discussion of how people can solve justificatory problems via devolution to individual and small group choice. D'Agostino appeals not only to a similar church-based analogy but also to a voucher system. See pp. 104–9, esp n. 64 (p. 120).
57. Lomasky 1987, p. 174.
58. McConnell 2001, p. 98.
59. Even if parents disagree about who those forces are.
60. McConnell 2001, p. 122.
61. Gaus 1996, pp. 151–58, provides an informative account of inconclusive public justifications.
62. See Gaus 2011, pp. 497–500, for an analysis of defeater reasons in these terms.
63. Gaus proposed this alternative to me in conversation.
64. Gutmann 1987, p. 61.
65. Lomasky 1987, p. 173.
66. McConnell 2001, pp. 87–8, discusses a similar proposal.
67. Mill 1978, p. 104.
68. Ibid., p. 104.
69. Ibid., p. 105.
70. Ibid., pp. 105–6.
71. McConnell 2001, p. 104. Emphasis mine. The latter societal point may be valid, but it is not part of my case in this section.
72. Lomasky 1987, p. 178.
73. Greenawalt 2008, p. 414.
74. Ibid.
75. Ibid., p. 415. The Court cited other factors as well, including concerns that funding will generate divisive conflict about religion. See pp. 414–24, for an extensive discussion.
76. The complaint might also be more plausible if the vast majority of the voucher money was clearly spent on religious activities. I thank Chad Van Schoelandt for this point.
77. A critic might worry that I have weakened my stricture against secondary coercion in Ch. 6, Sec. V, on the grounds that many arguably have defeaters for having their funds used to support causes they reject. But the issue in this case is whether their funds are used to support such causes. Their funds affect these causes, but in a voucher scheme it would be incorrect to claim that their funds are thereby deliberately used to support these causes.
78. Gutmann 2001b, p. 30.
79. Ibid., p. 35.
80. Gutmann 1987, p. 294.
81. Ibid, p. 75.
82. See Gaus 1996, pp. 179–91, for a discussion of inconclusive public reasoning.
83. Gutmann 1987, pp. 30–1.
84. Rosenblum 2001, p. 150.
85. Gutmann 2001a, p. 175.
86. Macedo 2000a, p. 234.

Conclusion

The best version of public reason liberalism protects religious citizens from the encroachments of the state and permits them to appeal to their most deeply held convictions in political life—or so I have argued throughout this book. Before my closing remarks, I offer a brief review of the argument. Some readers may prefer to skip to Section II.

I. Review of the Argument

Public reason liberals argue that, due to reasonable pluralism, the only respectful way in which free and equal persons can coerce one another is if those coerced have sufficient reason to accept the coercion in question. In other words, respect for persons requires the public justification of coercion. This idea is embodied in the Public Justification Principle, which holds:

> *Public Justification Principle (PJP)*: A coercive law L is justified only if each member *I* of the public P has some sufficient reason(s) R_i to endorse L.

The standard interpretation is a consensus conception of reasons R_i and a radically idealized public P. This view generates religious restraint via the Master Argument, which holds:

(1) Public Justification Principle → Accessibility/Shareability Requirement

(2) Accessibility/Shareability Requirement → Principle of Exclusion

(3) Principle of Exclusion → Principle of Restraint

In Chapter 2, I claimed that the case for religious restraint depends upon the mainstream, consensus interpretation of the Public Justification Principle, in conjunction with the Master Argument. Because religious reasons are not shared reasons, respectful citizens will either refuse to appeal to them in political discourse and activism, or they will subordinate religious advocacy to secular advocacy. I also reviewed the religiously based objections to restraint, specifically the integrity, fairness and divisiveness arguments. I concluded that the objections are by and large successful. If the Master Argument holds, then, the religious objectors have defeaters for the Public Justification Principle. Thus, contrary to providing a respectful reaction to religious diversity, public reason liberalism disrespects citizens by threatening their integrity and treating them unfairly. I then argued that we can deprive the religious objectors of their defeaters for the Public Justification Principle by denying at least one premise of the Master Argument. I admitted that premise (3) is suspect, but I built the rest of the book around rejecting premise (1), the justificatory premise.

In Chapter 3, I outlined a strategy for defeating the justificatory premise. First, I developed an account of public reason liberalism's foundational values, focusing on respect for integrity and reasonable pluralism. I then used the two values to construct desiderata for selecting among interpretations of the Public Justification Principle. Specifically, an interpretation is superior to another if (i) it better expresses respect for personal integrity and (ii) it recognizes a greater diversity of reasons as justificatory. Since public reason's foundational values provide reason to prefer one interpretation to another, public reason liberals must endorse the superior interpretation on pain of inconsistency. And if the superior interpretation involves rejecting the justificatory premise, then public reason liberals must reject the justificatory premise by their own lights. In this way, public reason liberals acquire a defeater for restraint and the religious objectors acquire a defeater for their arguments against public reason liberalism, bringing the two camps together.

We can interpret the general strategy of Chapter 3 in two ways. The first strategy seeks to minimize the amount of conflict between publicly justified laws and the free, religiously based actions of citizens, whereas the second strategy seeks to eliminate it. The first "truce" strategy is unattractive because it bases the social order on a modus vivendi. The second strategy aims for congruence, one that unites the practical reasons of each citizen such that the conflict between the demands of public reason and religious integrity disappears.

In Chapters 4 and 5 I developed alternative interpretations of reasons R_i and members of the public P in the Public Justification Principle. Chapter 4 develops and defends the convergence conception of justificatory reasons. On the convergence view, all intelligible reasons can figure into a public justification. I defined intelligibility as follows:

Intelligibility: A's reason X is intelligible to members of the public if and only if members of the public regard X as epistemically justified for A according to A's evaluative standards.

Intelligibility Requirement: A's reason X can justify coercing members of the public only if it is intelligible to them.

The intelligibility requirement is remarkably permissive: vast numbers of religious reasons suddenly become relevant to public justification. Convergence can therefore refute the justificatory premise and undermine the case for restraint, as it imposes basically no restriction on the employment of religious reasons. I then defended convergence against the mainstream consensus view on the grounds that it better protects the integrity of citizens (especially religious citizens) and better respects reasonable pluralism by acknowledging as justificatory the entire set of intelligible reasons endorsed by each citizen. After addressing some objections, I concluded that convergence blocks the Master Argument and establishes the thesis of the book. But a major concern remains: convergence can still impose restraint if combined with a radical conception of idealization. So we need an alternative interpretation of members of the public P as well.

Chapter 5 develops the alternative, moderate conception of idealization. Moderate idealization begins from citizens' present values and beliefs and upgrades them in accord with modest standards of rationality and information. I argued that a moderate conception of idealization better respects integrity and reasonable pluralism, specifically by acknowledging the great diversity of reasons among citizens. I concluded that convergence liberalism—the form of liberalism that combines convergence and moderate idealization—provides the theoretical reconciliation between public reason liberals and their religious critics by refuting the justificatory premise, thereby undermining the case for restraint.

But reconciliation in theory is not enough. Convergence liberalism must also provide reconciliation in practice. Chapter 6 applied convergence liberalism to public deliberation and religious accommodation. I developed a principle to aid this application derived from what I called the New Master Argument:

(1) Public Justification Principle → Intelligibility Requirement
(2) Intelligibility Requirement → Principle of Intelligible Exclusion
(3) Principle of Intelligible Exclusion → Principle of Convergent Restraint

The New Master Argument replaces the justificatory premise with premise (1), which connects intelligibility and the Public Justification Principle in light of convergence. Premise (2) connects intelligibility to a principle exclusion that determines how institutions should block and permit coercion. I called this the Principle of Intelligible Exclusion:

The Principle of Intelligible Exclusion (PIE): Law-making bodies must (i) only impose laws on members of the public that members of the public have sufficient intelligible reason to endorse and (ii) repeal or reform laws that members of the public have sufficient intelligible reason to reject.

The Principle of Intelligible Exclusion requires that institutions be sensitive to the intelligible defeaters of the citizenry, defeaters that are both diverse and dispersed. I argued that the Principle of Intelligible Exclusion imposes no restraint on citizens and only exacts limited proposal restraint from legislators. Legislators must only advocate proposals that they believe can be publicly justified, but they can act on whatever reasons they like. Judges are another matter, as delivering opinions collapses the reason-proposal distinction. I argued that judges should make decisions based on shared reasoning. I concluded by endorsing premise (3), but emphasizing that the restraint required is extremely limited, applying exclusively to legislators and judges, and imposing significant restraint only on the latter. The principle I defend is the Principle of Convergent Restraint, which takes different forms when applied to legislators and judges.

Intelligible Exclusion requires extensive religious accommodation, though by itself provides little information about how to assess particular accommodation claims. In light of this limitation, I appealed to considerations specific to religious freedom issues by defending versions of the Free Exercise and Establishment clauses of the U.S. Constitution. The Principle of Intelligible Exclusion requires that free exercise and non-establishment principles be used to block coercive laws defeated by intelligible reasons, the result of which is that constitutional law should be permissive with respect to accommodation. I then applied Intelligible Exclusion to *Yoder*, *Smith* and *Mozert*, arguing that in each case the burdened parties had sufficient religious reason to morally merit a legal accommodation, if not through the court system, then through the legislature.

In Chapter 7 I turned to the public school system. The mainstream, consensus approach to public education requires schools to produce citizens who can deliberate in shared terms and who prioritize shared values in their political lives. I developed the convergence liberal alternative, which allows citizens to support publicly justified institutions as they see fit. Consequently, convergence education does not prioritize deliberation or the teaching of shared values. More radically, the Principle of Intelligible Exclusion demonstrates that teaching any one substantive set of values in public schools cannot be publicly justified. Reasonable value conflicts over intelligent design and other issues mean that only a school choice education system can be publicly justified. Such a system should please religious citizens and their philosophical defenders, as it gives religious voices enormous weight in determining the shape of educational institutions. Once again, the shared must give way to the diverse, and monistic governmental institutions must give way to pluralistic ones. I conclude that convergence defeats the case for restraint in theory and practice. Public reason liberalism is friendly to religious voices in public life.

II. The Significance of the Argument

As I write this conclusion, American religious and secular elites are up in arms over the Obama Administration's Health and Human Services contraception mandate. Among other things, the mandate requires some Roman Catholic institutions (other than churches) to pay for contraception for their employees. Self-described liberals have rallied around the Obama Administration and against the Roman Catholic Church. Culturally, this was predictable. But public reason liberals must not succumb to popular prejudices. Instead, they must oppose the mandate as *illiberal* because many Roman Catholic groups possess clear intelligible defeaters for the coercion involved in the mandate.

A likely contributing factor to the American liberal's authoritarian stance on this issue derives from her consensus liberal proclivities. The consensus liberal responds to Catholic complaints as follows: "The Roman Catholic appeal to conscience is based on sectarian considerations that they cannot reasonably expect to override a woman's right to acquire contraception, a right that is based on the public value of gender equality and health considerations that derive from neutral, scientific reasoning." By opposing the mandate, Roman Catholics demand that the law be shaped by their private, sectarian reasons, whereas those who claim to defend women base their arguments on the shared political values of equality and public health.

The convergence liberal dissents, arguing that true liberalism treats religious and secular considerations the same, allowing both to serve as defeaters. Given the depth and care of the Catholic intellectual tradition, many Roman Catholics have intelligible defeaters for the coercion imposed upon them. As a result, they should be granted an exemption from the mandate on free exercise grounds.

At the same time, several state legislatures, including Virginia, have passed laws requiring women to get an ultrasound before they have an abortion. During early stage pregnancy, ultrasounds often require the use of physically invasive tools. While the law gives doctors discretion in this area, they still have the legal authority to override the wishes of women who would like to have an abortion. It is obvious that consensus liberals regard the Virginia law as illegitimate. And in this case, convergence liberals agree with them on the grounds that many women undoubtedly have clear intelligible defeaters for such invasive procedures. With respect to ultrasounds, some of public reason's religious critics are happy to employ illiberal coercion to promote their values at the expense of those who dissent. On this matter, self-proclaimed liberals are right to be outraged in no small part because women are coerced partly on the basis of religious considerations that they reject.

Convergence liberalism provides a true third way in American debates over the role of religion and religious reasoning in public life. It also helps us to understand the mistakes of both parties to the debate. The anti-liberals are right: consensus liberals have smuggled secularist bias into liberal political theory. However, the consensus liberals are also right: anti-liberals seek authoritarian power based on the false contention that liberalism is necessarily based on such smuggling. Convergence liberalism integrates these insights and so generates legal and policy recommendations that reorient this decades-old debate.

Convergence liberalism focuses like a laser on the core aim of the liberal tradition: justifying coercion to all. Thus, in an important sense, convergence liberalism deprives the categories of the religious and the secular of their political significance. The liberal political goal is to detect and respect all intelligible defeaters for coercion, regardless of their content. In one way, then, religion is not the issue. It is merely the most acute contemporary case of a more general conflict over what can and cannot be publicly justified.

Convergence liberalism is therefore a *post-secular* liberalism. It neither privileges a secular public sphere nor hopes that religious voices will dominate political activity and discussion. In some cases, liberals should support political secularization. In other cases, they must oppose it. Whether liberalism requires secularization is a contextual matter. On convergence, then, liberalism and secularism receive a much-needed divorce.

Liberals should welcome the opportunity to move beyond secularism, because liberalism has the resources to aid in reviving faith in liberal institutions. A massive portion of the American citizenry is disaffected by liberal political practice, in large part because they see liberal legislation and values as necessarily hostile to their most cherished and sacred forms of life. For instance, the HHS mandate has set the entire U.S. Council of Catholic Bishops against the putatively liberal Obama Administration, when only a few years before the USCCB largely supported the Affordable Care Act, the Obama Administration's capstone legislation. By imposing coercive mandates like these, can liberals really blame people of faith for fearing them? Convergence liberalism has great promise because it can quiet these fears by stridently opposing the destructive and divisive coercion that so often frames liberal administrations.

Part of the reason that consensus liberalism is so divisive is that it is infested with communitarian impulses. Many liberals wish to use state power to promote a shared civic community. Nicholas Wolterstorff has claimed that "the liberal is not willing to live with a politics of multiple communities," and when it comes to consensus liberals, he is correct.[1]

In contrast to most liberal political theorists, I have argued that public reason liberalism *clashes* with deliberative democratic doctrines that place great emphasis on shared civic values and consensus. Reasonable pluralism means the liberal dream of a shared civil life must be abandoned. Religious toleration applies to civil religions too.

I have spent much of this book criticizing traditional public reason liberalism. But I do so because I believe that public reason liberalism rests on a compelling, even moving, aspiration that we can live together on moral terms, despite our deep disagreements, and that politics can rest on reason rather than power, despite the fact that our ideals so sharply diverge. These are great goods, or so it seems to me. I am often upset when I recognize how much my values and ideals diverge from those of my friends and colleagues. I begrudgingly accept that we shall always be divided, and sometimes even opposed, on such important matters. But those of us who are liberals can create the next best thing: a world in which we recognize that neither has the right to coerce the other without justification. We can protect our treasured forms of life as free equals and live together on respectful, peaceful terms.

Public reason, as Rawls believed, has a quasi-theological aspect. It shows how human beings riven by pluralism can live together with great integrity. For if we cannot, "one might ask with Kant whether it is worthwhile for human begins to live on the earth."[2] Paul Weithman, a Christian and a student of Rawls, remarks, "political liberalism as Rawls develops it can help us to understand and affirm the very puzzling judgment that God is said to have passed upon the world."[3] The judgment is that the world should continue, despite the fact that some disbelieve, because we can live together well nonetheless. The faith of the public reason liberal is that we possess (created or no) a fundamentally moral nature that, while corrupted, allows us to build an earthly society that makes the human race worthy of continued existence. Within the bounds of public reason, this world can be so much more than a vale of tears.

Notes

1. Wolterstorff 1997a, p. 109.
2. Rawls 2002, p. 128.
3. Weithman 2010, p. 369.

Bibliography

Alston, William P. *Philosophy of Language.* Englewood Cliffs: Prentice-Hall, 1964.
————. *Perceiving God: The Epistemology of Religious Experience.* Ithaca: Cornell University Press, 1991.
Anderson, Lisa, and Charles Holt. "Information Cascades in the Laboratory." *The American Economic Review,* vol. 87 (1997): 847–62.
Aquinas, St. Thomas. *Summa Contra Gentiles, Book I: God.* New York: University of Notre Dame Press, [1268] 1975.
Audi, Robert. *Religious Commitment and Secular Reason.* Cambridge: Cambridge University Press, 2000.
————. "Natural Reason, Natural Rights, and Governmental Neutrality Toward Religion." *Religion and Human Rights,* vol. 4 (2009a): 157–75.
————. "Religion and the Politics of Science: Can Evolutionary Biology Be Religiously Neutral?" *Philosophy and Social Criticism,* vol. 35 (2009b): 23–50.
————. *Democratic Authority and the Separation of Church and State.* New York: Oxford University Press, 2011.
Audi, Robert, and Nicholas Wolterstorff. *Religion in the Public Square: The Place of Religious Convictions in Political Debate.* Lanham: Rowman and Littlefield, 1997.
Baier, Kurt. *The Rational and the Moral Order.* Chicago: Open Court, 1995.
Barrett, Justin L. *Why Would Anyone Believe in God?* New York: Alta Mira Press, 2004.
Bayle, Pierre. *Political Writings,* edited by Sally Jenkinson. New York: Cambridge University Press, 2000.
Bedi, Sonu. "Debate: What Is So Special About Religion? The Dilemma of Religious Exemption." *Journal of Political Philosophy,* vol. 15 (2007): 235–49.
Behe, Michael. *Darwin's Black Box: The Biochemical Challenge to Evolution.* New York: Simon and Schuster, 1996.
Bellah, Robert. *Religion in Human Evolution: From the Paleolithic to the Axial Age.* Cambridge: Belknap Press of Harvard University Press, 2011.
Benn, Stanley. *A Theory of Freedom.* New York: Cambridge University Press, 1988.

Bicchieri, Cristina. *The Grammar of Society*. New York: Cambridge University Press, 2006.

Bikhchandani, Sushil, David Hirshleifer, and Ivo Welch. "A Theory of Fads, Fashion, Custom, and Cultural Change in Informational Cascades." *Journal of Political Economy*, vol. 100 (1992): 992–1026.

Bloom, Paul. *Descartes' Baby: How the Science of Child Development Explains What Makes Us Human*. New York: Basic Books, 2005.

Bohman, James, and Henry Richardson. "Liberalism, Deliberative Democracy, and 'Reasons That All Can Accept.'" *Journal of Political Philosophy*, vol. 17 (2010): 253–74.

Boniface VIII, Pope. "Unam Sanctum." *Catholic Library*, 1302. Retrieved March 16th, 2010. From www.newadvent.org/library/docs_bo08us.htm.

Boswell, John. *Christianity, Social Tolerance, and Homosexuality: Gay People in Western Europe from the Beginning of the Christian Era to the Fourteenth Century*. Chicago: University of Chicago Press, 1981.

Boyd, Robert, and Peter Richerson. *The Origin and Evolution of Cultures*. New York: Oxford University Press, 2005.

Brecht, Martin. *Martin Luther: His Road to Reformation 1483–1521*. Chicago: Fortress Press, 1985.

Brennan, Jason. *The Ethics of Voting*. Princeton: Princeton University Press, 2011.

Bryk, Anthony, Valerie Lee, and Peter Holland. *Catholic Schools and the Common Good*. Cambridge: Harvard University Press, 1993.

Calhoun, Cheshire. "Standing for Something." *Journal of Philosophy*, vol. 92 (1995): 235–60.

Chisholm, Roderick. *Theory of Knowledge*. Upper Saddle River: Prentice Hall College Division, 1989.

Chomsky, Noam, and Edward S. Herman. *Manufacturing Consent: The Political Economy of Mass Media*. New York: Pantheon, 2002.

Cohen, Joshua. "Deliberation and Democratic Legitimacy." In *The Good Polity: Normative Analysis of the State*, edited by Alan Hamlin and Philip Pettit, 17–34. Oxford: Blackwell, 1989.

Cox, Damian, Marguerite La Caze, and Michael Levin. "Integrity." *Stanford Encyclopedia of Philosophy (Spring 2010 Edition)*, 2008. Retrieved October 22nd, 2010. From http://plato.stanford.edu/entries/integrity/.

D'Agostino, Fred. *Free Public Reason: Making It Up as We Go*. New York: Oxford University Press, 1996.

———. *Incommensurability and Commensuration: The Common Denominator*. Burlington: Ashgate, 2003.

D'Agostino, Fred, and Kevin Vallier, "Public Justification," *The Stanford Encyclopedia of Philosophy* (2013 Edition), Edward N. Zalta (ed.), URL = <http://plato.stanford.edu/entries/justification-public/>

Dawkins, Richard. *The God Delusion*. New York: Houghton Mifflin Harcourt, 2006.

DiCenso, James. *Kant, Religion, and Politics*. New York: Cambridge University Press, 2011.

Eberle, Christopher. *Religious Conviction in Liberal Politics*. New York: Cambridge University Press, 2002.

———. "What Does Respect Require?" In *Religion in the Liberal Polity*, edited by Terence Cuneo, 173–94. Notre Dame: University of Notre Dame Press, 2005.

————. "Consensus, Convergence, and Religiously Justified Coercion." *Public Affairs Quarterly*, vol. 25 (2012): 281–304.

Elster, Jon. "The Market and the Forum: Three Varieties of Political Theory." In *Deliberative Democracy: Essays on Reason and Politics*, edited by James Bohman and William Rehg, 3–34. New York: MIT Press, 1997.

Estlund, David. *Democratic Authority: A Philosophical Framework*. Princeton: Princeton University Press, 2009.

Feinberg, Joel. *Harm to Others: The Moral Limits of the Criminal Law*. New York: Oxford University Press, 1987.

Fish, Stanley. "Why We Can't All Just Get Along." *First Things*: 18–26, 1996.

Flaubert, Gustave. *Sentimental Education*. London: Penguin Books, 2004.

Frankfurt, Harry. "Identification and Wholeheartedness." In *Responsibility, Character, and the Emotions: New Essays in Moral Psychology*, edited by Ferdinand Schoeman, 27–45. New York: Cambridge University Press, 1988.

Gagnon, Robert. *The Bible and Homosexual Practice*. New York: Abingdon Press, 2004.

Galston, William. *Liberal Purposes: Goods, Virtues, and Diversity in the Liberal State*. New York: Cambridge University Press, 1991.

Gaus, Gerald. *Justificatory Liberalism: An Essay on Epistemology and Political Theory*. New York: Oxford University Press, 1996.

————. *Contemporary Theories of Liberalism: Public Reason as a Post-Enlightenment Project*. Minneapolis: Sage Publications, 2003.

————. "The Place of Religious Belief in Public Reason Liberalism." In *Multiculturalism and Moral Conflict*, edited by Maria Stirk Dimovia-Cookson, and Peter Stirk, 19–37. London: Routledge, 2010a.

————. "Coercion, Ownership, and the Redistributive State: Justificatory Liberalism's Classical Tile." *Social Philosophy & Policy*, vol. 27 (2010b): 233–75.

————. *The Order of Public Reason*. New York: Cambridge University Press, 2011.

————. "Hobbes' Challenge to Public Reason Liberalism: Public Reason and Religious Convictions in *Leviathan*." In *Hobbes Today: Insights for the 21st Century*, edited by Sharon Lloyd, 155–77. New York: Cambridge University Press, 2012.

Gaus, Gerald, and Kevin Vallier. "The Roles of Religious Conviction in a Publicly Justified Polity: The Implications of Convergence, Asymmetry and Political Institutions." *Philosophy and Social Criticism*, vol. 35 (2009): 51–76.

Gauthier, David. *Morals by Agreement*. New York: Oxford University Press, 1986.

Gintis, Herbert. *The Bounds of Reason: Game Theory and the Unification of the Behavioral Sciences*. Princeton: Princeton University Press, 2009.

Greenawalt, Kenneth. *Religious Convictions and Political Choice*. Oxford: Oxford University Press, 1988.

————. *Private Consciences and Public Reasons*. Oxford: Oxford University Press, 1995.

————. *Religion and the Constitution, Volume 1: Free Exercise and Fairness*. Princeton: Princeton University Press, 2006.

————. *Religion and the Constitution, Volume 2: Establishment and Fairness*. Princeton: Princeton University Press, 2008.

————. "The Significance of Conscience." *San Diego Law Review*, vol. 47 (2010): 901–18.

Greene, Abner. "The Political Balance of the Religion Clauses." *Yale Law Journal*, vol. 102 (1993): 1619–44.

————. "Uncommon Ground: A Review of Political Liberalism by John Rawls and Life's Dominion by Ronald Dworkin." *George Washington Law Review*, vol. 62 (1994): 646–73.

Gutmann, Amy. *Democratic Education.* Princeton: Princeton University Press, 1987.

————. "Can Publicly Funded Schools Legitimately Teach Values in a Constitutional Democracy? A Reply to McConnell and Eisgruber." In *Moral and Political Education (Nomos XLIII)*, edited by Stephen Macedo and Yael Tamir, 170–89. New York: New York University Press, 2001a.

————. "Civic Minimalism, Cosmopolitanism, and Patriotism: Where Does Democratic Education Stand in Relation to Each?" In *Moral and Political Education (Nomos XLIII)*, edited by Stephen Macedo and Yael Tamir, 23–57. New York: New York University Press, 2001b.

Gutmann, Amy, and Dennis Thompson. *Democracy and Disagreement.* Cambridge: Belknap Press of Harvard University Press, 1996.

Habermas, Jürgen. *Legitimation Crisis.* Boston: Beacon Press, 1975.

————. "Reconciliation through the Public Use of Reason: Remarks on John Rawls's Political Liberalism." *Journal of Philosophy*, vol. 92 (1995): 109–31.

————. *Moral Consciousness and Communicative Action.* Cambridge: MIT Press, 1999.

————. "Religion in the Public Sphere." *European Journal of Philosophy*, vol. 14 (2006): 1–25.

Harman, Gilbert. *Change in View: Principles of Reasoning.* Cambridge: MIT Press, 1986.

Hayek, F.A. *Law, Legislation and Liberty, Volume 1: Rules and Order.* Chicago: University of Chicago Press, 1973.

Hobbes, Thomas. *Leviathan*, edited by Edwin Curley. Indianapolis: Hackett, 1994.

James, Aaron. "Constructing Justice for Existing Practice: Rawls and the Status Quo." *Philosophy and Public Affairs*, vol. 33 (2005): 281–316.

Joyce, George Howard. *Principles of Natural Theology.* New York: Longmans, Green, and Co., 1922.

Korsgaard, Christine. *The Sources of Normativity.* New York: Cambridge University Press, 1996.

Kretzmann. *The Metaphysics of Theism: Aquinas' Natural Theology in Summa Contra Gentiles I.* Oxford: Clarendon Press, 1997.

Larmore, Charles. *Patterns of Moral Complexity.* New York: Cambridge University Press, 1987.

————. "The Moral Basis of Political Liberalism." *Journal of Philosophy*, vol. 96 (1999): 599–625.

————. *The Autonomy of Morality.* New York: Cambridge University Press, 2008.

————. "What is Political Philosophy?" *Journal of Moral Philosophy*, vol. 10, no. 3 (2013): 276–306.

Leiter, Brian. *Why Tolerate Religion?* Princeton: Princeton University Press, 2013.

Lister, Andrew. "Public Justification and the Limits of State Action." *Politics, Philosophy, and Economics*, vol. 9 (2010): 151–76.

————. "Public Justification of What? Coercion vs. Decision as Competing Frames for the Basic Principle of Justificatory Liberalism." *Public Affairs Quarterly*, vol. 25 (2011): 349–67.

Locke, John. *Two Treatises of Government and a Letter Concerning Toleration*, edited by Ian Shapiro. New Haven: Yale University Press, 2003.

Lomasky, Loren. *Persons, Rights, and the Moral Community*. New York: Oxford University Press, 1987.

Macedo, Stephen. *Liberal Virtues: Citizenship, Virtue and Community in Liberal Constitutionalism*. Oxford: Clarendon Press, 1990.

———. *Diversity and Distrust: Civic Education in a Multicultural Democracy*. Cambridge: Harvard University Press, 2000a.

———. "In Defense of Liberal Public Reason: Are Slavery and Abortion Hard Cases?" In *Natural Law and Public Reason*, edited by Robert P. George and Christopher Wolfe, 11–49. Washington, D.C.: Georgetown University Press, 2000b.

———. *Why Public Reason? Common Knowledge and Democratic Justice*: forthcoming (2014).

Martin, Rex. *A System of Rights*. New York: Oxford University Press, 1993.

McCabe, David. *Modus Vivendi Liberalism: Theory and Practice*. New York: Cambridge University Press, 2010.

McConnell, Michael. "Education Disestablishment: Why Democratic Values are Ill-Served by Democratic Control of Schooling." In *Moral and Political Education (Nomos XLIII)*, edited by Stephen Macedo and Yael Tamir, 87–146. New York: New York University Press, 2001.

McMahon, Christopher. *Collective Rationality and Collective Reasoning*. Cambridge: Cambridge University Press, 2001.

Mill, John Stuart. *On Liberty*, edited by Elizabeth Rapaport. Indianapolis: Hackett Publishing Company, 1978.

Mize, Sandra Y. "The Common Sense Argument for Papal Infallibility." *Theological Studies*, vol. 57 (1996): 252–63.

Moreland, J.P. *Consciousness and the Existence of God: A Theistic Argument*. London: Routledge Press, 2009.

Muldoon, Ryan. *Diversity and the Social Contract*. Unpublished dissertation, University of Pennsylvania, 2009.

Nagel, Thomas. *The View From Nowhere*. New York: Oxford University Press, 1986.

———. "Moral Conflict and Political Legitimacy." *Philosophy and Public Affairs*, vol. 16 (1987): 215–40.

———. *Equality and Partiality*. New York: Oxford University Press, 1991.

National Center for Education Statistics, *Fast Facts: Homeschooling*. Institute of Education Sciences, U.S. Department of Education, 2013. From http://nces.ed.gov/fastfacts/display.asp?id=91.

Neal, Patrick. "Is Political Liberalism Hostile to Religion?" In *Reflections on Rawls: An Assessment of His Legacy*, edited by Shaun P. Young, 153–77. Surrey, England: Ashgate, 2009.

Noddings, Nel. *Caring: A Feminine Approach to Ethics and Moral Education*. Los Angeles: University of California Press, 2003.

Nozick, Robert. *Anarchy, State and Utopia*. New York: Basic Books, 1974.

Pappas, George. "Internalist vs. Externalist Conceptions of Epistemic Justification." *Stanford Encyclopedia of Philosophy*, 2005. Retrieved October 13th, 2010. From http://plato.stanford.edu/entries/justep-intext/#3.

Perry, Michael. *Morality, Politics and Law*. New York: Oxford University Press, 1988.

———. *Love and Power: The Role of Religion and Morality in American Politics*. New York: Oxford University Press, 1991.

———. "From Religious Freedom to Moral Freedom." *San Diego Law Review*, vol. 47 (2010): 993–1013.

Pettit, Philip. *The Common Mind: An Essay on Psychology, Society and Politics*. New York: Oxford University Press, 1996.

Philpott, Daniel. *Revolutions in Sovereignty: How Ideas Shaped Modern International Relations*. Princeton: Princeton University Press, 2001.

Pincione, Guido, and Fernando Tesón. *Rational Choice and Democratic Deliberation: A Theory of Discourse Failure*. New York: Cambridge University Press, 2006.

Pincus, Steve. *1688: The First Modern Revolution*. New Haven: Yale University Press, 2009.

Plantinga, Alvin. *God and Other Minds: A Study of the Rational Justification of Belief in God*. Ithaca: Cornell University Press, 1990.

———. *Where The Conflict Really Lies: Science, Religion and Naturalism*. New York: Oxford University Press, 2011.

Pollock, John. *Thinking About Acting*. New York: Oxford University Press, 2006.

Pollock, John, and Joseph Cruz. *Contemporary Theories of Knowledge*. Lanham: Rowman and Littlefield, 1986.

Quinn, Philip. "Political Liberalisms and Their Exclusions of the Religious." In *Religion and Contemporary Liberalism*, edited by Paul J. Weithman, 138–61. Notre Dame: University of Notre Dame Press, 1997.

Quong, Jonathan. *Liberalism Without Perfection*. New York: Oxford University Press, 2011.

Railton, Peter. *Facts, Values, and Norms: Essays Towards a Morality of Consequence*. Cambridge: Cambridge University Press, 2003.

Rawls, John. "Outline of a Decision Procedure for Ethics." *Philosophical Review*, vol. 60 (1951): 177–97.

———. *A Theory of Justice*. New York: Oxford University Press, 1971.

———. "The Idea of Public Reason Revisited." *University of Chicago Law Review*, vol. 64 (1997): 765–807.

———. *Collected Papers*, edited by Samuel Freeman. Cambridge: Harvard University Press, 1999.

———. *Justice as Fairness: A Restatement*. Cambridge: Harvard University Press, 2001.

———. *The Law of Peoples with "The Idea of Public Reason Revisited."* Cambridge: Harvard University Press, 2002.

———. *Political Liberalism*. New York: Columbia University Press, 2005.

———. *Lectures on the History of Political Philosophy*, edited by Samuel Freeman. Cambridge: Belknap Press, 2007.

Raz, Joseph. *The Morality of Freedom*. Oxford: Oxford University Press, 1986.

Reid, Thomas. "Essay on the Intellectual Powers." In *Thomas Reid's Inquiry and Essays*, edited by Ronald E. Beanblossom and Keith Lehrer, 127–296. Boston: Hackett Publishing, 1983.

Reidy, David. "Rawls's Wide View of Public Reason: Not Wide Enough." *Res Publica*, vol. 6 (2000): 49–72.

Rorty, Richard. "Religion as a Conversation-Stopper." In *The Ethics of Citizenship: Liberal Democracy and Religious Convictions*, edited by J. Caleb Clanton. Waco: Baylor University Press, 2009.

Rosenblum, Nancy. "Pluralism and Democratic Education: Stopping Short by Stopping with Schools." In *Moral and Political Education (Nomos XLIII)*, edited by Stephen Macedo and Yael Tamir, 147–69. New York: New York University Press, 2001.

Rousseau, Jean-Jacques. *Rousseau: "The Social Contract" and Other Later Political Writings*, edited by Victor Gourevitch. New York: Cambridge University Press, 1997.

Scanlon, Thomas. *What We Owe to Each Other*. Cambridge: Harvard University Press, 1998.

Scheffler, Samuel. *The Rejection of Consequentialism: A Philosophical Investigation of the Considerations Underlying Rival Moral Conceptions*. New York: Oxford University Press, 1994.

Schmidtz, David. *Rational Choice and Moral Agency*. Princeton: Princeton University Press, 1996.

Schwartzman, Micah. "The Completeness of Public Reason." *Politics, Philosophy and Economics*, vol. 3 (2004): 191–220.

———. "The Sincerity of Public Reason." *Journal of Political Philosophy*, vol. 19 (2011): 375–98.

———. "What if Religion Isn't Special?" *University of Chicago Law Review*, vol. 79 (2013): 1351–1427.

Sen, Amartya. *The Idea of Justice*. Cambridge: Harvard University Press, 2011.

Smith, Steven D. *The Disenchantment of Secular Discourse*. Cambridge: Harvard University Press, 2010.

Solum, Lawrence. "Faith and Justice." *DePaul Law Review*, vol. 39 (1990): 1083–106.

Strawson, Peter. *Freedom and Resentment and Other Essays*. New York: Routledge, 2008.

Sunstein, Cass. *Going to Extremes: How Like Minds Unite and Divide*. New York: Oxford University Press, 2011.

Swinburne, Richard. *The Evolution of the Soul*. New York: Oxford University Press, 1997.

———. *The Existence of God*. Oxford: Oxford University Press, 2004.

———. *Revelation: From Metaphor to Analogy*. New York: Oxford University Press, 2007.

Taylor, Charles, and Jocelyn Maclure. *Secularism and Freedom of Conscience*. Boston: Harvard University Press, 2011.

Thomson, Judith Jarvis. "A Defense of Abortion." *Philosophy and Public Affairs*, vol. 1 (1971): 47–66.

Thrasher, John, and Kevin Vallier. "The Fragility of Consensus: Public Reason, Diversity and Stability." *European Journal of Philosophy* (2014), forthcoming.

Tomasi, John. *Liberalism Beyond Justice: Citizens, Society, and the Boundaries of Liberal Political Theory*. Princeton: Princeton University Press, 2001a.

———. "Civic Education and Ethical Subservience: From Mozert to Santa Fe and Beyond." In *Moral and Political Education (Nomos XLIII)*, edited by Stephen Macedo and Yael Tamir, 193–220. New York: New York University Press, 2001b.

Tutu, Desmond. *No Future Without Forgiveness*. New York: Doubleday, 1999.

Vallier, Kevin. "Against Public Reason's Accessibility Requirement." *Journal of Moral Philosophy*, vol. 8 (2011a): 366–89.

———. "Consensus and Convergence in Public Reason." *Public Affairs Quarterly*, vol. 25 (2011b): 261–79.

———. "Liberalism, Religion and Integrity." *Australasian Journal of Philosophy*, vol. 90 (2012): 149–65.

———. "On Jonathan Quong's Sectarian Political Liberalism." *Journal of Law and Criminology* (2014a), forthcoming.

———. "Political Libertarianism." Unpublished manuscript, 2014b.

Wall, Steven. *Liberalism, Perfectionism and Restraint.* Cambridge: Cambridge University Press, 1998.

————. "On Justificatory Liberalism." *Politics, Philosophy and Economics,* vol. 9 (2010): 123–49.

Weithman, Paul. *Religion and the Obligations of Citizenship.* New York: Cambridge University Press, 2002.

————. *Why Political Liberalism? On John Rawls's Political Turn.* New York: Oxford University Press, 2010.

Wenar, Leif. "Rights." *Stanford Encyclopedia of Philosophy,* 2010. Retrieved October 13th, 2010. From http://plato.stanford.edu/entries/rights/.

Williams, Bernard. *Moral Luck.* Cambridge: Cambridge University Press, 1981.

Williams, Roger. *On Religious Liberty: Selections from the Works of Roger Williams,* James Calvin Davis, ed., Belknap Press, 2008.

Wolterstorff, Nicholas. *John Locke and the Ethics of Belief.* New York: Cambridge University Press, 1996.

————. "The Role of Religion in Decision and Discussion of Political Issues." In *Religion in the Public Square: The Place of Religious Convictions in Political Debate.* Lanham: Rowman and Littlefield: 67–120, 1997a.

————. "Why We Should Reject What Liberalism Tells Us about Speaking and Acting in Public for Religious Reasons." In *Religion and Contemporary Liberalism,* edited by Paul Weithman, 162–81. Notre Dame: University of Notre Dame Press, 1997b.

————. "The Paradoxical Role of Coercion in the Theory of Political Liberalism." *Journal of Law, Philosophy and Culture,* vol. 1 (2007): 101–25.

Index

equality 32–4, 71
Establishment Clause of the First
    Amendment 197, 199,
    201–3, 237; and objections to
    vouchers 247–8
establishment of religion 113
evaluative standards 107–8, 118, 124,
    135; agent-relative 108
Everson v. Board of Education 246
evolution of norms 169–70; and the
    example of birth control 175
evolution, biological (Darwinism)
    232–41
exclusion, principles of: derivation
    of 50; direct and indirect
    methods of 51, 128; Principle
    of Intelligible Exclusion
    7, 184; as regulators of
    reasoning 50
exemption *see* religious accomodation

fairness objection to restraint 66–72,
    77; and convergence 129;
    forms of 198; and intelligible
    defeaters 209; resentment and
    127
faith: comparison of, with trust 47;
    definition of 47
federal funding for faith-related
    providers 202–3
Feinberg, Joel, Liberty Principle as
    formulated by 30–1, 42
feminist community, care ethics
    appealed to by 138
First Amendment 197, 199–200,
    201–3, 207–17
foreign policy: Congressional approval
    and 191; national 132–4
Frankfurt, Harry, on integrity as self-
    integration 80

Free Exercise Clause of the First
    Amendment 197, 199–200,
    207–17, 259; and the
    compelling interest test 210,
    212; as principle of exclusion
    200
free speech principle 249
free trade and government aid 188
freedom *see* liberty
Frost, Vicki 213
fundamentalist Christians 211

Galston, William 66
Gaus, Gerald 12, 25, 186; and the
    core problem of political
    philosophy 89; and free
    exercise 222; on public
    jusification 32–3; on
    rationality 149; on Rousseau
    and the normative bargain
    93; on rule internalization 91;
    and the sovereign (umpire)
    167; and sufficiency, coercion,
    and duties 41
Gauthier, David: bargaining scenario
    of 29; and decision theory
    150; and informational
    idealization 150; minimax
    relative-concession decision
    rule of 165–6
general equilibrium 15, 82
Gintis, Herbert, on common
    knowledge 76
Global South, religion in the 4
global warming policy and mild
    idealization 120
God: existence of 114; souls provided
    by 115
Greenawalt, Kent 78; and a "contingent
    limit" on science 237; and

integrity: accessibility failing to respect 120; and children's moral development 209; concerns about 228, 240; conscientious engagement as obstacle to 127; costs and benefits of 157–8; as a foundational value 88; justificatory reasons respecting 112; minimizing violating of the diverse 91; and the objection to convergence-based restraint 127, 129; respect for 87–8, 90, 101, 122, 125, 155; understanding of 80

integrity costs: and Convergent Restraint for Legislators 193; idealization imposing 155; morally significant 60; self-imposed 126

integrity objection to restraint 77, 80; Audi's reply to 65; convergence view as avoiding 129; normative interpretation of 59–60; psychological interpretation of 59; and Tutu 63; and the weight of it to public reason liberals 58; Wolterstorff's statement of 59

integrity-based reasons as robust defeaters of laws 88

Intelligent Design, teaching of 8, 120, 232–41

intelligibility, definition of 106, 257

Intelligible Exclusion, Principle of: formulation of 184; and institutional requirements 258; and political officials' choices 190; and religious accommodations 197; and

school choice 246; and *Yoder* 208

intelligibility of religious reasons 125

intelligibility requirement 231; argument for 108; and convergence 21; definition of 106, 257; and epicycle of recognition 106–7; illustration of 183; justificatory reasons circumscribed by 6; and *Mozert* 211, 213; public justification as entailing 111; religious reasons as meeting 125

Interest in Facilitating Practical Reasoning 156

Internet, the, and the media as tracking reasoning 175–6

intrapersonal conflict 95

Joyce, George Howard, on natural theology 141

judges 193–4, 258

justice: political conception of 17, 130; principles of 14; restorative 62–3; shared commitment to 134–5

Justice as Fairness 15–17, 96

justification, political 18, 28

justificatory liberalism *see* public reason liberalism

justificatory populism 29–30

justificatory premise 50, 83, 85, 90, 256–7

justificatory reasons: accessible reasons requirement and 28, 103–22; definition of 28; degrees of stringency of 105; and entry into the

restraint: coercive character of 53;
opportunity costs of 75;
promoting exclusion 72; as
setback 62; submission to
21–2, 37; uneven burdens of
64, 67, 69–70, 72, 198
restraint, principles of 4, 33–8, 63; as
applicable to nonreligious
moral doctrines 46, 49, 54; as
applied to citizens, legislators,
and judges 7; cognitive
compliance costs of 65,
68–70; as constitutive means
towards public justification
36; denial-of-truth objection
to 66; as distinguished from
principles of exclusion 50;
divisiveness objection to
72–7; and the duty of civility
16, 34, 75–6; empirical *versus*
normative stability arguments
for 72; fairness objection
to 5, 66–72; as grounded
in the Public Justification
Principle 37; and the ideal of
conscientious engagement 65;
integrity objection to 4, 57–66,
71–2; as not required by
other commitments 85; and
principle of secular rationale
55; on reasons *versus* on
proposals 184–5, 193, 195, 220;
religious citizens' objections
to 49, 60; as restriction on
private or comprehensive
reasons 34; and secularist bias
4, 67, 69; and the translation
requirement 68, 70
Rorty, Richard: on the empirical
stability argument 73;

on religious reasons as
conversation-stoppers 109
Rousseau, Jean-Jacques: on conflicts
between law and ideals 91;
and democracy 131; on
dignity diminished 93; and
the separation of politics and
religion 39
rule of law undermined by religious
accommodations 215

same-sex marriage 116–17, 127, 183
Scalia, Antonin 201, 210, 215
Scheffler, Samuel, on the agent-
centered prerogative and
impartiality 101
school choice 226, 244–50, 253; and
exposure to shared values
250; legitimacy of 232;
objections to 246–50; public
reason argument for 8, 216
Schwartzman, Micah: on public reason
129–30; on publicity's value
110; on restraint and public
justification 36
science and Intelligent Design 234–5,
238, 252
scientific method as common
evaluative standard 108
sectarianism 231
secular beliefs 81
secular rationale, principle of 55–7,
65–6; arguments for 57; and
secularity and adequacy 55
secularism 2, 229
secularist bias 4, 67, 69, 261
Secular Reason, Principle of 80
segregation and interracial marriage,
attitudinal shift on 168,
179

Made in the USA
Coppell, TX
17 July 2021